THE SPIRIT OF COUNSEL

MARY SWAINSON

The Spirit of Counsel

The Story of a Pioneer in Student Counselling

LONDON

NEVILLE SPEARMAN

First published in Great Britain in 1977 by
Neville Spearman Ltd
The Priory Gate, Friars Street, Sudbury, Suffolk

ISBN 85435 103 5

Set in 11 point Baskerville, 1½ point leaded, and printed and bound
in Great Britain by
The Garden City Press Limited, Letchworth, Hertfordshire SG6 1JS

To the memory of
Professor J. W. Tibble
who gave us freedom
to take responsibility,
to build,
to make mistakes,
and to learn.

CONTENTS

and its organization. Mental Health in the teaching profession: some modern trends. Students; teachers; staff. Where are we going?

ACKNOWLEDGEMENTS

I am grateful to all who have helped me to write this book : my parents for giving me the requisite heredity and upbringing; my friends, teachers, colleagues and students who have provided the experience; and especially Phoebe and Bill Carter for editorial advice, Vera Everitt for typing, Leslie Price for recommending books, and Ishbel McGain for help with the Index.

Thanks are also due to the editors of the many journals (acknowledged individually in the text) who have given permission for reproduction of published papers.

INTRODUCTION

This book is a story of building and learning, both outwardly and inwardly, on several levels of counselling and psychotherapy.

Outwardly, the events took place during a phase of rapid expansion in higher education. Expansion led to the introduction of more and diversified courses, and also of new attitudes, among them the recognition of the need for personal counselling and guidance in universities and colleges. Opportunities developed for the tutors themselves to study better methods of teaching, seminar-work and tutorial skills; also, if they wished, to participate in psychological group experience of various kinds. At the same time, however, the sheer weight of student numbers and the unwieldly size of the burgeoning institutions too often implied loss of the easy, informal, personal relationships characteristic of the older, smaller colleges. Now no more than a few students were known personally to a few staff, and many students, especially those in General or Combined Studies courses, felt they 'belonged' nowhere. Lost in the mass, and frequently unprepared for college life, they were crying out for guidance. So we find the anomaly that, just when a number of tutors were more than ever prepared to help their students personally, these tutors found themselves so over-driven by the paper-work, committees and formal administration which a large institution seems to make necessary, that they had little time or energy for informal talks either with students or indeed with one another. (Memos replaced the former leisurely, friendly chats over coffee!) This was one reason for the introduction of professional counselling services, often used by students and staff alike. At the present time, most universities and other colleges of higher education, and many schools, have their counsellors—an amazing development in twenty-five years.

Now we are in a (temporary?) phase of contraction. Although in many ways alarming and regrettable—for the pendulum is swinging too far to the other extreme—there is, at least, the possibility that units may become smaller, even within a collateral group of colleges. Let us hope that, when the next phase of expansion sets in, we may learn from mistakes, and that units may be formed of workable size, allowing scope and time for personal human relationships.

As regards the inward aspect, I have written the account in the form of an autobiography to show how one individual mirrored the changing attitudes and opportunities of the period, and (in a small way and in her own field) how she played her part in developing them. At each stage I have included an article or lecture which reflected the needs and ideas of the time.

This is not a text-book on student counselling, nor does it deal with techniques or offer detailed case-histories. (For a comprehensive description illustrated by plenty of case-material one cannot do better than refer to Audrey Newsome's account of the student counselling service at the University of Keele.[1]) Rather, this book is a case-history of myself *as* a counsellor during the difficult period of pioneering. It shows how a perfectly ordinary person, who might easily have become a complete failure during adolescence, was led, pushed and prepared by life for the task to be done. Everything that happened, both positive and negative, seems to have been used to urge me along. It is an instance of what a friend has called the 'plannish' pattern of happenings—something which occurs to so many people nowadays who are willing to 'be lived'. At certain critical turning points we recognize that a decision has already been taken on another level of being; yet always the incarnate ego has to take final responsibility for acceptance (and in minor choices—though never in major ones—I have sometimes said 'No!')

To write an autobiography can be, at one extreme, an 'ego-trip'—an opportunity for inflation and self-justification. At the other extreme, some find it indecent, preferring to use a small 'i', or the passive voice, or even to do away with the ego altogether. I feel that in loving oneself *as* one's neighbour—a necessity for counsellors—one can look at the ego fairly objectively as yet another 'I' among others, and use it. In one's later sixties, an autobiography is one of the best exercises in self-knowledge and

---

[1] Audrey Newsome, Brian J. Thorne and Keith L. Wyld: *Student Counselling in Practice*, Unibooks, University of London Press, 1973.

in letting the past go. So I have described myself as schoolgirl, student, tutor, and counsellor, not omitting the silly, over-anxious, and even 'morbid' bits, for they are all part of the whole.

As well as loving our neighbour and ourselves equally, we need first to 'love God', in whatever idiom that principle is perceived. I am interested in the change in basic assumptions underlying counselling practice over the last twenty-five years, and particularly in those pointers towards the climate of thought to come in the critical last quarter of this century. When I first started, after the war, even 'psychotherapy' was a 'bad word' in some academic circles, while the term 'counselling' was unheard of, or else misunderstood as giving directive advice, or as welfare work.

Counselling has stemmed from many theoretical sources: the analytic psychology of Freud, Jung, Klein and others; Behaviourism and Learning Theory leading to desensitization methods; and perhaps mainly from the non-directive approach of Carl Rogers, and many more. Recently, there has been a swing away from the psychodynamic, analytical orientation, which sought causes in the past, towards emphasis on the present, particularly in the 'New Therapies' of Humanistic Psychology (Gestalt Therapy, Transactional Psychology, and others) with its stress on 'sensitivity training' and on various types of encounter groups. As I shall show, during the 1950s and 1960s we experimented with some early variants of such groups. I advised my trainees to take part in carefully-chosen group experience as well as in two-person therapy. And I feel that, provided that such intensive groups do not stir up too quickly more than can be handled, they have a most important part to play, especially in resolving false personality patterns through re-living them in the here and now, and in horizontal relationships.

But there is also the inner, vertical dimension—that of relationship and communication between the different levels of our own being and those of others. Depending on the quality, group experience *can* enhance the subtler vibrations, and then much of the personality change is done at higher levels. In this way, counselling achieves a spiritual dimension which, in my opinion, is the pointer to future principles and practice. And here Jung (among others[2]) comes again into his own, for some of his recently published works provide a springboard for the spiritual psychology of the future. His outlook was always final rather than reductive: he worked towards the vision of the full-grown oak rather than the acorn. Moreover, his form of healing—whole-making—was intended not only for the sick but for all mankind, and in this age not an élite but all humanity must take the great stride into the new awareness. It is this aspect which I have stressed in Part IV of the book, and here there *are* some illustrations of case-material.

Recently a friend who has worked in this specific field for twenty-five years wrote:

> More and more people come my way who are primarily concerned with the problems of the inner journey, and whose tensions are largely transpersonal ones. These form a growing band of 'deprived' people; since their doctors put them straight on to antidepressants, while their NH psychiatrists as often as not tell them they are suffering from repressed sexual impulses, and help them to drug away some of the inner experiences they should be listening to.

Have we an answer?

[2] See pp. 239–43 and section (b) of New Age groups p. 249.

The Spirit of the Lord shall rest upon him, the spirit of wisdom and understanding, the spirit of counsel . . .

And he shall not judge after the sight of his eyes, neither reprove after the hearing of his ears . . .

The wolf also shall dwell with the lamb, and the leopard shall lie down with the kid . . . and a little child shall lead them . . .

They shall not hurt nor destroy in all my holy mountain : for the earth shall be full of the knowledge of the Lord, as the waters cover the sea.

From Isaiah, XI, 2–9

Part I: Patterns of Preparation

CHAPTER 1

Childhood and Adolescence

Why are we born to our particular parents in a certain place, time, and condition? In early life, when we are struggling to find ourselves, to survive as persons amidst moral, economic, and social pressures, it is often difficult to perceive the deeper meaning of incarnation. Yet even a glimpse helps. In my counselling work I have found that when an almost unbearable situation is recognized to be 'for something'—part of a significant pattern— then it can more easily be accepted and used constructively, the very insight releasing the energy of true incentive. Many young people, whom I meet, seem to be aware at an earlier age than we were of purpose in living, though as yet they may not know the detail. For myself, although a sense of purpose was always strong (sometimes even a burden), I have only been able to recognize each stage as it came, never to see the goal.

How are our life-tasks prepared for us? Those tests and problems which our parents have faced consciously, working them through into their own lives and attitudes, can be passed on, fulfilled and resolved, to the next generation in the process of natural upbringing. But those which remain largely unconscious or unresolved tend to become the children's heritage as a work-field. In my own case, all my life I have struggled with psychological anxiety, moral pressures, and conflicts of loyalty leading to the important lesson of mediating between and reconciling opposites. On the side of ready-made 'gifts', however, I was happily conditioned to work hard, to serve responsibly, and to build. Largely because of the specific function of a clergyman's family in a small organic community, there was little trouble outwardly concerning identity. Matters of appearance, money, and social class never seemed to me the overriding issues that they were to some of my friends. Above all, although later on I rebelled against the outer forms in order to find my own idiom, there was a firm grounding in spiritual values, and also in nature —in wonder, joy and play. Looking back now, I can begin to see the place of each patch of dark and light detail as it fits into the emerging picture.

Home background

My parents came from social strata moving in different directions—meeting as it were in the middle—so that I learned to see relative status, wealth, poverty, in close juxtaposition and perspective. 'Three generations up and three down,' my father, a keen student of genealogy, used to say with the implication: 'Does it matter?' And my mother, a most unorthodox parson's wife for those days, used to delight in 'naughty' parties to which she invited and mixed the 'wrong' people, partly from her genuinely democratic beliefs, partly from sheer devilment. So I grew up thinking social snobbishness all rather stupid. After all, the 'real' people of any class were never snobbish, and we, as the clergyman's family in the middle between county and villagers, were in a good position to judge.

The Swainsons had been socially and financially on the downgrade until the turning point in our generation. Originating from landed proprietors, clergy, army, and other professional people from the fifteenth to the eighteenth centuries in the upper Ribble valley of Lancashire, they moved to seafaring and manufacturing in Liverpool in the eighteenth and nineteenth centuries. My paternal grandfather migrated to Wells, Somerset, where he died when my father was only sixteen, so that my grandmother had a hard struggle and the large family was very poor. As the eldest son, my father, Samuel James Swainson, came up the hard way, developing a strong sense of responsibility to the others and to himself. He attended Wells Cathedral Grammar School (singing in the Cathedral choir) and later read in the evenings for an external London B.A. while teaching during the day. He then read Classics at Queen's College, Oxford, meanwhile supporting himself as Classics master at Oxford High School (where, incidentally, T. E. Lawrence was among his pupils.) At some stage—I think while teaching at King Edward

School, Bath—he trained at Wells Theological College for Holy Orders. He often spoke of the strain of those years, saying that it had affected the rest of his life.

The Kelways, on the other hand, were on the upgrade. My mother, Beatrice Kelway of Huish Episcopi, Langport, Somerset, was the granddaughter of the gardener who inaugurated Kelway's Nurseries. Her father, William Kelway, frequently travelling abroad, extended the business, built a big house, and became increasingly prosperous. I remember my mother telling me that when the new main railway line of the Great Western Railway was built (to shorten the 'Great Way Round' by Bristol) it cut right through 'paeony valley'—another asset. Her eldest brother carried on the business until the 1930s. All my Kelway uncles went to public schools (Sherborne, Winchester, Marlborough) while my mother studied music, practising her violin for many hours a day. Music and gardening were her life. In 1905 her father gave her a violin made by Alessandro Gagliano, which she worshipped; after her death in 1966 it was sold to Edward Downes of the New Philharmonia Orchestra for £1,000. (As an only child I was never troubled by sibling rivalry, but when I was training for child guidance, the picture of the boy with a violin in the T.A.T. test brought back a surprising degree of resentment and jealousy; it emerged that as a small child I had been convinced that if there were a fire my mother would rescue Alessandro before me!)

When my mother was only four, she lost her own mother in childbirth. Immediately she was sent away as a boarder to a dame-school in nearby Taunton, but to a small child it might have been thousands of miles away from home. However, as the youngest pupil she was much petted, so she experienced that unfortunate mixture of deprivation and spoiling which affected her subsequent life-pattern. After some years at the North London Collegiate School under Miss Buss (this school did not suit her as it was far too academic, though Miss Buss herself was kind and motherly) she went to a Swiss 'finishing school', returning to Langport after her stepmother died to bring up her two young half-brothers and to be mistress of her father's house, organizing the many servants. So it was quite a bump when, on the rebound from her first love, at thirty she married an impecunious curate and had to get up at dawn to clean old-fashioned grates herself. Yet she had the strong Kelway spirit; life had made her adaptable and resilient; she coped with spirit and courage, though bitterly resenting the little time and energy available for playing her beloved fiddle.

Throughout my childhood we were hard up. It was expected, and gratefully received, that the farmers and any rich parishioners would send us rabbits at harvest time and game in season; this was all in the tradition of tithe. Secondhand clothes given by society people to 'poor clergy' were a great delight; we never minded! My parents had worked through *that* experience, and so I am able to 'sit loose' to money matters provided that I have just enough. My mother's cousin James Toms[1] said to me as a teenager, 'Your first duty is to be self-supporting,' and my father always stressed that I must earn enough to keep myself and my mother after he died. (He was only two years older than my mother, but was always looking forward to an early death!) At the time I was glad of the excuse this provided to use my grandfather's allowance to my mother partly for my schooling, and not to have to remain at home as the unpaid skivvy or extra curate, as was the fate of so many clergy daughters I knew. Having brought up two boys, my mother wanted a daughter, but my father wanted a son. If there had been a second child—a boy—I doubt whether I should have been properly educated. As it was, I had to be son as well as daughter, and this situation played a big part in the pattern.

The area in which my parents did *not* resolve their difficulties was that of personal relationships, their temperamental and psychological problems spilling over into morals and religion. Here was the context for my life-task.

In temperament they were opposite: my father quiet, gentle, introverted, scholarly; my mother gay, dominating, extravert, practical. He had been a fatherless teenager; she a motherless

[1] The maker of John R. Toms's violin strings, of Wellington, Somerset. Cousin James, a brilliant yet afflicted son of the marriage of first cousins, was stone deaf, making every string separately by the touch of his fingers. His strings were used by many performers of the day, for example Kreisler. As a child, I loved visiting his home workshop and hearing my great uncle John play the organ he had built himself. Music was supremely important to all this side of the family.

child. I will not, for obvious reasons, describe the depths of their conflicts which were largely sexual; it is enough to say that they did not get on. My mother was angry and driving, my father withdrawn and depressed. They tended to sit in separate rooms. I felt terribly torn between them, as a young child identifying with my mother's 'cause', but in later adolescence seeing my father's point of view. For me, the challenge was also intrapsychic; I was endowed with the over-sensitivity, fear of rows (leading to escapism), and inner awareness of the Swainsons; at the same time I had something of the drive and pioneering energy of the tough, long-lived Kelways. The spiritual and pastoral attitudes of my father had to be earthed in the hyperactivity and perfectionism of my mother's practical standards. It was not easy. To my Kelway cousins who went to Cheltenham Ladies' College I was 'a silly little thing'—doubtless true; anyway I was certainly very shy of them. The person who (implicitly) helped me most to synthesize these opposites was my mother's younger half-brother Ian Kelway (later Drama Organizer for Devon County). He was an ideal figure to me in my childhood, more like an elder brother than an uncle. He had both the strength *and* the inner awareness, combined with a sense of humour. Though we met seldom, and then mainly during crises, I knew he was a friend of the spirit as well as a blood relation—to me a rare thing.

Painful as it was, psychologically this pattern laid the foundation for my future work, and *now* I am truly grateful for it. Some such pattern in childhood is, I suggest, an invaluable experience for a psychotherapist, *provided* that it can be worked on (as I did later in analysis), understood in feeling as well as intellectually, and used.[2]

As an only child, was I spoiled? I don't know. I was often ill, introjecting the atmosphere; but my memory is mainly of overanxiety and responsibility rather than spoiling: anxiety to fulfil

[2] Only after this chapter was written did I read Laurens van der Post's *The Face beside the Fire* (Hogarth Press, 1953). On p. 285 is the passage: 'How clear it was to him now: whatever the parents left of themselves unlived, the children had to live for them before they were free to take up their own proper and special burden for which they were born.' How true! Yet can it also be possible that the parents' unlived life in itself provides the necessary setting for the life-task for which the child was born? I think of Eliot's *Family Reunion*.

my parents' expectations (usually at variance) and responsibility towards them. There was constant tension and great pressure. This fatal compulsion to try to be what people require of me has been a lifelong weakness with which I have struggled. I longed for a brother or sister with whom to dilute the intensity and share the half-comprehended problems.

Although I had no identity problem outwardly, there certainly was an inward one mirrored (as is frequently the case) in change of name or assumption of nickname. The two names Beatrice Mary, given at my christening, in themselves indicated duality, for Beatrice was my mother's name, Mary a standard name throughout the Swainson family tree (also I was expected to be born on Lady Day but characteristically came two days beforehand). During the early period of mother-dominance I was called Beatrice (or Bee—a happier aspect). Later I rebelled, especially when my great aunt Delia Toms called my mother 'B major' and myself 'B minor'. Too horribly near the truth, and made worse by the musical idiom! There was also the complication that my father—identified with Dante—had idealized my beautiful mother, marrying a projected image. In his frustration he was liable to concentrate too much on me. The picture of Dante's meeting with Beatrice hung on his study wall. Dimly I felt the need to live up to the image : to bless, inspire, lead people through journeys. At the same time, in all fairness I must record that consciously my father did all he could to set me free from the home atmosphere. Released at nineteen into the freedom of university, I broke away and lived my own life. In the exaggerated joy of reaction, I went 'mad as a March hare' and so was called 'Bunny'. Not until my late thirties and the move to Leicester did I identify with the more serious 'Mary' aspect, which I have retained until now.

That is the general picture. Now for the detail.

Beatrice (and Bee)

I was born on March 23rd 1908 at Weston-super-Mare, Somerset, where my father had his third curacy at the Parish Church. When I was nearly five, he was preferred to the vicarage of Blackford, near Wedmore. Here, on the edge of one of the Sedgemoor 'islands', in winter we were often flooded; I well remember my father being taken to the church in a flat-bottomed boat, and my mother sweeping the water out of the back door. It was hard for her; she was often ill and so was I. Yet my memories of Blackford are happy ones: a wonderful immense garden filled with cedars and other beloved trees which were like people to me, particularly my very special juniper tree. In a countryside full of the magic of Arthurian legends we used to hunt for Excalibur among the rhines. I practically lived with the farmer's family across the road; we had a gang, built houses in trees, ran wild with animals, studied birds and insects; in this respect it was an ideal childhood. Because I was 'not strong' I did not go to school until the age of eleven, but was taught by my mother on the P.N.E.U. method.[3] So, though backward in some ways, I was forward in others. From the age of three I could read; my mother, who was very good with young children, read to me a great deal; I had a thorough grounding in all children's classics (such as Andrew Lang's *Tales of Troy and Greece*; books on Norse Myths, the Knights of the Round Table, Robin Hood and many historical novels, including most of Scott; Kingsley's *Water Babies*, *Swiss Family Robinson*, and many, many more). By six I spoke German fluently but unfortunately when the first war began my beloved Fräulein had to go, and I forgot it all. But I lacked orthodox primary schooling, and the P.N.E.U. system bound me still more closely to my mother.

In 1919 we moved from the lowlands to the hills of West Somerset near the Devon border where my father became vicar of the small parish of Langford Budville (later with Runnington), remaining there until his death in 1948. Here, even more, were great beauty, freedom, and that space of wild land to explore that so many town children lack. I cannot be sufficiently thankful for a country upbringing—always in close touch with the realities of nature and hard rural life. For in those days it was hard. At Blackford we had only a pump with very questionable live creatures in the water! At Langford there was piped water except when it ran out, but for thirty years we had no electricity, using oil lamps and cookers. Both vicarages were immense—damp

---

3 Parents' National Educational Union: a postal course issued from the Charlotte Mason College, Ambleside.

and cold in winter though grand in summer—ideal for children, with outbuildings, a tennis court, orchard, paddock, wild shrubberies, all that could be desired for play. But the upkeep was a nightmare. We were in a constant state of exhaustion due to the sheer physical toil and financial worry about 'dilapidations'. Picking and preserving all the fruit alone was a major job. It was a case of survival; my father strained his heart, and my mother, though slaving away with her usual drive in the garden which she loved, was almost invariably ill in the holidays when I returned, and ended up with arthritis. I still have a horror of not being able to muster the physical strength to keep up with overwhelming material chores. It did not help my mother that at first I was going through the animal craze : rabbits, then ducks, fowls, and many, many cats! All these had to be cared for during school terms. And of course we had a series of ponies—an absolute necessity before the days of cars. I rode; my mother drove my father in the trap on his visits to outlying farms; but mainly we walked or cycled everywhere. There were no buses or telephones for a long time. I well remember being called urgently from the garden (barefoot as usual) to cycle down to Wellington —which I did in record time without bothering to put on shoes —to fetch the doctor for our postmaster who had been taken seriously ill.

My memories of early adolescence are of cycling for miles over the Brendon hills, mainly with my school friend Vi Bonsey, also a clergyman's daughter, whose father had a parish four miles away. This rural background had a profound effect, later to be expressed in settlement studies and in an outcry against the depopulation of the South-west where, owing to the migration of young people to the industrial Midlands, there were not enough inhabitants left to keep life going in the more isolated parishes. But all these memories concern the holidays.

Boarding school

From the age of eleven to seventeen I went to Gardenhurst at Burnham-on-Sea, Somerset, where the absence of parental stress and the healthy life did wonders for me physically. In the summer we swam in the sea; in winter we played hockey on the sands—a much faster game than on grass, the pitch being marked out afresh each time after the receding tide by running the lines and circles with a hockey stick. When older, we played lacrosse, a wonderfully free game. I enjoyed school, never had any difficulty in making friends, and gloried in group life. At first there was plenty of bullying, but I soon learned to give as good as I got, and then outgrew it. (For a short time at the outset I was unhappy and asked to be taken away, but my mother— who knew from experience—said firmly, 'It is just when things are difficult that you must learn to stick them out'. I respected her immensely for saying that, and it stood me in good stead in later life.) Soon I found a role as story-teller to the dormitory at night, for I could always produce stories at will. Lessons were easy, especially Geography, which was very well taught, and English with Miss C. who gave us a sound basis of grammar yet plenty of freedom to write verse, plays, and let rip imaginatively. There was, however, no Science. Gardenhurst, at that time, was not an academic school; when I was there only two of us went on to take School Certificate, and that not until seventeen. Among the girls it was 'not done' to be 'brainy' which was a label akin to 'mental'! That didn't worry me, but emotionally I was still immature and terribly tied up with anxiety about parents, religion, and morality, not helped by the unhealthily pious talks we were given by one of the headmistresses every Sunday about our sins and our 'characters'. Of course I was fair game, taking the talks far too seriously. In a school exercise book, camouflaged as 'History Form V', I kept a secret 'thought book' addressed to God, in which I wrote all my problems, puzzles about right and wrong, life and death.

The moral conflict came to a head over music. Naturally my mother wished me to follow in her footsteps, my father in his. So I studied the violin with my mother's former master, Herr Milani of Taunton, who taught at the school, but after a couple of years I had to give it up because rapid physical growth and a weak back gave me too much pain and exhaustion when trying to hold up the fiddle for long periods. My first failure. (I have always suffered with my back.) The piano I studied with Miss R., the very able senior music mistress, called 'Churn' by the girls because of the way in which she kept going on ceaselessly at us. Brilliant herself and very impatient, she could be cruel;

when we were older we realized she must have been a sadist. One comfort was that we *all* suffered; to come out crying from music lessons was a regular thing. So at first I did not feel extra bad; concern for the others enabled me at least to try to feel some degree of detachment and forgiveness. In my thought book to God I wrote :

> You said once, 'Vengeance is mine, I will repay.' It is not for me to judge but for you. Oh God do deal justly with Miss R., and if she ought to be punished please show her how very awful it is to have a bad music lesson. When you were dying you prayed for your murderers, but I think it is very difficult to forgive Miss R. for what she said to K., P., and E. But still I will say it. Please don't punish her very hard, but only show her gently how she is unkind occasionally. I suppose it must be very hard to be a music mistress.

A year later, however, I was less objective. I began to come in for a worse deal than most because (so I learned long afterwards) I was one of the more naturally gifted girls musically in the school but was too paralysed by fear to play. I must indeed have been a sore trial to her! At first I had been able to throw it off, but by the time I was fifteen she was having an insidious effect; I was falling into a state of what I now know to be depression. Just after my sixteenth birthday I wrote :

> In my music lesson today Churn said that I didn't learn music to play the piano, as I shall never do that, but to make me determined and to give me some backbone which I haven't got. 'You are so dreamy,' said Churn, 'you have no will-power, no force of character to *make* yourself do anything. Now if you had seen me at your age . . .' I really don't know what to do, it is so awful. The harder I try the more she says I don't try. If it was for myself I wouldn't care a hang, but Mummy wants me so badly to play her accompaniments when I am older. I hate to tell her how badly I am getting on because it makes her so disappointed. I know that Churn is perfectly right and that I am dreadful, and never can be any good at anything but no one shall ever say I don't try.

Three months later :

What an awful thing it is to have remarks made about you, your character and your future, regularly twice a week. Oh Churn, you are making me so hopeless, so despairing of my life and everything! You have taken away my self-respect. Whenever I think about what I shall do in my life a sudden feeling of despair comes over me. I can't be sure of myself, she has made me distrust myself so much that I can no longer say 'I will do that' but only 'I suppose I shan't be able to'.

She says I can never excel in anything, never have the will-power to do anything, but always lean on other people, and go on in my feeble way getting lower and lower until I die. I shall never make a success of my life. I shall go under.

Of course at first I tried not to believe it, but slowly and surely it impressed itself on my mind, telling me with a peculiar insistence that I was no good, no good, a failure, worthless, backboneless—with an 'odious' character. Odious —and weak. At first when she said I didn't try I argued. 'Oh yes,' she says, 'you try in your feeble way.' She puts on a face to copy me and says, 'I don't know what that note is, Miss R., but I am trying to find out!' So I have given up arguing. What is the use? You only get reported to Miss W. and called conceited, self-satisfied and impertinent ... I try not to believe her. But have I the right to do that? She is older than me, she knows my (odious) character; she is so positive that she has to say it twice a week that I shall never be any good at anything. I say, "I don't care, I will be good at something. I hate you, I will be of value in the world. I will try to live up to my name, Beatrice ...'

At *that* stage the Kelway fighting spirit overcame the Swainson depression.

For a future therapist, it is probably valuable to go through such an experience of feeling a complete failure in life. I composed some music (in a minor key)—an expression of despair— and played it in the holidays, nearly driving my poor father up the wall! But at the time I worshipped my beautiful and talented mother, and consciously only wanted to be all she wished of me; so when she asked me how the music lessons were going I replied, 'Just ordinarily.' I *could not* bring myself to tell her the appalling truth, especially in view of what she had said much earlier about sticking things out. Later, however, when Miss R. started to call me 'insane' and succeeded in convincing me that I was morally 'in the wrong' as well as being a failure in life, I began to lose all power to fight. There was a time when I contemplated suicide, standing on the high vicarage wall overlooking the drop to the sunken road, and thinking, '*Then* they would be sorry!' Of course this was a hysterical reaction to 'show Them' and make 'Them' take notice, rather than the pattern of a true depressive. All the same I have made use of the experience on many occasions in therapy with people who have suffered similarly.

Eventually, the solution was quite simple. My friend Vi Bonsey, who had also suffered with Churn, told her own mother that she refused to continue with her any more; she was transferred at once to the second mistress who was not really good enough for Vi. Then Vi told my mother about me. My mother took it very sensibly, wishing she had known earlier. She asked for me also to be transferred to the second mistress with whom I got on much better. But the critical break had yet to be made. In my seventeenth year, with School Certificate looming, I decided to give up music altogether and to follow my father's pattern of academic work.

I have written fully about this episode because I feel it to be one of the most traumatic experiences of my life. Later, in psychological analysis, I worked over it a good deal, seeing how unconsciously I had used the situation to effect a break from my mother's immense power over me. But, despite this insight, and the early attempts at forgiveness, I remained extremely vindictive towards Miss R., longing to inflict on her what she had inflicted on so many of us. I realize that I shall need to come to terms with her before I die—both for my own sake and hers. Here is one of the reasons for writing an autobiography such as this; I can now see events more in proportion. It would seem that she had to be the agent of very severe pruning so that I could be cut right away from the bonds that bound me to my mother's values (her shadow—B minor—her accompanist) and be set free for the path that was mine to fulfil in this life. Even my vindictiveness can be accepted as giving me the energy to 'show *her*!' Acceptance and understanding are, I hope, at least the preliminary stages to forgiveness.

Other patterns of pruning were radical, but none was as cruel or destructive as those music lessons. At sixteen I was engaged to be married to Freddy Spencer Chapman who was then seventeen. From the time he was fourteen and I thirteen we had been friends during those holidays from Sedbergh which he spent with his guardian, the rector of the neighbouring parish of Runnington. He called me 'Bee'. We had a gloriously happy time exploring, bird-watching, playing tennis and talking of our teenage ideals and problems, for if I had parent trouble he had the worse problem of being an orphan. But this friendship, of which my parents thoroughly approved, was firmly stopped by his guardians, in consultation with my parents, when they found out about the 'engagement'. Of course, neither of us was ready for a mature relationship.[4] Anyway, although I think my mother would have liked me to be married, especially to Freddy, all of whose books she read later with great interest, my father instilled into me that it was my duty never to marry but to look after my mother after he died. I remember him saying once, 'Your father should be sufficient for you.'(!) This responsibility I fulfilled, with Vi Bonsey's and her sister's help latterly, until my mother died at ninety. Although naturally to some extent the assignment was a burden, it seemed to me a perfectly normal and acceptable commitment on the personality level. It never touched the depths of Miss R.'s continuous assault over those six crucial years of adolescence. Towards the end she reached beyond the personality into my soul. For a time I felt that this incarnation had been wasted and that I was utterly damned.

To return to the final rejection of music and the choice of academic work : my father, as a Classics teacher, had been horrified by the late date of starting Latin at Gardenhurst. Personally I think this was a good thing, for it came to me at fifteen as

4 For the full story, see Ralph Barker : *One Man's Jungle: A Biography of F. Spencer Chapman D.S.O.*, Chatto and Windus, 1975, pp. 35–39.

fresh and exciting. In the holidays he coached me himself, and I pleased him by getting a distinction in School Certificate after only two years of study. (I pleased *myself* by a distinction in my own chosen subject of Geography which I had loved from P.N.E.U. days.)

At seventeen I went for two years, again as a boarder, into the sixth form at Redland High School, Bristol, where they allowed me to use the Higher Certificate course to prepare for London Intermediate in four subjects: Latin, Geography, English, and French. Redland was memorable chiefly for the excellent quality of the teaching and for the joy of finding my 'brainy' interests to be perfectly average—nothing to be ashamed of. On the human side it was memorable for my friendship with Phoebe Ashburner (now Carter), another clergyman's daughter, with whom, for the first time, except to some extent with Freddy, I could share the inner world of mystical imagination and poetry. We have had an extraordinarily 'plannish' relationship since then, meeting only at rare intervals but—when we do—very meaningfully; and now she helps me with my books. At the boarding-house we both endured similar 'pi-jaws' to those at Gardenhurst on 'character'. On one of my reports was the label from the boarding-house mistress: 'Self-centred'. Doubtless true, but no wonder! I was trying far too hard to 'be good'.

* *

CHAPTER 2

Early Training and Experience

Student days—Bunny

In 1927 at nineteen I was accepted for the three-year London External Honours course in Geography at the University College of the South West (as it was then.) When asked to play the game of remembering the happiest period of my life, I always go back to Exeter; it was like waking to a daylight world of sanity after a bad dream. Of course I still worried about my parents, especially in vacations. Once my father visited me in term-time, absolutely at the end of his tether; he said that he wished they could separate but such a solution was impossible both financially and because he was a clergyman. (He sometimes did escape from the house for a week or so to avoid the rows.) Personally, I would have preferred separation; I have often thought there is less strain on the children. But the home problem was put in proportion as life in Devon became full and joyous. We were surrounded with freedom and beauty. It was enough to live. We canoed on the river, swam in the sea, walked along the cliffs and on the moor. I was resident in Hall, and our set soon established itself in college activities. As for me, in a literary phase, I first wrote for, then edited, the college magazine. I even joined a choir and loved singing. Gone were the exaggerated religious and moral pressures of school about 'character'. The pettiness and intensity of an all-female community faded; it was fun to get to know men. We played and laughed in guiltless joy; in fact some of us reacted by being quite childish. So I have always understood first-year students who ran wild after the pressures of school, and I have not taken their tutors' anxiety too seriously.

We also worked hard. Professor W. Stanley Lewis ('Uncle Stan' as we called him), a close friend of Professor Fleure, was a most imaginative Geographer, the first of many people to inspire me. 'Don't just sit and swot', he would say, strolling into the old army hut (dating from the First World War) that was our domain; 'Talk, discuss, explore, *live* it!' And we did. I shall always remember the wonder of my first field course, when what we had studied came alive in reality. After his first wife died, Stanley Lewis married Eve Macaulay, a beautiful Irish lecturer at the college. There is a nice story about Eve: when she gave some voluntary lectures at the local prison, one prisoner said to her, 'Don't you worry, Miss. 'Tisn't what you says, 'tis what you looks like!' It was through Eve that later on I was to be led to psychological and eventually also to psychic interests.

Teaching would never have been my own choice of career, although my father advocated it for security reasons. (At seventeen my choice had been poultry farming—firmly suppressed!) But it was essential to be independent financially, and in those days, when we applied for the four-year Board of Education grant, we literally had to 'swear' to teach. So, after finals in 1930 I put in a year in the Education Department for the Cambridge Teachers' Diploma, combined with two terms of unpaid part-time teaching at Truro Training College and Truro Boys' School, which counted as my own teaching practice. The weekly trip to Cornwall made life very pleasant; when supervising the students' teaching practice I might spend half a day—a huge pasty tucked under my arm for sustenance—at tiny isolated schools with names such as 'Five Lanes' End', or sneaking a swim at Feoch on the Fal. But it was also exceedingly arduous since I had registered at the same time for the London M.A. to be completed in 1932. Then came a financial crisis: in 1931 my grant expired; there was no money with which to complete the M.A., and at that time students were required to study in vacations and not to take paid outside work. My grandfather, who had paid for my schooling, had been forced to stop all allowances owing to the financial state of Kelway's Nurseries, so my parents were living on my father's stipend of less than £300 a year. Ought I to take a teaching post and give up research? It was a major turning point. My mother's cousin Arthur Toms (brother of James), a master at Clifton College, was consulted. 'Put everything you've got on her *now*,' he advised. My parents had nothing to put, but my father

took the problem to a parishioner who very kindly gave £100—
a good deal in those days—and Stanley Lewis managed to get
me some part-time work in the Geography Department to 'earn
my keep'. So, thanks to them, I made it.

From 1932 to 1934 I was appointed as Assistant Lecturer in
the Department, though there was no security of tenure, and
hence no pension scheme. In the second year the Principal,
John Murray, advised me to 'leave the nest' and try other parts
of the country. Was I, he suggested, afraid of responsibility?
That struck home. (One assistant lecturer remained happily in
that status for thirteen years without promotion, so pleasant
and leisurely was university teaching in Devon in the thirties.
How very different it was from the competitive rat-race for promotion—the 'publish or get out' attitude—of universities today!
Two extremes?)

Not that we failed to publish, but we did so when ready;
there was no great pressure, no form to fill in annually. My own
research was in Rural Settlement[1] which involved cycling over
Somerset and Devon as well as map-work in local museums. At
this stage I was in love with the earth and the landscape, feeling
that in some way I was giving back, in joy and recognition,
what the South-west had given to me.

It was also a period of foreign travel—essential for a Geographer. In spite of our low salaries, going abroad was then
relatively inexpensive. My first trip was to Czechoslovakia in 1930
while we were waiting for the results of finals. Through the
N.U.S. a party of students, half Geographers and half Historians,
organized a tour by way of Holland, Leipzig, and Prague right
into the Tatra mountains, returning via Bavaria and the Rhine
valley—all for £10 per head. Of course we 'slept rough', some
of us on luggage racks in the third-class compartments, and we
were well supplied with Keating's powder, but I shall never forget the wonder of the experience.

Later, with my colleague in the Geography Department, Ethel
Patterson, I explored Belgium, Luxemburg, North-east France,

[1] 'Rural Settlement in Somerset', *Geography*, June 1935. (An abstract of
my M.A. thesis, a paper on which had been read by Professor Lewis at a
meeting of the International Commission on Rural Settlement in Paris.)
'Rural Settlement in North West Devon, England', *Economic Geography*,
1935. (An American publication.)

Paris, and Chartres. Subsequently, when at Lincoln, a colleague and I went with the Le Play Society (which arranged opportunities for visiting areas where tourists did not usually go) to the Basque country, and again to Luxemburg, this time on a field course with Lincoln and Homerton students. It was a grand feeling when I was able to pay for my parents, taking them on a (more civilized) cruise to Madeira, Morocco, and Lisbon, again for not much more than the cost of the Czech trip. My father was so popular on board that the following year the firm offered him and my mother a free cruise with a first-class cabin to the Baltic Ports, provided that he acted as Chaplain, which he was only too glad to do. (This was on that happy ship the *Vandyke*, later to be sunk during the war.) Those were the days! The intensive travel period in my twenties, accompanied by several field courses and survey work in Britain, came at the right time, and was supremely satisfying.

Lincoln and Oxford

The Principal's advice to move was sound. In 1934 I started applying for jobs. It was a period of acute unemployment in the teaching profession; some people applied for sixty or seventy jobs before getting one. However, I was lucky. In view of the three post-graduate years working with students, and especially the experience at Truro Training College before that, I was interviewed both at Bingley and at Lincoln Training Colleges. At Lincoln they appointed me as Lecturer in Geography and Librarian (not a separate post in the small colleges of that period, nor did it seem to matter that I 'did' the Library by the light of nature and with a little help from my friend the Librarian at Exeter University College). Further, since Lincoln was a Church college, every member of staff was required to take a share in 'Scripture Method' and to supervise the students' lessons in Religious Knowledge. At first I refused, on principle. But after my father had put me through an intensive course on the whole Bible in one vacation, I agreed to try! The Principal, Miss Constance Stewart, inspired us and gave us freedom. I was young, inexperienced, but always ready for new ideas. 'Those who ask, get,' said Miss Stewart, so I tried out experiments in teaching Geography, and asked for plenty of books and equipment. In view of the present emphasis on visual and auditory aids, it may seem strange that at the time, and at least in our area, films were practically unheard of. We obtained a 16 mm projector for silent films and toured the local schools, training the students to use films in their lessons, if they could find a bare white wall, for we had no screen. I was never very practical with machinery, and I well remember running the wretched thing for a student's lesson, feeling an increasingly snaky sensation as the reel of used film wound itself round my ankles! These early efforts attracted the attention of an inspector who came to watch me give a film lesson to a very bright class of ten plus, whom I had taught before, so thought I knew their mental range. But the headmaster had put them so much on their mettle that they saw infinitely more in the film than I did. It was difficult to know who was teaching whom, and the lesson ended in chaos. However, it was all good fun.

During the five years I spent at Lincoln, the educational aspect —especially child guidance—began to fascinate me.[2] Much against the advice of some of my Geography friends (for I was beginning to make a corner in Rural Settlement) I decided to give up Geography and move to Educational Psychology. Further, having been at a provincial university college, I wanted to experience life in one of the older universities, and I knew that it would please my father if I chose his own. The post at Lincoln had been residential, light duties providing free board and lodging. In five years I easily saved enough to finance myself for two years of research and further study (grants were more difficult to obtain than nowadays, especially for post-graduate work). So in 1939 I went to Oxford, at first to take a B.Litt. in Educational Psychology, but soon this was changed to the two-year course for the D.Phil. My tutor was Dr. Basil Yeaxlee who helped me very much both personally and academically. He supervised my thesis on *The Moral Development of Children and Adolescents.* (Of course I *would* choose that subject, but I needed to

[2] Shown by the trend in investigations. (Note that this was before the reorganization of elementary education into primary and secondary modern schools.) 'An Enquiry into the Likes and Dislikes of Elementary School Children in Geography', *Geography*, June 1939. 'Elementary School Children and Ideas of God', *Religion in Education*, April 1939. 'The Preferences of Elementary School Children in Scripture', *Religion in Education*, June 1939.

work it out of my system.)[3] I was based on the Oxford Department of Education where he lectured, but not confined to it. After the departmentalized syllabus of a provincial university, the Oxford system of free access to almost any course going seemed a marvellous opportunity. I attended courses at the Institute of Experimental Psychology, and others in Ethics and Philosophy. We were fortunate in that year of the 'phoney war' to have many scholars from the Continent and elsewhere, some waiting for a visa to go on to America. It was a privilege to be included in a small seminar taken by Koffka on Kohler's *Gestalt Psychology*. Radhakrishnan started a course on Eastern Philosophy in a tiny room at Oriel which soon became packed with people sitting on the floor. As the great shadow spread over the world, knowledge and wisdom became unutterably precious.

Exeter during the war

Now the war began in earnest. We were granted extension 'for the duration'. I broke off to go home as assistant billeting officer, since the problems of evacuees in our village were becoming acute. For nearly a year I worked harder physically than ever before, also growing vegetables (to my mother's delight and my father's sorrow at a broken career). We had nineteen evacuees altogether at the vicarage, and they had to be fed; I certainly learned a great deal about children which was a direct help to the research.

In early 1941 Eve Lewis wrote from Exeter: what on earth did I think I was doing at home looking after evacuees and growing vegetables? In true Irish fashion she made various unflattering remarks about race-horses trying to be ineffectual carthorses. Many staff were called up; they were desperate. So in April I returned to Exeter to replace a man leaving for the Admiralty—and this time was warmly welcomed back by Principal John Murray.

---

[3] Apart from a couple of articles in *Home and School*, 1951, this thesis was never published, though it was often on loan to those doing similar research. I think I couldn't face the labour of re-writing it for publication after passing on to other interests, and I felt a little guilty! So it was a great bonus when William Kay in his *Moral Development: A Psychological Study of Moral Growth from Childhood to Adolescence* (Allen and Unwin, 1968) did it more than justice, placing it in its—by then—historical setting. I am very grateful to him.

Throughout the rest of the war I worked as Lecturer in the Geography Department, with Stanley Lewis (who had to spend a great deal of his time running the Observer Corps) and Ethel Patterson (then part-time as she had a child). In view of this staffing situation, it was not easy to cover the whole syllabus, but we managed. Our students were mostly women, with a sprinkling of men unfit for service. We had our 'blitz'—one of the Baedeker raids—when the city burned for three days because they could get no water to it. Yet although we took our full share in civil defence jobs, I remember the period mainly for its constructive aspects which, in some strange way, the war seemed to stimulate.

One of these was making a survey of the South-west Peninsula for the Ministry of Town and Country Planning. Several members of the college staff took part. My share was the section on population.[4] The problem of depopulation, especially in the less accessible parts of West Devon and North Cornwall, was becoming serious. Able-bodied young people were emigrating to that 'coffin-shaped area' (as it appeared on the map) of the industrial Midlands—where I was so soon to go myself. We were concerned to provide data so that the Ministry could help existing communities to become viable by introducing some form of industry. After the book was published, I really felt I had given all I could in love to my homeland. Some earlier settlement research was also written up.[5]

Psychological analysis and child guidance

My interest was now mainly in psychology and in training for psychotherapy. At the Exeter Child Guidance Clinic Eve Lewis was working as psychologist. Many psychiatrists from Europe were coming to England, and we were fortunate to have the services, for a short time, of Dr. S. H. Foulkes (later of the Institute of Group Analysis). It was at Exeter that he started experimenting with groups, working with Eve. As well as attending one of these groups, in 1942 I started personal analysis with him (then at the reduced fee of 7s. 6d. ($37\frac{1}{2}$p) per hour!) When

4 'The Distribution, Trends and Local Movements of Population in Devon and Cornwall', part of *Devon and Cornwall: A Preliminary Survey*, Wheaton, Exeter, 1947.
5 'Dispersion and Agglomeration of Rural Settlement in Somerset', *Geography*, March 1944.

he left us for Northfield, I had a year's formal and very sound Freudian analysis with Miss Helen Sheehan-Dare, a member of the Institute of Psycho-Analysis, who was then living in Exeter. Although I am mainly a Jungian, I shall always be glad of that Freudian year; with her I plumbed some of the depths of the infantile material connected with my mother. When she left, after a rather frightening gap I went on to Dr. Hardy Gaussen with whom I remained, off and on, until 1947. (He is a Jungian and he also has insight into Steiner and the deeper spiritual issues which were to help me so much in future years.) At this time I was working mainly on my relationship with men. My father was ill and slowly dying. Towards the end of the war I had a very important love affair which taught me a great deal and which I shall never cease to value; yet in many ways it was 'in trust' and (rightly) had to be given up. At the same time the 'Mary' aspect in me was beginning to emerge. All this I worked through with Dr. Gaussen's constructive care.

Meanwhile, in every available spare moment I worked and studied at the Child Guidance Clinic. During the war it was more like a first-aid station, so that I gained experience of every aspect of the work. Eve taught me psychological testing and ascertainment, but trained me particularly in play therapy where she was very skilled. She herself, I believe, had been a pupil of Flugel, yet she had both Jungian and Freudian training and experience.[6] Although we had many psychiatrists, we lacked social workers, so that there was plenty to do on that side. In this way I had a wide, realistic, though (compared with modern training courses) informal, part-time training for three years. It is good to work from child therapy towards adult therapy, for it is the 'damaged child' in the adult who needs care. Dr. Gaussen advised me in one or two adult cases. By 1945 the time had come to apply what I had learned to students.

Plans for student counselling

I had already met Mr. J. W. Tibble—Billy as we called him —casually and typically silently (he was a man of few words

[6] Her own research had been in the same field as mine, in fact was one of the reasons leading to my choice of subject. See Eve Macaulay and Stanley H. Watkins: 'An Investigation into the Development of the Moral Conceptions of Children', *Forum of Education*, 1926, Nos. 1 and 2.

unless speaking of essentials) in the common room and at lunch.
He was then Senior Lecturer in the Department of Education at
the college. I remember that we once travelled back to Exeter
from Newton Abbot by train together; he had been on teaching
practice supervision, I on the survey. We never exchanged a
word, yet we related.

One night we both happened to be on the rota for firewatch-
ing in the college buildings. For once there was no alert. Suddenly we talked, and continued the whole night through : he of
his plans for the education of teachers, I of my ideas for building
a counselling service for students. I had been very aware of the
waste of energy which could have gone into their studies and
their living; both psychological help with personal problems and
educational guidance were needed. Concerning the latter, I remember when I returned to Exeter in 1941 being asked to coach
a fourth-year student who had failed finals. I found that she had
not yet mastered some of the elementary learning skills necessary
in the first year.

'I wish you would teach the first-years this,' she said when
we had worked through the normal know-how of library use,
summarizing articles, planning of study, and so on.

'I wouldn't dare. They'd be insulted.'

She assured me they would not. So for the first two terms of
each first-year group I experimented with a course ostensibly
labelled 'Human Geography', partly to discuss a basic overall
view of the subject and its philosophy, but mainly to pool study
skills in a group setting where, by comparing notes, they taught
each other. In some departments of universities there is still a
need for such guidance, especially for those students who have
not been trained in self-education in school sixth forms.

Anyway, after that night's talk, Billy and I determined to put
our ideas into practice—somehow—sometime—somewhere.

The first move came in 1945 when the man I had replaced
returned from the Admiralty. Fortunately at the same time a
vacancy occurred in the Education Department when Patrick
Meredith went to Leeds, and I was able to transfer to the post of
Lecturer in Education with Geography Method. For a year Billy
and I worked closely with students in teacher-training, both the
young post-graduates and the mature ex-service men who were

beginning to return in increasing numbers and who needed a very different approach. Implicitly he was training me. We experimented with group-work, and I did a little tentative individual counselling.

Then in 1946 Billy was appointed to the Chair at University College, Leicester, from which he was to do such radical and widespread work in the field of teacher education during the next twenty years. For another year I stayed on at Exeter, then returned to Oxford—a very different Oxford after the war—to complete my D.Phil. In 1948 Billy advertised for a Lecturer in Educational Psychology and Geography Method. Although there was some stiff competition I was glad that I managed to get the post without his having to open his mouth during the interview! One of the most difficult questions to answer came from the Principal, Mr. F. L. Attenborough: why had I chosen to leave a university college which was twenty years older and (at that time) twice the size of the Leicester college? Why indeed?

It certainly had been a wrench. There would have been a promising future academically, and environmentally more seductive conditions. We knew that I should be pioneering in something I was not appointed to do, and that the East Midlands would be hard—'sodden and unkind'. Before he left, one glorious evening on our way back from supervising teaching practice at Torquay, Billy had driven me to the top of the Haldon Hills from which one can see over half Devon, to Exmoor and Dartmoor.

'All the kingdoms of the world ... To give up all *this* for an idea?'

'Yes, oh yes.'

I had soaked up enough beauty and joy to last a lifetime. It felt right to go. North and east once more. Even then I was very aware that the main decisions are taken by our deeper selves and that all we have to do is to say 'Yes'. So I gave up 'Bunny' and became my 'Mary' self. But I did not realize then that the exile would last for nearly thirty years.

My father died in February 1948, and in July my mother and I moved to the house which Billy and Anne Tibble had just vacated in Oadby, near Leicester. A word about Anne. It had not been easy either for her or her children to leave their beautiful old house at Topsham for the little surburban 'semi' which was all they could get in 1946, and which Anne called 'Box'. In 1948 they moved into a larger house with an extensive garden, rented from the university, and we bought 'Box'. At Leicester Anne was a tower of strength to us all in the tiny but rapidly growing new Department of Education. It is not for me to write of her books, her support of young writers, and her understanding friendship with all the overseas students, especially the Sudanese.[7] I can ony add my own tribute which perhaps is best shown in one of those colourful premonitory dreams, before leaving Exeter. In this dream, all the difficulties of Leicester appeared in exaggerated detail, but, throughout them all, Anne fed me steadily with poached eggs! I shall always value her stimulating, critical, yet constructive and *believing* support. When I first came to Leicester, after my father's death, the ending of the love affair, leaving my analyst, and having the responsibility of my ageing mother now living with me, I felt ill and only 'half there'. But it was Anne who told me that Billy had said to her, 'I would rather have half of Mary than the whole of some people'. That helped, and steadily life came back.

Retrospect

Reading through these two chapters, now that I have written them, I can see how thoroughly—though largely unconsciously—I had been prepared by the age of forty for the work I was to do. The home and school situations; the five years of personal analysis, with the training in child guidance; the knowledge of student life in two universities and two training colleges; the love experience; the practice in research and writing : all these and many other things could be 'fed in'. Further, I have always believed that the best way to outgrow a phase or a need is to live it through fully. The fulfilment of a country upbringing in areas of great natural beauty freed me to be able to settle and work whole-heartedly in an industrial Midland city. The itch for outer travel and exploration had been satisfied, so that I could turn inwards to exploration of the psyche.

One lack worried me : that of no experience of marriage and children. With a family, however, it is very doubtful if I could

[7] See Anne Tibble: *One Woman's Story*, Peter Owen, 1976.

have carried the job through. And the very fact that I saw my single status in the light of a possible disqualification for the work is surely in itself a sign that I would not have made a very suitable wife! I would have welcomed the mutual love and companionship, but not the ties, nor the never-ending household chores, for I am not domesticated. As for maternal needs, in the early days I thought of all my writings as my 'children'—a different father inspiring each! Later, I felt more like the old woman in the shoe, since I have taken nearly 1,000 clients. (Here, of course, it is important to be as objective and unidentified as possible, but in order to achieve objectivity one's natural feelings must first be made fully conscious and accepted.) In practice I never had any complaints; perhaps for student counselling I was sufficiently experienced. Even marriage problems are basically the reflections of the two personalities in close relationship. Only P. W. Martin, with whom I worked in some group research on Jungian archetypes, once said, 'The trouble is that you are "Miss" not "Mrs.".' Yet there is the other side of the coin: single status can be a challenge in strengthening the inner 'marriage' of the *Logos* and *Eros* principles within the Self, a balance which is hard to achieve and even harder to keep. And being single need not stop one loving; ever since the age of seven (when the first impact broke in on me with startling wonder) I had rarely ceased to be in love with someone or something. 'That,' Billy once told me, 'is what keeps you sweet.'

I mention this problem in detail because I have never seen it dealt with openly, yet I know that many counsellors are single, separated, or divorced, and not all have children. I would submit that such a situation is not *necessarily* a disadvantage, in fact it *can* provide other lessons; as always in therapeutic work everything depends on how we use the situation. Later on, deeper insights were to throw more light on the issue (see p. 204).

For those whose language is that of symbolism, in conclusion I would like to tell of an integrating image—a potential mandala —which has always accompanied me, especially during my later periods of personal analysis (1956 to 1958 and 1961 to 1962) with a Jungian analyst, Dr. Lola Paulsen. The image links Geography with Psychology, outer places with inner experience. It takes the form of a St. Andrew's cross over Britain, the diag-

onal lines running north-west to south-east and south-west to
north-east, crossing at Oxford. I was conceived at Oxford, at the
Mitre hotel, during my parents' honeymoon. I have returned to
Oxford twice, at changing points in my life. It will be interesting
to see whether I shall die in or near there. In personal free
association, the west symbolizes to me the feminine principle, the
east the masculine. The north stands for the hard, cold, and
testing; the south for the soft, warm, and nourishing. So the
south-west was the gentle, beautiful, feminine nursery, fruitful
and feeding, yet potentially seductive and reductive; I had to
keep leaving it for the north-east (Lincoln and Leicester) where
all I had been given was to be put into practice. The south-east
represents to me male values in their positive, dynamic aspect:
inspiring and stimulating; I visit many friends and groups in
London and the south-east to get recharged. The north-west still
remains partially a mystery; I have never lived there, only visited.
Just as Leicester felt 'thick' for many years, so the north-west
feels 'thin'—transparent to the spirit—symbolized by Iona. Perhaps it signifies the aspect described in Part IV of this book
which I am developing in older age.

Others have told me that they have experienced variations of
this powerful symbol with, of course, their own personal interpretations. At least it gives the possibility of a mandala of wholeness to be completed one day.

Part II: Pioneering in Student Counselling

CHAPTER 3

The First Seven Years: 1948 to 1955

Now that the value of counselling in universities and other colleges of higher education is so widely recognized, student counsellors having a professional association of their own,[1] it is difficult to realize how hard were the early days. College authorities were not then aware of the possibilities. There were no posts for which to apply. Counselling and any allied personality work had to be introduced *sub rosa* and steadily proved by results.

Building the Psychological Advisory Service
  With Professor Tibble's full backing and approval, I began in a small way within our Post-graduate Department of Education to offer opportunity for personal counselling, over and above my normal lecture schedule. This was relatively easy. The rub came when we made it available also to those undergraduates who were still under the system of the Ministry of Education four-year grant, and for whom we had some responsibility. Although a few members of staff in the academic departments were sympathetic, the majority were unconcerned or even hostile. Any advisory function was seen to be the job of the 'moral tutor'; yet although some of these tutors were most human and caring, a good many avoided personal contact and a few were afraid of it. I sometimes felt that, despite the University College's motto: *Ut Vitam Habeant,* there was a prevalent attitude that universities (and not only Leicester) did not exist to help students to 'have life' and 'have it more abundantly'. They existed to train *minds.* (Fair enough, but one or two lecturers did not

[1] The Association for Student Counselling was established in 1970.

seem to be aware even of the 'minds' before them, addressing a point on the wall!) It is only just, however, to say that over the last thirty years the attitude has changed considerably. As for the students, they were far more open, though understandably in the initial stages they were wary of anyone resembling a 'head shrinker'.

Politically, it could not have been a worse time to stress values other than the purely academic. The University College was struggling towards university status, to be achieved in 1957. The Department of Education and the School of Social Studies were considered, by some, to be too 'professional' in outlook—their courses being 'applied' rather than 'pure'—and hence perhaps better relegated to a technical institution. There was no department even of academic psychology until 1960, and anything verging on the practical application of psychodynamic theory was not then acceptable, neither was it (by most) understood. After the more open attitudes at Exeter, where at least my *academic* status had been unquestioned, all this was at first quite a test; but I learned to 'sit loose' to it and bide my time.

It was even harder, in those days, to obtain recognition from the medical profession, especially for those of us who were psychologically and educationally but not medically qualified, and hence were technically 'lay' practitioners. I learned that terms such as 'treatment', 'psychotherapy', 'diagnosis', and 'patient' were the prerogative of doctors and must never find their way into letters or reports. Used to the easy give-and-take with doctors at the Exeter Child Guidance Clinic, I once wrote a confidential report to a general practitioner about his patient, using a few (to me) innocuous terms such as 'mother-fixation', only to be told later by a mutal acquaintance that my letter had been considered 'obscene'! By some I was referred to as a quack, and one elderly doctor went as far as to say to a patient of his (and later of mine), 'Don't go near that woman, it's just witchcraft.' So I learned to write harmless little notes to the G.P.s, asking whether they minded their patients coming 'for a few talks'. At that period, 'welfare work' would have been a more acceptable term. But again, it is only fair to say that in later years this attitude has changed very markedly.

The fact that I had a professional association behind me cut no ice at all at first, although in due course it was fully recognized.[2] Naturally, as a non-medical member of this association, I was very careful to abide by our regulations which rightly demanded that we should work closely with the client's doctor, for 'medical coverage'. However, in view of the difficulties with most G.P.s, it was paramount to have contact with an understanding psychiatrist and the resources of a mental hospital behind him. Here we were fortunate to obtain the services of Dr. C. E. H. Turner of the Towers Hospital, Leicester, who agreed to be our consultant psychiatrist right from the start. He visited monthly under the National Health scheme, interviewing and then discussing with me the more difficult cases, occasionally taking one or two on himself, or into hospital in the rare cases when this was necessary. He also advised me on the careful wording of reports and letters. So we came to call our work 'The Psychological Advisory Service'. 'Counselling' was then 'one of those American terms', not fully understood. At that time it would have been unwise to use it. Of course, as any modern counsellor will know, straight advice was rarely used except where indicated in a few 'management' cases. But this title was right for the period. Dr. Turner was a great friend in need. In later years, as I gained in experience, he visited only on request; yet altogether he stood by us for nineteen years, until I joined the doctors in the University Student Health Service in 1967, and I cannot thank him enough.

During the first few years I carried on the teaching work for which I had been appointed and kept as quiet as possible about the rest. At first, counselling had to be done in a tiny room possessing only two hard chairs which I shared with a colleague. However, as we were then a small and self-contained department, the authorities kept moving us; soon I was given a very pleasant larger room all to myself in an extension of the old building which (because it used to be a mental asylum) we called the 'luniversity'. This room was big enough to contain a couch, and there is a nice story about this. After my own analysis and

[2] In 1953 I was elected a full member of the (then) Provisional Association of Professional Psychotherapists (now the British Association of Psychotherapists.) I served on their executive committee from 1954 to 1961. My membership of the British Psychological Society from 1946 onwards was more 'respectable', but in fact was far less relevant for the work in question.

training at Exeter (where a couch was a normal item of furniture) neither I nor Billy thought there would be any problem when I asked him to requisition one for the use of those students (or staff—who were now beginning to use the Service) if they needed to relax. We were surprised by the resulting alarm. The Principal, Mr. F. L. Attenborough, finally said, 'Well, I don't want the idea to spread, but I *suppose* it's all right with Dr. Swainson?' I wasn't quite sure how to take that one! Anyway, the couch arrived, and by that time it was I who needed to relax.

The only disadvantage of this lovely room was that it opened off the main hall where students congregated round the notice boards, so that when I hung an ENGAGED notice on the door handle, people would watch to see who came out. Privacy of access is essential for a counsellor's room, and in 1955, when the transfer to the Institute of Education took place, I moved to a quiet and beautiful room in the Tibbles' private house. After my mother left me for an old people's home in 1958, I saw clients in my own house at Oadby until I retired in 1972—a relatively informal arrangement about which I never had any complaints, even though it was four miles from the university site. (Here, in a south-facing room, in the summer we looked out on the sunlit garden; in the winter sat either side of a coal or wood fire. This focus on the *third* aspect, symbolized by living sunlight and fire, is especially significant in Jungian therapy.)

Nowadays, many student counsellors have a suite of rooms and a receptionist/secretary. Right to the end I was never able to obtain clerical assistance except for the usual help with material for teaching, as did the other lecturers. All the confidential records, letters, and annual reports I typed myself, or paid privately at first for a part-time confidential secretary (much later I was able to charge up some of this to expenses). To obtain equipment (typewriter, duplicator, filing cabinet, and cupboard) was relatively easy, but not the clerical personnel to use them. However, this was the understandable price to pay for the opportunity to do unofficial pioneering, and I accepted it accordingly. I know that many other counsellors are still in a similar situation.

Reactions to the growing Service were by no means all negative. Some university departments valued it, notably the School of Social Studies, where I did a certain amount of teaching work. I gave courses also at Vaughan College, the University Adult Education Centre, and we had a few clients from there. We were welcomed also by those local authority colleges concerned with professional training. In 1951–2 the City of Leicester Training College (later College of Education) started to refer students—and here I would like to thank my friend Kathleen Douet who co-operated so fully throughout her time there as Senior (later Principal) Lecturer in Education. In the next few years three other City of Leicester colleges came into the scheme: in 1953–4 the School of Speech Therapy, followed in 1954–5 by the College of Art School of Teacher Training, and the Domestic Science College. (The last-named college sent relatively few clients; a member of their staff told me that the students 'worked it out in the pastry'!) Another local college to join, later in 1962–3, was the National College for the Training of Youth Leaders, founded in 1960. There were also a few staff from these various colleges, and some in-service teachers.

The Service had expanded spontaneously as the demand arose. This, I felt, was a natural and healthy process in the early stages, but without Billy Tibble's faith and steady support it would have been impossible. Increasingly it became valued as a background to courses in training teachers and workers in kindred 'helping' professions. For we all found that the best time for personality work was during the formative years of training, before any potentially neurotic patterns became fixed in middle life.

Application for official recognition

By 1955 I had taken over 150 clients. After a preliminary consultation with Billy, I felt in a strong enough position to ask the Principal, Mr. C. H. (later Sir Charles) Wilson, for official recognition of the Psychological Advisory Service. This caused a big storm in Senate which fell on Billy's head. Everything came out. I had made the usual mistakes, often not going about things the best way, learning by experience; but the chief error was to publish an article with an unfortunate title[3] which (in all innocence—I must have been naïve) I thought would be liked! Of

[3] 'Building a University Psychological Service: The First Three Years', *Mental Health*, Winter 1951. Summarized in *Education Today*, April 1952.

course I was told that I had *not* been appointed to build a 'University Psychological Service'. True.

After Mr. Wilson had been appointed in 1952, he used to sit in the senior common room, ready to *listen*—giving us all an opportunity to talk to him—something that was immensely appreciated. So I had already told him roughly what I was up to. When in 1955 I asked for recognition, he discussed with the authorities at the London School of Economics (where he had previously taught) the value of the psychiatric service which had been started there three years earlier by Dr. John Read. In our own case, Billy Tibble had emphasized to him the use of my work *as an intrinsic part of teacher training*, so finally Mr. Wilson felt prepared to allow me to continue provided that I restricted the Service to those in professional courses, and left the undergraduates alone, unless they should be specifically referred by the head of department concerned.[4]

In view of the increasing connection with other colleges in the area, the solution was clearly to move me to the Institute of Education. The McNair Report on the Training of Teachers had provided for the setting up of these institutes catering for the needs of teachers both in training and in service. The University College had agreed in 1948 to set up such an institute, for which Professor Tibble was responsible, though suitable premises were not ready until 1950. In September 1955 the Psychological Advisory Service was recognized as one of the many educational services provided for the constituent colleges of the Leicester Institute of Education, including of course the University College Post-graduate Department. From my point of view the move could not have been better. It gave an ideal setting for the organically growing pattern of need, so that I was very grateful to Mr. Wilson. My great regret was that so much of the storm caused by my request should have fallen on Billy. However, one of the many things he had taught us was that we inevitably hurt one another, and that this was to be accepted. 'Children suffer,' he used to say, 'that students may learn; students suffer that we may learn.' And also the other way

---

[4] Later on, the Students' Union kept asking for a psychiatric or counselling service, finally fulfilled by the Student Health Service from 1967 onwards.

round. It had taken me many years to get over my mother's description (told to me at the age of eight) of how much she suffered at my birth. And now, in order to be true to what I felt (as far as I could see then) to be my life-task, I had been a partly unwitting source of severe trouble to the very man who had given the Service life. Yet I knew inwardly that the Service must be openly established. At the time Billy said very little to me about the repercussions on himself. It was only later that I felt a sense of profound sorrow and even some guilt at the inevitability of being me. Yet all this had to be accepted.

Work within the Department of Education

One of the conditions of transfer was that I should continue to fulfil that part of the post-graduate course for which I was appointed; but the course had been changing all the time as the number of students and staff increased and our programme became more diversified, so my share kept changing too. Here is a brief sketch of the history.[5]

To go back to the war : by 1942 the number of students had fallen to seven, so understandably the Board of Education discontinued its recognition, with resultant closure of the department until 1946 when the Ministry (as it had then become) resumed recognition. From 1946, therefore, Professor Tibble had to build a new department from nothing. Two tutors were appointed in 1947 (in which year I came over from Oxford for a few weeks to give a crash course in Educational Psychology to a handful of students) and one or two others were found to give part-time specialist help. Two more full-time tutors—one of them myself—were appointed in 1948, one in 1949, and three in 1950. From then on, steady expansion took place so that a more comprehensive course and greater specialization were increasingly possible. After 1951 a part-time tutor took over from me the Geography Method. Later I was able to share the Educational Psychology courses with a full-time colleague, concentrating myself on Developmental Psychology with Child-studies, and initiating special topic groups (for voluntary choice) on Child Guidance, Vocational Guidance, and 'Psychological Discussion

5 See Jack Simmons: *New University*, Leicester University Press, 1958, pp. 127, 137 and 217.

Groups'—all of which were closely allied to the personality aspect.[6]

This early period, 1948 to 1955, was largely one of experimenting in bringing the values of mental health into the course itself, as contemporary articles show.[7] It was a time of great happiness within our small team of colleagues. Billy provided an atmosphere of freedom to experiment combined with individual responsibility for what we undertook to do. There was a sense of challenge and adventure.

Perhaps this is the place to give a detailed picture of what we were aiming at. The next chapter is a reprint of an article initially requested by Dr. Peggy Volkov, then editor of *The New Era*.[8] After being used at a UNESCO conference, it was quoted fairly fully in Dr. W. D. Wall's *Education and Mental Health* (UNESCO, 1955, pp. 265–9). Peggy had suggested that I should consider fantasy and reality in a teacher's idea of himself. So, sitting in a beach hut in the Isle of Wight during a somewhat chilly holiday in the summer of 1952, I meditated on the subject and wrote this.

[6] From 1950 to 1955, on my weekly free afternoon, I worked as non-medical child therapist at the City of Leicester School Psychological Service, then in charge of Olive Sampson, whom I had known at Exeter. This kept me in touch with the practice, gave great enjoyment in itself, and was useful for student visits. I had also attended an intensive course in vocational guidance at the National Institute of Industrial Psychology in the late 1930s.

[7] 'Psychological Climates and the New Education', *The New Era*, November 1953. 'Group Work and Personality Change', *Education for Teaching*, February 1954.

[8] Reproduced from *The New Era*, December 1952, by kind permission of the present editor.

CHAPTER 4

The Training of Teachers and Their Mental Health

[*A working paper written for the UNESCO conference on the Mental Health of Normal School Children held in Paris in November 1952*]

One of the clearest indices of a teacher's mental health is the quality of his relationship to his idea of himself in the teaching role. A mature relationship implies detachment from fantasies so that whilst remaining at one with himself the teacher can play any role at will. According to the degree of freedom attained he will be able to meet with objective insight the child's idea of him, thus helping the child to liberate himself from his own fantasies.

Let us look first at some instances of immature relationships and later examine the means by which they can be changed.

Immature relationships

Some teachers, although they do not fully realize it, are in bondage to compulsive ideas, and appear to be inwardly driven to play certain roles but to have no insight into the fact that they are driven. We all know the power-seeking dictator, the all-providing mother, the encyclopaedia of knowledge who dares not confess ignorance, the 'successful' teacher whose pupils always excel in examinations, the buffoon who feels uneasy unless he gets a laugh, and so on. Such compulsive patterns create problems which may be perceived at three levels :

(1) *Overt signs and symptoms* which catch the attention of tutor or headmaster. A teacher may show lack of human

57

contact with his pupils, ineffective class control, inability to adjust to modern teaching situations, or excessive reliance on repressive discipline. When children are aggressive he may become frightened or angry, being obviously involved emotionally at the pupils' level so that he regards himself as persecuted or insulted and retaliates in kind. If he depends on the children's approval for his own emotional satisfaction he dare not risk unpopularity; indeed he (or more likely she) may encourage 'pashes' or hero-worship. He cannot 'take' aggression and hatred with equanimity since he is not yet able to discriminate between that difficult behaviour on the part of his pupils which is due to transference from relationships with parents and other teachers (paying off old scores) and that which is due to his own handling of the class. Thus he becomes discouraged and laden with a crippling sense of guilt. In the staff room he may show inability to co-operate on equal terms with colleagues, or to relate sensibly to the authority of the headmaster, finding it impossible to adjust easily to the contrasting roles which a school society demands. During his training he may give evidence of an ambivalent attitude to his tutors, complaining bitterly at any firm external framework of direction, yet objecting that he is given insufficient guidance when provided with freedom and responsibility. In his personal life he may suffer from a variety of neurotic symptoms such as feelings of inferiority, depression, insecurity, or even from psychosomatic conditions such as blushing, speech defects, headaches, minor heart troubles.

(2) *Underlying attitudes which give rise to overt problems.* Usually the teacher is only partly conscious of these and, in the past, most tutors also have been unaware of them. Thus, a teacher's reaction pattern to the child's idea of him may be determined by unconscious identification with his pupil. He has not yet learned to relate *to* the child in himself because he still *is* that child. And, until he can gain insight into this situation, becoming able to accept his own child-self in tolerance and love, he will be unable to relate dispassionately to children. One way in which this kind of difficulty shows itself is in the teacher who sides unconsciously with the very children whom he is reprimanding severely. No wonder that he finds it difficult to understand why he is not the effective disciplinarian he imagines himself to

be! Another way is his relationships with colleagues when, without realizing it, he may transfer to them feeling-patterns which originated in connection with his brothers and sisters. Perfectionism and compulsive rivalry are often due to such a mechanism.

A student teacher is usually unaware of it when he projects the fantasy image of a parent or previous teacher on to a tutor or headmaster, and when his apparently sound reasons for his mixed attitudes to them are in reality the rationalization of emotional needs incidental to the working out of delayed adolescence. On the one hand, he may identify unconsciously with images of parents or teachers and thus be compelled to imitate them, playing to others the 'good' roles which they played to him. (Some teachers even perpetuate a system, with which they consciously disagree, from unconscious motives of resentment and revenge, dealing out to children 'for the good of their souls' the repressive methods from which they suffered themselves. Hence one reason for the extremely slow progress in liberalizing educational techniques.) On the other hand, a teacher who has experienced very repressive authority may be forced equally compulsively to swing right to the opposite extreme, finding himself unable to relate positively to the role of authority at all, since to him the concept is tainted by so unfortunate a fantasy image. (Hence the exaggeration and abuse of modern teaching methods by certain extremists who are, in fact, working out their own problems. 'I will give a child all that I never had' can be a useful pattern of compensation, but it is dangerous unless carried out in full awareness of motive.)

(3) *The basic problem states.* Deeper than the level of specific patterns of identification and transference, and even more disregarded in traditional teacher training, are the relatively few basic problem states which make up the foundations of our behaviour and attitudes. As far as the mental health of teachers is concerned, the most obvious need is for *emotional maturity,* which will manifest itself in the extent to which the young teacher has broken free from family ties and is capable not only of relatively independent living but of behaving satisfactorily as an authority or parent-substitute himself. Many student teachers have not yet emerged from adolescent or even pre-adolescent

attitudes and have little or no insight into their own motives. Again, particularly in the case of university graduates, their growth has often been one-sided, too great an emphasis on intellectual cramming resulting in relative starvation of the practical, artistic, emotional and social life. Such uneven development may cause acute tension within the personality, predisposing the individual to a schizoid attitude and rendering harmonious integration of the personality extremely difficult.

Deeper than the problem of the individual lies that of society. If teachers grow up in a society which is itself somewhat schizoid, where the education of the emotions lags far behind that of the intellect, where individuals are conditioned to a competitive system which enhances undesirable emotional attitudes such as fear, aggression, perfectionism, desire for dominance, and self-centredness, then naturally they find a greater difficulty in leaving the security of family ties and in growing a balanced personality.

The role of the training college and of older colleagues in school in helping young teachers to sort out reality and fantasy

Since the confusion between reality and fantasy in the teacher's mind is seen to be due fundamentally to lack of growth and unbalanced development, the obvious basic need is to provide for that growth and all-round development.

The first approach must be diagnostic: the tutor or older colleague finds out what aspect of the young teacher's personality is still in bondage and studies the best method of release. Then the environment of college or school is so arranged as (1) to activate awareness in the young teacher of his disability as a problem to be tackled, (2) to give him sufficient motivation for tackling it, and (3) to provide facilities for the desired change.

The keynote of the process is this: those insights which we hope the young teacher will use with children must first be experienced practically in relation to himself. Thus, if we want him to understand children's fantasies about himself (tyrant, beast, angel, hero, fool!) in an objective way, we must understand his own fantasies about his tutors and about himself, and help him to understand them and himself in an equally objective way. Again, it has been seen that one of the most common problems with which the young teacher must come to terms is his relationship to his idea of himself as an authority. Let us assume that though intellectually he believes in democratic theories of government, emotionally he has been conditioned by home and school to a large measure of autocratic authority. Being unable to imagine democratic authority *in practice*, he is therefore compelled to perpetuate the autocratic system in the classroom despite his theoretical convictions. It is a revelation to such a student to be in a college in which the community is a co-operative group, where the Principal deliberately abrogates a good deal of authority, and where students study the implications of freedom and responsibility by living them. The establishment of such a college environment is not easy since, to be effective in a dynamic way, it can be planned only to a limited extent; rather must it grow organically, altering its quality with each new member of staff and with each influx of students, and taking several years to mature. But when it is informed throughout by psychological insight and co-operative understanding, the emotional atmosphere of college or school is the chief factor in the teacher's psychological release and growth.

Methods employed in training establishments at present

(1) *Initial 'shock treatment'*. To turn to more specific techniques, some colleges and departments of education organize a short introductory period at the beginning of the course in which as many of the new aims and attitudes as are considered suitable at this stage are presented to the students both by word and by situation. The aim is to challenge students' attitudes both to the acquisition of knowledge and to themselves right from the start. Fruitful themes of study during these periods have been: 'Our changing pattern within and without' and 'A job-analysis of teaching'. Graduate students who for the past three years have imagined that only the intellect is valued by 'the powers that be' are faced now with a different set of values.

(2) *Organization of the main course*. Courses are planned deliberately so as to challenge automatic assumptions and to put the student in the position of having to do something about these matters if he is to survive (teaching practice can be a most useful test and activator!) At the same time students are helped to take a hopeful and constructive attitude towards their own

development and a belief in the possibility of change. These aims are carried out by means both of *content* and *methods*. Some examples are quoted below:

Content

(a) *Widening of the course* to cater for those aspects of the personality which have been starved. Emotions are released and educated through the medium of arts and crafts, drama, music, gardening—practical and artistic activities of all kinds.

(b) *The course in psychology.* In traditional training establishments psychology courses are largely theoretical. In progressive colleges a certain amount of lecture time is saved by giving essential information, bibliographies, and suggestions for study in the form of duplicated notes. Psychological attitudes can be assimilated at a deeper level by means of films, group discussions, projects, and surveys, visits of observation, and child-studies. The course is broadened to include considerable emphasis on the principles of mental health and given a more dynamic orientation. First, far greater place than in the past is given to social psychology, stressing the development of inter-personal and inter-group relations with particular reference to the family group, the play group, the psychology of the classroom and the school as society. Secondly, the course includes a survey of child and adolescent development with particular reference to emotional growth and to the significance for the healthy development of personality of the early years of infancy. A study of the dynamics of personality should include some outline of the psychology of the unconscious, which is clearly essential to an understanding of problems of behaviour and adjustment. Such a course tacitly leads a student to gain insight into his own attitudes; indeed some students choose to make retrospective studies of themselves or of each other instead of a child-study, thus learning to relate to the child in themselves. The idea is not to make the students morbidly introspective, nor to train them as therapists, but to lead them to become at least to some degree 'transparent to themselves' so that they can begin to free themselves from their own illusions and deal realistically with the fantasies of their charges.

(c) *A psychological service.* Some students need personal psychological advice of a more specific kind than the tutors can give, or, in certain cases, psychiatric treatment. It is essential that such cases be ascertained as early in the course as possible. In the past a good many young teachers went into the schools with neuroses untouched by the training course—neuroses which frequently led to a breakdown during the first few years of teaching or to severe personality problems in later life, with consequent unfortunate repercussions on the children. It is important to realize that sensitive and intelligent neurotics, *provided* that they have tackled their problem, can become of more value to the educational profession than can insensitive mentally robust types, since they are more understanding of children's difficulties. At the student stage a good many problems which cause severe anxiety are relatively slight and yield to help from a psychological adviser. For the more severe cases some colleges and university departments are developing a service run by a trained therapist and/or social worker with the assistance of a visiting psychiatrist.

Methods

As regards mental health, the way in which the course is presented is as important as the content. Educational situations are arranged so as to activate, release, feed, and heal.

(a) *Individual development* is a primary aim. There is the widest possible freedom of individual choice (including research topic) so that rarely do two students carry out an identical programme. Since the issue of freedom and authority is so crucial, students are encouraged to take progressively more responsibility for the course until towards the end they plan it largely themselves. Free criticism of the course and of the tutors is encouraged and at certain times even rebellion is found valuable so that the student can become aware of the processes going on his own psyche, learning to discriminate between rational and emotionally induced criticism. The whole purpose of such techniques

63

is to strengthen the ego in its work of making choices and accepting responsibility in contrast to the older super-ego type of training based largely on introjection of external standards. By this means the individual is helped to develop all his potentialities, to grow from his own roots, to find himself and discover that inner security which frees him from compulsive dependence upon the opinion of society.

(b) *Groups.* No one, of course, can develop himself fully except in relation to a free group; hence, since socialization and individuation go hand in hand, stress is laid on group life as much as on individual development.

(i) *Tutorial discussion groups* in a large college provide the necessary intimate unit in which each student is known well as a person and the shyest feels he is valued. The family set-up provides that feeling of 'belonging' which is so necessary, particularly at the outset, to give a sense of emotional security. In this informal environment students can exchange experience and learn to understand themselves and each other. Sibling problems are worked out in relation to other students, and parent problems in relation to the tutor. A wise tutor can help an immature student to free himself from parent-fixations by playing deliberately whatever form of parental role is required. Throughout the course he may purposely adopt different roles, according to need, ranging from that of the strong leader providing information, advice, inspiration, and encouragement, to the colleague who shares equally in discussion, the guide, the detached observer, the guinea-pig training them by using his own personality as example, or the servant of the group. This change of roles precipitates awareness in the student of the deeper principles involved in the idea of 'teacher'. A great deal depends on the experience and insight of the tutor; it is his function to make sure that the students are gaining awareness of these matters exactly when they become ready for them.

One of the most profitable techniques is that of interpretative discussion in a leaderless group where the tutor acts as experienced observer, his role being to point out what is happening in the group. Used early in the course, this method challenges the assumption on the part of the students that the tutor 'ought' to do the work; indeed that he is failing in his job unless he is constantly giving them secondhand information. Such discussions, with their pregnant silences, have great value in evoking the emergence of the more significant, deeper patterns of feeling, imagination, and intuitive insight.

(ii) *Activity groups* differ from purely discussion groups in that they tend to be more closely structured, the group working actively towards some practical end, e.g. survey or project. In such a co-operative group neurotic traits born of a competitive environment are allowed to die away. Shy students come to feel that they have an essential contribution to make to the group; potential rebels find that the group puts them into positions of responsibility; and those with inferiority/superiority patterns can relax and be blessedly ordinary. The centre of consciousness begins to shift from the individual to the group. If the group structure is fairly fluid the student learns to take any role which he sees to be necessary to the whole. Status is perceived to be merely a dress for specific occasions. He therefore begins to question his previous valuation of human beings according to their status, and this goes a long way in helping him to sort out reality from fantasy in his image of himself as a teacher.

(iii) *The transference to the child.* A useful bridge between the student's relation to his idea of himself and his relation to the child's idea of him is achieved by transferring the co-operative group idea, preferably fairly early in the course, to the context of school practice. A group of students (the tutorial group) carries out a project with a class of children, each student being responsible for six or eight pupils only, engaged on a specific branch of the work. In this way two projects are being run simultaneously: the overt

65

project with the children on (say) a local survey, and a less explicit project with the students on learning how to teach and on human relationships. All kinds of problems in mental health arise, and in the tutorial group the children's fantasies about the students and the staff in the school are discussed and seen for what they are. Thus, in a safe laboratory situation which is not so overwhelming as to frighten him, the student learns to apply to the children in his own small 'tutorial group' (making allowance for age differences) these insights which have been applied to him, and to begin to handle children's fantasies with detachment, humour, and impersonal love.

Note for practising teachers

This ability is naturally not acquired in a couple of years, since it depends on emotional maturity and personality integration. Useful suggestions for in-service teachers might be: (1) to attend a short course on mental health and particularly on the attitudes adopted towards children by those engaged in child guidance; (2) to initiate staff discussion groups in school (try the leaderless technique!); and (3) to join an interprofessional group of those interested in the mental health of children or adults.

The following questions merit consideration:

(1) To what extent is the slow process in liberalizing educational techniques caused by the tremendous strength of conscious and unconscious resistance to change in the personality structure? In what way should the ideas and techniques outlined above be presented to students so as to minimize resistance?

(2) Some of the modern methods used in the training of teachers to sort out reality and fantasy have been described, but this work is still in its infancy. Where do we go from here?

CHAPTER 5

Serving the Needs of the Area: 1955 to 1967

The Service was recognized in 1955 as an integral part of the Institute work. From 1957 (when we were granted full university status) it was described as 'The University of Leicester Institute of Education Psychological Advisory Service'—rather a mouthful, but a carefully exact title, this time! Childishly, I enjoyed using the specially printed notepaper. Here was the ideal framework for expansion.

The ebb: further personal analysis

However, as so often happens before a strong flood tide, the year 1955–6 marked for me an equivalent ebb, this time due to physical illness worsening throughout the winter and ending in a major operation in March 1956. Understandably, the number of clients dropped (see tables, pp. 145–7). Afterwards I found I needed more analysis myself, but there were no Jungian analysts in the area. So, for eighteen months (June 1956 to January 1958) I spent one night each week in London for two sessions (one in the evening, the other early the following morning) with Dr. Lola Paulsen, a training analyst on the committee of the Society of Analytical Psychology. (I was not, of course, in a position to take the full formal Jungian training.)

About the time of starting this second period of analysis, I had a colourful dream. There was a large, square, flower-filled courtyard which had been beautifully paved by Billy Tibble. I had to take up these well-laid stone slabs. Underneath was horrid mud containing some yellowish plants starved of life and light. It needs no special skill to interpret *that* dream! For many

67

years afterwards I had to work at a much deeper level of the psyche than that of my first period of analysis. To justify the trips to London, in my annual report of 1956–7 I wrote:

> Every therapist needs constantly to work on herself, just as a trainer of teachers needs to keep in touch with education, or a university lecturer with research in his own subject. Her personality is her main tool and it needs maintainance . . . To make up for the two half-days in London, I see clients for the whole of Saturdays, an arrangement which suits teachers and students on teaching practice.

Incidentally, at that time one had to finance oneself for such work; no grants were available as are sometimes nowadays.

To look forward a little: when in 1961 I became too involved with a long-term and difficult case, I returned to my analyst for a further period of eighteen sessions during the autumn and winter, followed by an intensive three weeks' course in the next summer vacation. I doubt whether I could have come through without all this help from Lola Paulsen, to whom I owe a very great deal. Counselling is extremely demanding work; every counsellor needs the opportunity to receive help as well as to give it, and ideally from a trained therapist or suitable group in the locality.

This is the place also to give a big 'thank you' to my friend John Read, for eighteen years Psychiatric Adviser to the London School of Economics. I made contact with him first in 1952 when his service was still experimental, sponsored by the Maudsley Institute of Psychiatry, and I visited him at the L.S.E. in April 1953. Since then we had corresponded, discussing mutual problems and exchanging reports and papers, meeting also at several conferences on student mental health. Later he saw two of my students for diagnosis and advice. One of the great difficulties of pioneering in counselling is the completely confidential nature of the work, so that—except when referring a client with his or her full permission—one can never share the personal details with anyone else. Yet it helped to talk over some of the more general problems with someone who was also committed to this lonely path, and above all I valued John's moral support; as a

medical man appointed specifically to do research and treatment, he was (at first) in a far stronger position than was I.[1]

The flow: personality work in the local colleges

Gradually my strength returned and the number of clients
coming to me for advice increased rapidly. Since the terms of
reference of institutes of education were 'to serve the needs of
the area' I maintained contact with the local colleges not only
by counselling but also by visits to explain the Service, lectures,
and group discussions.

In teaching, I tried to concentrate on the more specific topics
which would have direct relevance to personality work. Thus, in
the University Department of Education, by 1961 I managed to
pass over to colleagues my share in the general course, taking
'psychological discussion groups' instead. At the Institute itself,
I gave an annual course on depth psychology as part of the
Further Diploma course (later called the Diploma in the Sociology and Psychology of Education) for practising teachers, plus
an optional course on counselling (well attended), the latter from
1960 onwards. I also shared in some of my colleagues' courses
for in-service teachers; here we experimented in psychological
role-playing and many similar group techniques so much in vogue
at the present time.

As regards the City of Leicester colleges: several of us took
part in lectures to the College of Art's School of Teacher Training. I visited the Training College (later the College of Education) for three or four talks to various student groups each year
until 1965 when, owing to the pressure of counselling work, the
talks were converted into tape-recordings. All these lectures
covered a range of topics varying from normal child development, through psychological and personal problems in schools—
especially those of the teacher's first year out from college—to
more specific talks on dreams, art therapy, play therapy, and
straightforward applied Jungian theory.

It was with the City of Leicester School of Speech Therapy
that I had the closest link because these students were in training

[1] See John Read: *Warnings from the Left, Essays in Autobiography*, Pica
Editorials, 1974, Chapter 11: 'Psychiatric Adviser at the London School
of Economics'.

for actual *therapy* with handicapped—and in many cases also emotionally disturbed—children and adults. The students were most co-operative, my contribution being regarded as an integral part of the course. From 1957 I gave an annual course of twelve meetings on the theory and practice of therapeutic play, until 1961, after which the course was converted into a set of duplicated notes for future generations. (How useful are tapes and duplicated notes!) But they did not let me off the hook. The Principal, Miss Kathleen Allen, suggested a course of informal group discussions on 'personal psychology', at the beginning of the second year of the three-year course. In the long run, she said, it would be more economical of my time to take this modified form of group therapy, as it might well save the referral of individuals. This argument was irrefutable. (It was produced again by a tutor in the final year of existence of the University School of Social Studies (1962–3), when he asked me to take the larger part of their second-year group *en bloc* as an experiment in group therapy. 'Otherwise,' he threatened, 'you will have them all separately!')

I continued the groups in the School of Speech Therapy until 1966, using some of them as group experience for the trainee counsellors. (Muriel Kay took a group during her sabbatical year with us in 1967, and my colleague Tony Grainger took them after that.) Since I had known the aims and needs of the school for so long, in 1964 I was co-opted on to their governing body, remaining until 1967 when the school merged with the College of Education, and I transferred to the Student Health Service.

Should counsellors also teach?

I mention the teaching work in this detail because it raises an important principle for counsellors. Of course, according to the terms of my transfer, I was required to do it. But the question arises: to what extent it is advisable for a counsellor to be seen in the role of tutor by the students? On the one hand, these contacts with the colleges made for good relations with the staff. Further, the students saw me as a person (not as some fantasy witch!) and heard my ideas and values, so that recruitment to the Service was facilitated, especially for those who were shy or bottled up. Indeed, much later on when the University Department had grown so large that it was divided into sections, a student advised me to make at least *one* appearance in his section. 'We want to get to know you as an ordinary human being.' So in that year I took a series of free discussions with each tutorial group, and this brought in twice as many clients to the Service from the Department as in the previous year, all but three being self-referred.

On the other hand, before 1955 my tutorial involvement with the post-graduate course had raised difficulties. Whilst I was assessing their work, some students who needed personal help would not trust me for fear of prejudicing their results. (This is understandable, though, if they had only known it, often it worked the other way!) Again, it can be very awkward for a student who is in deeper therapy to meet his therapist in a different context, and this is partly why I worked at home and attended only the essential minimum of social functions. There is much to be said on both sides.

So far, I have not described exactly how the Service was run. In 1959 Dr. J. R. Rees asked me to contribute a paper, as a follow-up of my previous one (see Chapter 4), for World Mental Health Year in 1960. In England, this was subsequently printed in the journal of the A.T.C.D.E. (Association of Teachers in Colleges and Departments of Education).[2] In the next chapter, this paper gives the whole picture as it was at the time.

2 'Mental Health and the Education of Teachers: A Contribution of an Institute of Education', *Education for Teaching*, November 1960. I am grateful to the present editor for permission to reproduce the greater part of this article.

CHAPTER 6

Contribution of an Institute of Education

[A paper written for UNESCO's use in 1960]

The World Mental Health Year is taking as one of its objectives the improvement of teaching mental health in schools of professional training. Among the most numerous and important of such schools are those catering for the training of teachers. Social workers and medical therapists meet only the few who need special help, whereas through the hands of the teachers passes the entire next generation. If, then, we hope for an increasing level of mental health in the population as a whole, an immense opportunity awaits the teachers who go forth each year from the colleges. Since, however, they are able to pass on only what they have and are, much depends on the growth and change in personality that can take place during the crucial periods of one year in university or college of art education departments, and two (soon happily to be three) years in teacher training colleges, together with any subsequent courses offered by institutes of education and other bodies to practising teachers.

My previous article [*see Chapter 4*] contained a survey of some of the ways in which the principles and practice of mental health are incorporated into the education course by tutors in various colleges and departments. In the present paper I shall suggest some possible contributions that can be made by institutes of education. For, if the declared purpose of an institute is to serve the needs of all teachers in its area—and these include students in training, staffs of colleges and departments, as well as teachers in schools—then one branch of such service may well be that of mental health. If I start with an outline of the work I know, this is because it is the best contribution that I can make, and is not to be taken in any sense as a blueprint, since each institute area is different in its varying needs, opportunities and personnel.

How the Psychological Advisory Service came into being

The first obvious need, in our case, was for remedial work in a few acute cases among students in the Education Department of the University College of Leicester (as it was then), and among undergraduates in training under the old system of the four-year grant who were found to be suffering from psychological troubles which prevented them taking full advantage of their courses. Further, as potential teachers, many other students needed considerable personality adjustment before they could function adequately, freely and happily, in the classroom; indeed one or two would possibly have become a menace to children if they had remained as they were. Such students were referred to me, then a lecturer in education, for confidential personal help. From these small beginnings (nine in 1948–9) the Service has grown steadily until now (1960) 341 people have been interviewed, the annual intake of new cases over the last four years ranging from 38 to 48.

[*I then described the move to the Institute of Education and the expansion to colleges in the area.*]

How the Service runs

The Service is entirely free of charge. Some psychotherapists would feel this to be a bad principle which might have adverse effects, but personally, in an educational setting where nearly all students receive grants and regard psychological advice as an 'extra' that helps in their training, I have never experienced any difficulty. Even in the case of college staff and teachers, who could pay, it is found to be profoundly therapeutic that, for once, they should be given something with nothing expected in return—no strings attached. In such an atmosphere they come to realize that they *want* to make an equivalent contribution to life themselves, indeed that they cannot help it, because any change in them is bound to affect all the colleagues, students,

73

and children with whom they come into contact. It must be remembered that most teachers are normal citizens who are engaged in an exacting social job and who may have temporary problems and breakdowns; they are not the sick neurotics for whom, perhaps, the discipline of payment is a therapeutic necessity. Indeed, as they have recovered, two or three have said that they felt very deeply, 'Freely ye have received : freely give.'

Techniques of notification vary according to age. In the case of practising teachers and the older university post-graduate and college of art post-diploma students, a notice describing the Service and stressing its completely confidential nature is sufficient, with the result that the majority of such people are self-referred. In the colleges, where most of the students are under twenty-one, referral is made by the principal or tutor with the knowledge of the college medical officer if medical symptoms should be involved. One of the most important and rewarding aspects of the work is the building of co-operative relationships with principals and tutors so that, without anything of a confidential nature being divulged, the adults concerned with the student are all working together in their several roles. In the early stages of making contacts it is advisable to stress, as the notice states, that the Service 'is not meant to overlap with any tutorial system but is intended for those students who have some nervous trouble, however slight, or some personality problem which may be hampering them in their work or in college life, causing unnecessary suffering and anxiety'. We envisage, as it were, three 'lines of defence'. First come the 'moral' or 'personal' tutors and wardens in each college who deal with all normal personal problems— and it is impossible to over-value the great work done by these people who have all the responsibility of making initial contacts, recognizing needs, softening resistances, watching and guiding, and above all knowing when to act and when to wait for natural growth. Behind these is the non-medical therapist who has had considerable experience of student life as a former teacher in both universities and training colleges yet who, working at the institute, is felt by the students to be outside their particular college involvements and not directly concerned with their studies and assessments. The trained therapist tackles those deeper psychological problems with which no untrained tutor or warden should be expected to deal, even if there were time available, and also acts as liaison between the educational and medical worlds. Thirdly, behind the non-medical therapist stands the consultant psychiatrist with the facilities of the local mental hospital at hand in case of possible need for in-patient treatment.

Troubles brought to us are of every degree from a 'nervous breakdown'—and even a very occasional psychosis—to a worry over a boy-friend or over college work that the student would rather discuss with a complete stranger. In kind, too, symptoms cover the whole range from all varieties of psychosomatic disorders, through depressions, nervous fears and anxieties, nightmares and sleeplessness, delinquency (rare) and inability to concentrate (extremely common) to problems of behaviour and personality such as 'cannot make contact with her class', 'gets across the headmaster', 'has ability but can't give in work', and the all too frequent complaint of exaggerated perfectionism. Now, in many student health services, even where a psychiatric unit is available, students will rarely refer themselves for personality defects unless some physical symptom also is present. But in a setting which includes professional training, such as ours and the Psychiatric Services of the London School of Economics and the London Institute of Education, a good deal of emotional immaturity is spotted through attitudes and behaviour 'on the job', for the professions of teaching, social work, and medical therapy tend to throw a searchlight on to personality weaknesses that, in other walks of life, may well go unremarked. Since these professions all involve work both with and under discipline and also constant exposure to the raw emotions of immature human beings, the fundamental challenges underlying the diversity of symptoms are found to be those of coming to terms with authority, external and internal, and with the child both within the student himself and in his pupil, client, or patient. Otherwise he will be unable to function freely in human relationships, but will become compulsively involved. Therapy, then, consists basically in the liberation of emotional energy that has remained fixed at early levels and in the re-growth of the personality through all the unfaced challenges of adolescence into full adulthood.

Duration of treatment again shows a wide range. At one

extreme is a referral for diagnosis only—usually not more than one to four sessions. Here a principal or tutor may refer a student towards the end of his first year, saying, 'We are undecided whether he will make the grade next year and would like your view as to whether his poor work is due to psychological disturbance or not.' Investigation may show that the student is (1) in the wrong career, (2) of relatively poor intelligence but not much disturbed, (3) disturbed and will not face it nor accept help, so that it may be wiser to recommend that he leaves the profession, or (4) disturbed but will accept therapy so that we can take a risk on his coming through his problem in the second year. (Such cases often need scientific vocational guidance. From vocational guidance it would be only a step to offer help in selection procedures; this, I believe, is done at some institutes.) At the other extreme are cases, usually of good students, referred for anxiety symptoms. These need deeper psychotherapy, which may possibly last for one or two years or even longer, including follow-up supportive help, if time allows. It is difficult to speak of averages, but generally speaking, the majority of such cases fall into the class of about eight to fifteen sessions; in these there is a definite problem but it is not very deep and it clears up fairly rapidly. (Some, of course, do not clear up; we have to accept that a small proportion of cases show little or no improvement.) Treatment, then, is at all levels from advice to deeper psychotherapy with the middle of the range in what may be described as responsive listening. From experience I do not believe in taking the work more deeply than is necessary at the student stage of life, and considering all the commitments of their courses. If the immediate block is cleared and the strong forces of life are liberated, creative living in an enlightened college environment will do the rest. With regard to frequency of visits, most students come once a week, but in severe cases twice or even three times. Towards the end of the course, or in follow-up and supportive work, the frequency lessens to fortnightly, monthly, or even less. So far, therapy has been carried out individually, but in future there will probably be more group work. One of my trainees has experimented very successfully with an art therapy group in which six students meet weekly to paint freely instead of, or as well as, their weekly individual session. Since many students, particularly those from universities, tend to function too much at the conscious, intellectual level, future developments may well lie in the direction of further non-verbal techniques.

Mental health and the teaching profession: some modern trends

Experience gained through the Psychological Service has shown only too clearly the crucial importance for future generations of the mental health, maturity, and adjustment of teachers in the present-day community. Recognition of this fact has been indicated by the rapidly growing interest among educationists in personality work in the training of teachers and social workers. Recent developments appear to lie in three directions: (1) in the application of mental health principles to the actual content and methods of the curriculum of students in training, (2) in comparable work with teachers in service, and (3) in meeting the increasing demand from the staffs—college, department, and institute teachers—for helping them to work more effectively with their students' personal problems and, further, for creative group work amongst themselves.

(1) *The students.* Following the present trend towards prophylaxis—'stopping the rot before it sets in'—and towards the more positive goals of liberation and discovery (or re-discovery) of creative relationships, a large number of education and other courses include mental health attitudes, principles, and practice as an integral part of the curriculum for *all* students, not merely as remedial measures for deviates. Social psychology and depth psychology are studied in a practical way, being applied in activities such as the writing of self-studies and family-studies and in creative group experience, both non-verbally in art, craft, drama, and movement, and verbally in free discussions such as those based on the fundamental challenges of life or on education for family life in connection with the National Marriage Guidance Council. At Leicester, a recent experiment in optional 'Self-Discovery Groups' (called 'Psychological Discussion Groups' on the timetable) has been offered to post-graduates, comprising not more than eight or nine in each year. It is difficult to describe the programme because the atmosphere is so permissive that each group has developed in a different way according to the specific needs of the persons within it. But in such situations students feel

free to observe themselves in relationship, to gain insight, to grow and change—all with considerable benefit to themselves and to the children they will teach. Indeed, many have said that they have found this to be one of the most valuable parts of the course. For we think that certain students need, above all, the time and opportunity to think and to *be*—to work on the fundamentals of living. 'If only I could know what it is all for, then I could throw myself into it,' said a student referred for apparent apathy and lack of involvement in her work. In such groups they can become committed, in fellowship with others, to the search for meaning in life.

The effect of courses based on these principles is not always recognized until much later in life, as letters from former students often show. Yet some are aware at the time. Writing of herself in the third person, a post-graduate student took as the theme of her self-study 'a character steeped in perfectionism' who found that the unfortunate effects of school and home were mitigated during the university stage : 'It was the first feeling of encouragement that she had ever experienced. At school she had none from the mistresses who tried to suppress her high spirits, and hitherto her home life had been constantly subjected to criticism. In contrast to this, her year of study in education has been so interesting, encouraging, and full of human understanding, so unlike anything she had previously experienced, that her self-confidence which had been slowly ebbing away from the age of sixteen has been almost fully restored, and a little of her "real self" is beginning to overcome her reticence and stoicism.' An infant teacher, during her first year out from college, wrote that she was now engaged to be married and was very happy teaching in a slum area. 'When you are right within yourself,' she said, 'the place is not so important, is it?' From being a problem student who ran away from work and responsibility in her first year, she had come a good deal of the way through into commitment to life.

(2) *The teachers.* Much the same is being done, particularly by institutes of education, in the case of in-service teachers, many of whom, being older, have missed the experience while at college. In further diploma and similar courses, conferences and small groups, the principles of mental health and creativity are implicit in the work done. A recent development which fills a

great need is that of the free discussion group for teachers in their first and second years out. A group of women teachers in their twenties and thirties, together with their husbands and boy-friends, has now been in operation for several years, meeting monthly at the home of a training college tutor in Leicester. These teachers have already experienced an education course on the lines described, and they have chosen not to discuss psychology further but to go more deeply into spiritual values—religion and the way to live. Here is a pointer towards the future.

(3) *The staff.* This is the crux of the problem. Tutors, lecturers and principals *want* to be of service to their students. They know that for most of the time these young people find their own way through their problems by living; they also know that, for many, the relationship possible between the tutor and learner with a common love for a special field of knowledge is itself a creative relationship which makes for personal growth. Can we do any more? Can we become the kind of people who, having lived in some deep way, are sufficiently mature, open, loving, and understanding to be able to use our experience with the youth of the race? In the last resort this is a matter of our own commitment to life, our own personal philosophy. While not everyone's way, many tutors have found the dynamic life of small informal discussion groups to be a great source of help, inspiration and growth. In such groups, a sense of fellowship and togetherness develops; everyone alike is committed to the common purpose of gaining insights, of discovering the nature of self and other, and of understanding the way in which human beings behave in social group relationships. The climate is open; whatever comes up is looked at, assimilated, and often transformed in the group, for the only way to make an effective relationship in depth is to put all our cards on the table, to meet as whole persons, each with our own light and dark sides, admitting our tendency to refuse our own darkness and to see it instead in the other person. Then finally, we come to accept the darkness in the other, and even (how difficult!) in ourselves, with understanding, humour, and love. Such a setting and such an attitude facilitate the work of the creative process, for it is found in practice that more occurs 'between man and man' than can be accounted for by the sum of the capacities of the group members; or, in the words of Christ,

79

'Where two or three are gathered together in my name, there am I in the midst of them'.

Several experimental groups of various kinds have been tried out or are in operation, and institutes of education have an obvious part to play in facilitating such meetings. On a rather wider scale, an association of those interested in mental health in the area has a stimulating effect, especially where college tutors meet mental health workers in other professions.

[*Here I gave detailed references to current projects, e.g. P. W. Martin's working groups in depth psychology at Oxted; the conferences and seminars of the New Education Fellowship, the National Association for Mental Health, and the Association of Psychotherapists. Local examples were the residential seminars at Leicester of the Tavistock Institute of Human Relations, and our own Inter-Professional Association for Mental Health.*]

More specifically, there has been a recent demand from the training colleges, especially in view of the three-year course, for the training of staff in student psychotherapy and 'counselling'. Here we are still in the very earliest stages of experiment, and the issue is full of confusion and danger, which the following questions may serve to clarify. First, do tutors want to train themselves as 'psychotherapists'? If so, they are contemplating undertaking an entirely new profession from that of education, and would need a long training involving personal analysis, theory and supervised casework by a recognized professional body. If, on the other hand, they seek to increase their efficiency as personal tutors, what exactly is the position for which training is required? Should there be one full-time (or part-time) specialist 'counsellor' in each college? But this might lead to difficulties among the staff which would rebound unfavourably upon the students. Or now that 'counselling' attitudes and methods are becoming more and more integrated with the curriculum, should *all* tutors who are interested and suitable carry out such activities as a dynamic part of the ordinary work of teacher training rather than as a specialist function? In this case, would the students feel sufficiently safe and free to discuss their intimate problems with the same tutor who gives them their grades? And what is the nature of the training needed for such work?

Each college and A.T.O. [*area training organization*] will

come to its own conclusion on these vital issues. My own experience, for what it is worth, suggests that under the care of a wise tutor, and in a group situation where all are equally committed, most healthy students will co-operate freely and with considerable incentive in personality work if it is presented as a normal part of the course. At the same time, the more reserved and disturbed students, those in fear of failure, and those who happen not to be in tune with their particular tutor, definitely need someone outside the college set-up to whom they can bring more serious issues in complete confidence. I would suggest, therefore, that a suitable scheme, based on co-operative team-work, might well include :

(a) A trained psychotherapist who, if possible, should have had some experience in the teacher training field. Operating *outside* the colleges at some central point, preferably the institute of education, the therapist would deal confidentially with the more difficult cases and would work in close consultation with all the college counsellors in the area and with the doctors and the consultant psychiatrist. (Judging by the proportion of students referred even in a small A.T.O. such as ours, there is plenty of need for a considerable number of such trained people in this country.)

(b) The tutor-counsellors *within* the colleges and departments. (The term 'tutor-counsellor' is perhaps undesirable but inevitable.) These would not necessarily have undergone long personal analysis, but would have taken part in some such creative group experience as has been described, and/or a short course of personal psychotherapy, so that, having achieved the essential insights of mental health in themselves, they could pass them on to all whom they contact. Training for such work, then, might well consist of dynamic group experience together with seminars on counselling methods in student education and casework, with opportunity provided for personal psychotherapy where necessary, and at the right moment for each individual in the course.

If such a scheme is to be living and workable, it will show

typical English flexibility even at the price of untidiness. For example, if some therapists have had teaching experience, they might well do occasional educational work with students and teachers—a welcome refreshment after dealing with disturbed individuals all day long! Conversely, if some tutors have had analytic experience and training, they could, if they wish, share some of the work of the therapist, taking a case or two from a college other than their own. At Leicester, two senior lecturers in education from training colleges are at present in training. After some years of personal psychotherapy, their course consists of a weekly session with a client, followed by a weekly discussion on casework and relevant theory, linked, of course, with considerable reading. (If there were more trainees, we could organize a programme of groups, lectures and seminars, but we are still on the very fringe of this work.) Whatever the pattern, it is an undoubted advantage when at least one tutor in each college has practised in mental health work, since there is so much that can be done, not only in co-operation with the institute therapist through preliminary work with problem students, but, more important, in affecting the attitude of all the students in the college community.

Where are we going?

Four general principles arising from our experimental findings in England may be of universal interest.

Fundamental to everything else is *the recognition of the vital importance of the mental health of teachers* who, through their ordinary work and contacts with children, can impart healthy attitudes to the whole of the rising generation. It follows that an immense opportunity lies in the hands of those responsible for teacher training in colleges, departments, and institutes of education. This opportunity is enhanced in the light of the second principle: *prevention is better than cure*. The organic growth of our own service shows the same progression as do marriage guidance and mental health work generally: from remedy for the few to prophylaxis for all. Perhaps the goal to be aimed at is that one day the remedial therapist will be replaced by the enlightened teacher, while the one-to-one situation will give way to the small creative group in which there is less emphasis on 'my individual problem', since teachers and pupils alike will learn and take counsel together.

Thirdly, it is found that *the principle of healing—of making whole—operates as a living fire from the creative centre deep within the human psyche.* Historically, the theory and practice of 'counselling' show three phases :

(1) The early counsellors gave advice based on an accepted code of values.

(2) Non-directive counselling, the current method, puts the emphasis on the client himself. In a permissive relationship with a mirror-like counsellor he achieves insights which enable him to see the truth of his thoughts, feelings, and behaviour, and so to strengthen his conscious ego and cure his ills. This is a great advance on external advice, but both of these approaches, *if* they start from what is wrong with the person, can be somewhat negative.

(3) The most modern form of counselling begins with what is healthy and right in the person : the positive, creative forces at work in the depths; when these are activated —perhaps in the day-to-day work of a special subject group —the 'problem' aspects will be resolved, accepted and integrated, through the strength of the deep centre beyond the ego, as the person moves towards wholeness. For it is wholeness that is now needed and being sought—even if only unconsciously—by everyone, not only by the sick. We have moved a long way from diagnosis of ills, release of aggression, and even strengthening of the conscious ego, as the only answers, though all these have a most important place in the earlier stages of the healing process. It is now not enough to achieve a workable existence at the ego level, curing ills or even preventing them by coming to terms with the primitive forces within and with the claims of society without; instead of mere *existence,* the adult human being seeks to liberate and experience the more abundant *life.*

Finally, *to be mentally healthy implies not only aiming at becoming whole in oneself but also learning to relate to the greater whole of which we are a part,* and this in a far deeper sense than adjustment only to society. As we begin to experience the transforming effect of that greater life within ourselves, we come to want to relate to it beyond ourselves, so that the emphasis shifts from psychotherapy to metaphysics—from 'how we work' to 'who we are' and 'what life is'. Is it by accident that a group of teachers should wish to go on from psychology to ask what life is about and the way to live it? Or that, after two conferences on the teaching of personality development to students and the problems arising in the course of such work, the third (Keele, 1960) should be on moral issues? 'How often,' writes Jung, 'have I heard a patient exclaim: "If only I knew my life had some meaning and purpose, then there would be no silly story about my nerves." ' Surely this search for meaning and purpose, for the primordial truths and values, is the essential concern of educationists, and particularly of those training teachers, not only in Britain but in every country in the world.

CHAPTER 7

Some Special Aspects

The 1960 paper, reprinted in Chapter 6, was in a sense my 'theme song'. The rest of my time at Leicester was spent endeavouring to put into practice the ideas advocated in it. Chapters 7 to 12 tell this story.

In 1962 the Department and the Institute were united in the University of Leicester School of Education. Not that this made much difference except perhaps that we all worked still more closely together, taking our share in the many specialized areas of activity. Here is my part of the picture.

Higher degree supervision, research, and publications

All tutors in the school were required to supervise, in their own specific fields, candidates for the M.Ed. and Ph.D. (Leicester) higher degrees. The four in my field, during the eleven years from 1961 to 1972, included one tutor from the school and three from various colleges of education, two enrolling for the M.Ed. and two for Ph.D. Among the latter was Muriel Kay (1964 to 1968), then Senior Lecturer in Education at Furzedown College of Education, whose thesis[1] included a chapter based on data concerning the students who had attended my Psychological Service from the Leicester College of Education. (The records were carefully processed beforehand by myself to ensure confidentiality, and the research was carried out with the permission of the Principal of the College, then Mr. Francis Cammaerts.) Miss Kay spent a sabbatical year in 1966–7 working intensively on this material and taking my experimental training course in

[1] Dr. M. M. Kay: *Personality and Adjustment Problems of Students in Training for Teaching: A Contribution to Developmental Psychology.* Unpub. thesis for Ph.D. (Leicester), 1968, Chapter 7.

student counselling (see Chapter 8.) In January 1968 she was appointed to the newly established post of Student Counsellor at the University of Hull, where she built up the service from the beginning.

I am very grateful to Muriel for analysing at least some of our immense number of records, for I had no time to do this. I was well aware that we needed a confidential research assistant, and I commend this suggestion to any well-staffed service of the future!

Already by 1960 I was overworked. In the annual report of 1960–1 I mentioned that I felt inundated by practical casework, needing a sabbatical year (or even only one term) to analyse and write up the increasing volume of data. But, of course, while I was working alone it was impossible to desert ongoing cases, so that I did not achieve a term of study leave until 1970, after joining the Student Health Service team. The 1962–3 report stated :

> This has been a year of 'survival'. Apart from one review there has been no writing or research. From questions put to me by visitors, or when being interviewed about the establishment of a University Mental Health Service, I have realized how much data I have which is most significant but I have not had the time to work on it. I can only give general impressions, or at most a few superficial figures. I am aware that vacations are intended for research, but it is not generally realized that in psychotherapy, especially when there are severe cases who cannot be left for long at a time, it is difficult to do the essential reading and preparation for the theoretical part of the training course (e.g. this year I prepared twelve sets of duplicated notes on clinical types for the trainees), or even to take a proper holiday, let alone to do the research which is what I should like to do.

And later, in 1966–7 :

> It was not until Miss Kay embarked on her Ph.D. that some actual research was done in direct connection with the Service. If we are to provide evidence we must have time,

people and opportunity to get this data evaluated and published. The need for more research in the field of student problems and counselling at the present time is great. There are so few of us in the field, and most of us are snowed under with casework.

Only now (1975), after three years of retirement, can I write up the whole story—but not alas! the case material—for after retirement I destroyed all detailed records for safety. Still, these problems would now be dated. Perhaps present services can collect and process more relevant current data.

However, apart from that reprehensible gap between 1960 and 1964 when I wrote only the usual few reviews, I managed to keep up that fairly steady flow of articles which is expected of every university tutor.[2]

External activities: visits and surveys, lectures and conferences

Starting with the first paper for UNESCO in 1952, this spate of articles soon attracted numerous visitors from universities (old and new), institutes and colleges of education, all seeking to establish their own services. Some came from overseas (U.S.A., Australia, Hong Kong, South Africa, Sweden). Since we were an experimental and pioneer service, there were also many letters of enquiry. Beginning with Cato Hambro's 1958 international survey for UNESCO, investigating techniques

---

[2] 'When I may as well Walk at Liberty' (with Kathleen Douet), *The New Era*, September/October 1957. 'The Experiential Approach', *Education for Teaching*, November 1959. (This was part of a symposium organized by P.W. Martin on 'God, Sex, and Society'.) 'University of Leicester Institute of Education', Contribution to a symposium on 'The Neurotic Student'. *Cambridge Review*, May 1960. 'Learning the Art of Training', *Bulletin of the Association of Psychotherapists*, No. 2, September 1960. (A survey of facilities for training psychotherapists and counsellors, and an account of the early days of my training scheme.) 'Mental Health and the Education of Teachers', *Education for Teaching*, November 1960. (Reproduced in Chapter 6 of this book.) 'Deeper Levels of Counselling', Chapter 8 in *Healing Through Counselling*, Ed. by William Kyle, Epworth Press, 1964. 'A Counselling Service for Teachers', *Journal of Education*, University of Hong Kong, 1965. (Requested by Miss Beryl Wright, Counsellor in the Department of Education, Hong Kong University, when she visited us.) 'Art Therapy', *Proceedings of the 1966 Conference of the Radionic Association*, 1967. 'Training for Student Counselling', *Bulletin of the Association of Psychotherapists*, No. 7, 1967. (Reproduced in Chapter 8 of this book.)

of education in mental health in teacher training, I was asked to furnish data for several other surveys and a few research theses in counselling and mental health, again both at home and overseas. Soon it became imperative to print a descriptive eight-page brochure, brought out in 1960 and revised in 1962.

Visits and literature, of course, formed a two-way exchange. I—and later my trainees—learned much from the early-established services in this country, especially L.S.E., University College London, the London Institute of Education, the Universities of Leeds and Bristol, and later of Keele and Sussex. Each service seems to have developed in a different way, producing its own distinctive pattern—a typically British phenomenon.

I was asked to visit some universities (including Oxford), and a large number of colleges of education all over the country, for staff discussions on staff-student relationships or on the role of the tutor in counselling; to describe our service; to advise on the setting up of a service; even sometimes to interview a problem student; and often, while I was there, to give a talk to the students as well.

In the late 1950s and early 1960s I was also working closely with my own professional association (now the British Association of Psychotherapists). Starting in 1958 with a paper to members (including visiting university student health officers) on 'A Survey of the Theory and Practice of Counselling', I then took a few seminars organized for social workers in 1958, followed by some for training college tutors in 1959. After one seminar on 'Directive and Non-directive Techniques in Casework' for Part I of the Association's programme of training social workers in counselling, in 1961–2 a fellow-member of the Association and I together led a course of sixteen sessions in group experience for Part II of this course. (All these meetings were, of course, in London, so I managed to fit in the group sessions with further work with my analyst.) In attending a course of seminars on Jungian and Freudian theory for members of the Association, I contributed a paper on 'Introversion and Extraversion in Health and Disease' (reproduced in Chapter 13).

There was also the usual number of single lectures, e.g. to the Open Way Clinic, the Counsellors' Training Scheme at the

Highgate Centre; even one on group methods at H.M. Prison Service Staff College at Wakefield; and many others to local groups.

The widespread interest in student mental health at this time was reflected in conferences, most of which I attended. Among these was the 1958 meeting at Keele on 'The Teaching of Personality to Students in Training for Teaching and Social Work', and its follow-up in 1959 at Leicester; a couple in London organized by the World University Service on 'Student Mental Health' in April and December 1961; a seminar at Bristol University in 1963 to discuss the setting up on a national scale of counselling services for schools; and the sixth international congress of psychotherapy on 'New Developments in Psychotherapy' in London in 1964. Together with Billy Tibble and one or two other colleagues, I served from 1958 to 1963 on a small committee of the National Association for Mental Health to discuss the contribution which the N.A.M.H. could make to promote mental health in training colleges. We organized two residential conferences for tutors, in 1961 and 1963. (We were still experimenting with group methods—feeling our way—so that, although they provided useful experience, these intensive weeks were not entirely successful.)

I have listed these external contacts and activities for the sake of the record and to show the climate of the period. They *did* take up a good deal of time, but it felt right to expand in this way. As usual, Billy Tibble not only gave me freedom, but took an active part in some of the events; he was as keen as I was to introduce the principles of mental health into teacher training.

Another great time-consumer (though enjoyable and rewarding) was the unofficial experiment in training student counsellors.

The training course in student counselling

Already, mention has been made of the 'trainees'. In the 1950s I had grown very concerned by the existence of an apparent bottle-neck. At one end, many well-qualified and experienced people such as tutors, teachers, and social workers were interested in student counselling; they kept inquiring where they could find full-time or part-time training courses. At the other end, universities and other colleges of higher education were now increasingly looking for trained counsellors, but finding the field very poor.

I wanted to find out more about the nature of training schemes. There was a good deal of American literature on the subject, but although I learned much from it, it seemed doubtful whether it would fit our own particular needs if *directly* applied. In Britain I failed to find any provision, at that time, for training counsellors in work with adults except for the Marriage Guidance Council. I studied their methods—indeed we had worked closely with them in the two N.A.M.H. conferences already mentioned —and there were some local examples. But, understandably, their training seemed to be more specific, and my experience of cases shared locally showed that, if any degree of deeper psychological probing were required, the clients were passed on to others. (The same was true, later, of the Samaritans.) So I turned to explore methods of training for psychotherapy, endeavouring to make a small survey of existing schools which trained psychotherapists—non-medical as well as medical—for I was concerned mainly with opportunities for candidates qualified in education and psychology; and further I believed that it is always better to be trained at a level deeper than that at which one actually practises. Possibly I missed some schools, but it may interest readers that in an article on 'Learning the Art of Training' published in 1960 in Bulletin No. 2 of the Association of Psychotherapists—largely to raise discussion on the matter—this list contained all the training schools I could find:

Existing schools of training in psychotherapy

There appears to be no universally recognized system of training psychotherapists for adult clients in this country, although a few schools are experimenting in different ways. I am grateful to all who have contributed information from the following groups:

(1) *Schools training medical and non-medical psychotherapists*

The Association of Psychotherapists, London.

The Open Way, London.

The Davidson Clinic, Edinburgh.

(2) *Schools training medical psychotherapists only*
    The Tavistock Clinic, London.
(3) *Schools training psychiatrists* (who take a course in
    psychotherapy as part of their psychiatric training)
    The Maudsley Institute of Psychiatry, London.
    The Department of Psychiatry, University of Leeds.

Since we were not concerned with training medically qualified
people, I wrote only to the two schools mentioned in this last
section. Neither were we venturing to embark on anything like
the long, expensive, and arduous training of formal analysis;
yet I felt that a knowledge of the thorough courses and high
standards of analytic training might be a useful guide, so I wrote
for details to the Institute of Psycho-Analysis and also to the
Society of Analytical Psychology, both in London.

The most experienced and (to us) relevant school of all these
we found to be the Davidson Clinic, Edinburgh, where non-
medical as well as medical psychotherapists were throughly
trained. In 1960 I spent a rewarding time at a summer school
there, taking the opportunity to discuss the training programme
in detail with the staff.

Where local facilities for qualifying in group experience were
concerned, I must mention the work of Professor Emeritus John
Allaway, until 1967 Head of the Department of Adult Education, who was for many years a close associate of Billy Tibble.[3]
His co-operation with the Tavistock Institute of Human Relations for a decade from 1957 is mentioned in the next chapter.

How could local facilities, my own training and experience,

---

[3] Professor Allaway has arranged and directed several courses annually,
principally in Leicester, Northampton and Nottingham, in Group Dynamics,
viewed from the theoretical perspective of W. R. Bion (*Experiences in
Groups*, Tavistock, London, 1961), Transactional Analysis, viewed from
that of Eric Berne (*Transactional Analysis in Psychotherapy*, Grove Press,
N.Y., 1961, through to *What Do You Say After You Say Hello?* Bantam
Books, N.Y., 1973), and also conducted Encounter Groups, the latest of
which consist of days without words. Whilst membership of almost all these
courses has been open to the general public, the majority of the participants
have come from the helping professions—social workers, teachers, clergy,
medical practitioners and their auxiliaries. Of recent years the number of
these participants has averaged 250. John has the assistance of six fellow
counsellors and each year an equal number of trainees in the group counselling role.

and all the written information that had been gathered, be adapted to our specific needs? Could the suggestion which I had made so rashly in the 1960 UNESCO paper, concerning the training of tutor/counsellors in the colleges, be implemented? (See p. 81.) One can find out only by trial and error, and it is always wise to start quietly by experimenting at home. So I carried out an unofficial course, using it as a learning experience for us all, for twelve years, between 1955 and 1967. Since I was in my sixtieth year when leaving the School of Education in 1967, there was never any question of its establishment as a recognized course, but I fed all our experience into a paper[4] which came to be distributed fairly widely, both at home and abroad, to those concerned with setting up official courses in the future.[5] It is reprinted in the following chapter.

[4] 'Training for Student Counselling', *The Association of Psychotherapists' Bulletin*, No. 7, 1967. Thanks are due to the editor for permission to reproduce this article.

[5] The development of training courses since the 1960s has been phenomenal. Mrs. Jean Mackintosh, formerly Student Progress Officer at Aberdeen University, and Research Officer of the Association for Student Counselling until 1974, was the first to produce a *Survey of Training Courses*, 1973 (obtainable from the A.S.C.). Interested readers are advised to write to The British Association for Counselling for the up-to-date and comprehensive booklet: *Careers, Opportunities and Courses in Counselling*, 1975. A companion booklet on courses in psychotherapy is in preparation, and should be available by the time this book is published. (For addresses of the A.S.C. and B.A.C., see pp. 148–9.)

CHAPTER 8

Training for Student Counselling

An experiment in the University of Leicester School of Education Psychological Advisory Service

The term counselling covers many forms and levels. In this article, the kind of counselling to which I refer, while not psychotherapy, is yet analytically orientated. To me it seems essential that those who will soon be expected to counsel the next generation should have the opportunity during their college life to make personal contact with older people who have some experience and understanding, both with heart and head, of the psychology of the unconscious.

The need in Britain for counselling in *schools* is slowly being recognized. Selected, experienced teachers are now trained as counsellors at the universities of Keele, Reading and Exeter; social workers have been introduced experimentally into some schools; there is talk of inter-disciplinary training of teachers and social workers to their mutual advantage, while one college of education has started to train teacher/social workers. Does not the need for training extend into the *colleges*? Are there enough facilities for helping the teachers of teachers—the tutors in university departments and colleges of education—to acquire modern counselling attitudes?

Leicester, a pioneer outpost in several areas of psychological education, possesses two particular background resources for such work. First, group experience has been available for university and college tutors (together with personnel workers from other professions) since 1957, when the Tavistock Institute of Human Relations, in conjunction with Leicester University Department of Adult Education, started intensive residential conferences in inter-personal and inter-group relations in Leicester. Several tutors have since applied this experience in modified form to their own student groups. Secondly, two-person counselling and psychotherapy have been provided for the last nineteen years at the Psychological Advisory Service for students in training for teaching, social work, youth leadership and speech therapy, for school teachers, and for the university and college teachers concerned, with the result that many of the training staff in the area are now thoroughly familiar with therapeutic attitudes either through personal experience of psychotherapy or through consultation about a student. It was in response to a demand from some tutors that, from small beginnings in 1955, the training experiment arose.

An experience rather than a formal course

As yet, the training offered is developing and unofficial; there is no named award. It is not designed to qualify people as official 'counsellors'; only one—my colleague—of the twelve trainees up to date has taken up student counselling professionally.[1] Rather, the training is intended to help those tutors who feel drawn to such work to develop further understanding about themselves and about students' problems so that their more insightful attitudes may be caught and passed on, directly or indirectly, to these students and hence to their pupils. It follows that, during this experimental twelve-year period, whilst learning myself about both the need and art of training, I have not been unduly selective; it is as important on a college staff to help a member who is in difficulty to gain some insights as it is to help one with considerable awareness to go still further. If, however, the experiment ever became an official course, selection would need to be rigorous.

Qualifications of trainees

Of the twelve trainees, seven are men and five women. On enrolment five were college of education tutors (all lecturers in education), four university tutors (in teacher or social work training), two school teachers and one psychiatric social worker responsible for training others. Most of these have a first degree in

[1] After this was published, another did so.

a teaching subject and/or a further degree or diploma in education which provides an academic background of educational and developmental psychology and of the major authorities on the psychology of the unconscious. P.S.W.s have their own qualifications, stronger on the clinical, less strong on the academic side. Since student teachers are a highly selected body of supposedly 'normal' and healthy people, examined by the medical officer in charge of each college, the general emphasis in student counselling is more on development, emotional education, and character aspects of personality work than on the clinical, although it is most essential for trainees to know both.

Before starting training, candidates are required to take a course either of group experience or of personal psychotherapy, and preferably both. Of the twelve, eleven have had group experience, mostly at the Tavistock conferences. All except one underwent personal psychotherapy or analysis (and this one had group experience). One of the difficulties in a pioneer area is that of finding people qualified to provide psychotherapy. Since I have been responsible for the training and supervision of all twelve, I have been reluctant also to be their therapist. Fortunately, five had been analysed elsewhere, but in the other six cases there was no alternative but to take them. Therapy, however, always precedes training, although in two or three cases there has been some overlap. Personal psychotherapy may last from six months to several years, according to need or opportunity. With some, a short period is enough to achieve the essential insights; others, with longer analysis behind them, are capable of more fundamental work provided that they are far enough away from their own deeper work to be able to adjust to emergency short-term counselling, and to refrain from stirring up more than the youthful ego can take in the short time available.

The training experience

The duration of training has varied from the extremes of six months to ten years, but the average is two to three years. In term-time, two periods of one and a half hours each week are usual, one for theory and one for casework supervision, the trainees taking their control clients in their own time.

(1) *Course A: Introductory.* We plunge straight into discussion of the basic issues of counselling, looking at our own motivation and deeply-felt philosophies. As in teacher training, secondhand skills do not work; the counsellor must function from what he *is*, and each functions differently. For instance, the position of each counsellor on the scale ranging from directive advice to the completely non-directive approach is related to his concept of the nature of man. Therefore I never present techniques until trainees have achieved at least some degree of conscious responsibility for their use.

In discussing techniques, we begin with group personality-work as an aspect of the total educational process in the class-room and with the whole range of students. Many educational skills can be used with a double reference: typological studies, self-rating and other-rating, child-studies, family-studies, and self-studies, social surveys—all these and many others can help students to understand themselves and each other as well as being a necessary preparation for teaching children. It is here that methods modified from the trainees' group experience can be applied to the students' own ways of learning, for the modern education of teachers includes social and emotional as well as intellectual and practical experience and growth. Indeed, most tutors in education already employ many of these methods, but not always with clear understanding of what they may stir up.

Individual counselling begins with a study of interviewing skills with particular reference to the first interview, since trainees will be starting with a control client about this time. Later on, we look at deeper ways of communicating with the unconscious, among them art therapy and the study of dreams. Here is a debatable point: should counsellors study dream-work? Although most trainees will not be employing dream and picture interpretation in their actual casework, yet in view of their own personal experience during analysis, and of the need always to understand at a deeper level than one practises, I believe that these ways of communication should be understood.

All the above, though broad in outlook, including Rogerian, Freudian, and other theories where appropriate, has a mainly Jungian slant.

My father and me

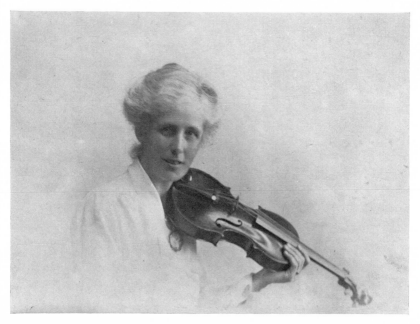

My mother and 'Alessandro'

Myself at eleven—
outgoing and happy

Myself at sixteen—
the introvert period
of adolescence

(2) *Course B: a formal survey of clinical types* is based primarily on Fairbairn's model of the psyche. Fairbairnian theory was chosen partly to make a bridge for those trainees who had already been given this conceptual basis at the Tavistock conferences, but mainly because, as presented by Guntrip,[2] it would appear to offer the clearest pattern for classifying neuroses and psychoses analytically. In my opinion, it is more far-reaching than Kleinian theory and is the closest to fundamental Jungian concepts of all the neo-Freudian schools, so in this way I have aimed at achieving a balance and as much integration as possible between Freudian and Jungian theory. Here again is a debatable issue, but it must be remembered that most of these trainees already teach the theory of the main schools of the psychology of the unconscious in simplified form, and particularly as applied to child development, to their students; so that integration, at least intellectually, presents little difficulty. Although studied at a deeper level than will be used in practice, Course B is justified, I feel, both generally on the ground of comprehensive training, and specifically so that the trainees may be better able to distinguish between those who can or cannot be helped at a counselling level, and to know when to refer elsewhere.

(3) *Course C* is fluid, geared to the particular interests of individuals, and may involve a paper to be given by the trainee to the group.

Methods of presenting theory

Under the older training methods emphasizing bookwork and particularly systematic clinical theory, those trainees who had difficulty in abstract thinking tended to find the ideas meaningless, whereas those who shunned feeling seized on them too eagerly, attempting to fit neat, preconceived concepts on to human nature (which obstinately refused to be thus pigeon-holed). Certain modern methods of group training with a consultant, therefore, show a swing of the pendulum towards learning by emotional experience based on concrete casework in the here-and-now. In attempting to find and follow the middle way here, I have discovered that, since 'readiness is all', real learning

[2] Harry Guntrip: *Personality Structure and Human Interaction*, International Psycho-Analytic Library, Hogarth Press, 1961.

depends on careful timing. Too early presentation of abstract theory is unwise, but, introduced at a later stage, exactly when the trainee has become fogged by the confused mind of his client, then 'there is nothing so practical as a good theory' (as Dr. J. Sutherland used to say) to explain the contradictions he finds.

Again, much depends on the way in which the theory is presented. It must be remembered that most of the trainees are themselves expert educationists, living by the cardinal principle : 'It isn't what we teach, it's what they learn'; and they expect the same dynamic learning situation to be applied to them. Obviously, with only four or fewer people in the training group at a time, formal lectures are out of the question. Instead, the theoretical material is given in the form of duplicated notes, containing lists for further reading, and the learning problem centres round the use of these notes. Most trainees prefer to take them home, to read them first and then spend the following session in discussion, but here, as also in relating theory to practice, there is a difference between the more academic 'thinking' people and the more personally oriented 'feeling-intuitive' types. The thinking types would read anything, discuss fluently, and work by *deductive* reasoning, applying from first principles to a particular case, but they found practical work more of a strain than did the others. Those approaching from feeling, intuition and the more personal angle, however, tended to enjoy case-work and to be good at it, but to find books and notes useless unless preceded by live cases. No matter how many specimen case-histories were provided to illustrate each clinical type, they found it difficult to work from idea to case so that it was real to them. They learned *inductively*, and, when given conceptual consolidation after the living experience, though slow, their learning often showed greater integration of heart and head and greater permanence than that of the thinkers. Ideally, with this type, the trainer should gear their head-learning to their case-work, no matter how disorderly the syllabus becomes. This means that the requisite theory must be available 'on demand', which is not always easy for the trainer. These people do excellent work, but often have no idea why they do it, and will ask afterwards, 'Why did I feel I had to say that?' This is the moment that must be seized to discuss the reason behind the action. In our world of today which puts so much value on thinking and verbal expression, they often feel unwarrantably inferior, being slow to verbalize their feelings and values, compared with their more glib colleagues, and it is extremely difficult to get them to write. The same applies to reading-lists; they will not read unless the book is completely relevant to their need at the moment. The best way to achieve incentive is to allow a certain degree of muddle with a client and then refer to a helpful book on it.

These two types, of course, are highlighted as extremes. One trainee hit the happy medium when he said that he liked the theory presented systematically first, then he has it for reference, and when he has a case he reads the relevant note 'and it becomes real'. By whatever approach, the aim is that the trainees should learn to see and to analyse what is involved in their own roles so that, in achieving some understanding and detachment, they will avoid becoming either unduly inflated or discouraged.

Supervised casework

After some initial practice in personality work with the whole range of students in their education groups, trainees study specimen case-histories and then proceed to take disturbed clients in two-person sessions. It is here that the exigencies of a pioneer set-up, in which we still have to establish our cause fully, create problems which I do not find mentioned in reports from the more ideal training conditions in London.[3] First there may well be suspicion of the validity of depth psychology—and even hostility to it—among some of the trainees' colleagues, especially academics at the university. Some trainees even wish to keep their association with the Service secret since they fear it might be detrimental to their careers. Others in more liberal environments consider it an advantage. Secondly, the pressures brought to bear by college authorities that we should 'get the students cured' as soon as possible involve the prestige both of the Service and of the trainee, interfering with the freedom to move naturally between counsellor and client. Of course we resist these pressures firmly, and most tutors know now that time and early referral

---

[3] 'Symposium on Training', *The Journal of Analytical Psychology*, Vol. 6, No. 2, July 1961, and Vol. 7, Nos 1 and 2, January and July 1962.

are essential. Nevertheless, emergency short-term cases do not make good control cases because there is too high a level of anxiety in everyone concerned and too little time for consolidation. Whenever possible, therefore, I attempt to find control clients where such external demands do not arise. In the early days I aim to create adequate safeguards for the trainee to work in his own way and rhythm, yet without over-protection. Later on he needs to be exposed progressively to outer pressures because, being part of reality, they are also part of the training process.

Choice of control clients, especially the first, is very important. For a first client I try to find a student who is near the trainee's own personality type, preferably showing a disturbance pattern similar to the one with which the trainee has come to terms in himself sufficiently long ago to be reasonably objective about it, yet to have plenty of empathy. (Here is one of the few advantages of my having taken a trainee previously for psychotherapy.) If the trainee is still in analysis, and if the client's problem is too near his present self-work, he may become too identified; if, on the other hand, the client's problem is too remote from his own experience, he may either feel helpless or be hearty or uncomprehending. It is vital that his first experience of counselling should give him reasonable confidence as it may well set his attitude for subsequent work. Second and third clients, however, can well be more difficult—opposite types, less familiar problems —presenting a challenge. But one cannot always achieve this desirable gradation in practice!

To facilitate such selection, and also because, personally, I feel it very difficult to supervise adequately when I do not first 'have the feel of' a client, I interview the client beforehand; I am perfectly open about the situation, asking permission that we should work as a team. This appears to be another debatable point in training, some trainers considering that control clients should not be told that their counsellor is still in training because it weakens his prestige. I can only say that we have never experienced any difficulty either from trainees or from clients in this respect, but here perhaps our pioneer situation is actually an advantage, since control clients are often students from outside the Service area who otherwise would be turned away. Accustomed to the modern team system with their doctors, they are thankful to be accepted at all. A very useful device, especially later on in the training, is that in which the trainee and I take a married couple between us, discussing on equal terms, supervising each other. One of the trainees (the P.S.W.) in her own work is experimenting with four-person interviewing—two counsellors and two clients—and I hope to learn and practise this with her in marital situations.

From experience I have come to recognize three stages of learning-problems in supervised casework. In the first stage, the beginner tends to be dependent, asks what to do, easily becomes alarmed and over-responsible, yet not objectively self-critical. If he has had a deep analysis and is still close to it, he may apply his analyst's methods regardless, and often these are quite unsuitable for counselling. It takes a good deal of experience to handle short-term cases. Further, just as he identifies consciously with his analyst, so he may project his own patient-self unconsciously on to his client, becoming involved. Or, if social pressure should be strong, he may come too near to the sort of counselling that is brainwashing so as to achieve social norms. Success in his first few cases is very important to him. It is in the second stage that he grows sufficiently confident to let go the compulsive need for success and to take risks. Mistakes happen to us all, and our keynote is: 'Whatever happens *use* it!' Here is a razor's edge between my responsibility for the trainee's learning, and for the client's progress; as in all training we have to let the guinea pigs suffer to some extent that we may learn. And now there comes a phase—beneath all techniques and roles—of exposure of the trainee himself in relation to another human being, together with the realization that basically no one can help him very much. He asks himself, 'Should I be doing this work at all? *Who* needs help? To what extent are we separate entities or changing parts of a pattern in a field of patterns?' He may rebel in face of these questions. In one case, a trainee deliberately went against the advice of both his analyst and his supervisor in a control case and, judging by the outcome, he was perfectly right. He could handle it in his way because he was himself, and this was a valuable growing point in the experience of us all. So, finally, in stage three, the trainee comes to realize that he cannot be other than he is in the pattern; with real humility he allows himself to be used in relationship; then things really begin to work. And all concerned in the training experience—trainer, trainees, and clients alike—begin to find that problems are not things to be got rid of or solved; rather they are ways of learning, processes to be lived with, until, in the end, perhaps the problems will solve us.

CHAPTER 9

Counsellor in the Area Student Health Service: 1967 to 1972

Establishment and staffing

First, a brief retrospect. Until 1964 I had no assistance with the increasing casework, although I was glad of any voluntary help available. A few cases were taken by the trainees, and here I am particularly grateful to Kathleen Douet who was for several years an associate member of the Association of Psychotherapists. Apart from casework, one of her main contributions was to take an art therapy group of my clients from 1957 to 1961 when it was continued by one of the former members, Jean-Marie Roberts, until she left Leicester in 1968. Some students who find verbal expression difficult are able to tap unconscious material more readily through free painting. If they wished, they brought their paintings to their regular interviews with me for mutual interpretation, and we found that insights were gained more directly than by words alone.

Occasionally suitable clients were referred to local services (e.g. Canon E. N. Ducker's Diocesan Clinic) especially if they had left college and needed further help. However, by the early 1960s I was overwhelmed. The crucial need was for a salaried therapist, even if only part-time, and preferably male so as to make a balanced team. Understandably, there was great difficulty in obtaining official establishment (once more I had to put Billy in an awkward position) but eventually in 1964 Mr. Anthony ('Tony') Grainger, previously head of the English department of a local school, was appointed on a part-time basis, renewable annually, to take up to 300 interviews a year. Tony had just completed two years of training with me. (Later he

103

travelled regularly to London to take the training course of the Association of Psychotherapists, being elected an associate member in 1972 and a full member in 1975.) He worked with us until 1968, then built up a private practice in Leicester, thus fulfilling a great need. It was a joy to have a colleague to work with, and we had a very happy partnership throughout. But the case-load was not lightened for this was the period of rapid expansion of student (and staff) population in higher education.

During the sixties, however, came a most important development. In 1962 Dr. Hugh Binnie became the first full-time Medical Officer to the University Health Service (a general practitioner service). This was just before the post-Robbins expansion.[1] In the next few years not only did the increase warrant the appointment of a second practitioner, Dr. J. L. Crighton, but the students were clamouring for a mental health service of some kind. Representatives of the Students' Union interviewed me; the Registrar requested a summary of data on our Service; and then I had a very helpful talk with Mr. (now Sir) Fraser Noble, the Vice-Chancellor, who advised me to co-operate closely with Dr. Binnie. This I was only too glad to do. There was mutual referral of cases, particularly of one very difficult case in the School of Education with which he helped us; in return, Tony and I began to take undergraduates again—twenty-three in all between 1964 and 1967.

And now the authorities asked us to stop the free service previously given to teachers and college staff; we should concentrate more on the needs of the university students since, after all, it was the university which paid us. (So there was a reversal of policy from that of 1955!) The recommendation was understandable enough in view of the fact that from 1963–4 the rapidly expanding College of Education had become our chief customer; indeed in 1965–6 almost half (49 per cent) of the interviewing hours were spent on students from that college. Aware of this problem, for some time we had tried to work for the establishment of a separate counsellor there. The Principal, Francis Cammaerts, was in favour of the idea, and we nearly got it through, but during the critical period of the negotiations he

[1] Between 1962 and 1966 the number of students increased from about 1,800 to nearly 3,000.

left for Africa. The issue was finally solved by the college's merger with the University Health Service in 1968.

All this time, since my appointment in 1948, I had remained on the ordinary lecturer grade of salary. In view of the current amount of policy-making, organization and responsibility, I thought it only fair, both to myself and to my successor, to apply —before Billy Tibble left in 1966—for senior lecturer status. (By that time I was by far the most long-standing member of staff in the school who had not been promoted.) Promotion would have helped my pension at retirement, but Billy was unable to get it through, so I remained on the ordinary grade until retirement in 1972. Once again I realized that this was part of the price to pay for having been able to build the Service; also that, compared with some counsellors appointed elsewhere, and although I had fulfilled the teaching commitments until the last few years, I was fortunate to have academic conditions of employment.[2] To be honest, as I told Billy at the time, I had mixed feelings. Despite the pioneer work that I had felt inwardly impelled to do, I am not by nature an empire builder; my heart has always been in research and writing, which are more important to me than money and status. Senior lecturers in a university are expected to do quite a lot of administration; this can be a responsible and lonely job, and not my strong suit. I love sharing and longed to be a member of a team again, as in the Exeter and Leicester clinics, or in the early years of the Department. The answer to all this tangle came in the move to the Student Health Service.

I join the doctors

After Billy retired in 1966, the School of Education changed its policy to some extent, and I felt rather a liability! In many ways I was sorry to leave, and have been most appreciative of the way my colleagues continued to carry the Service for so long, especially in the last three or four years when I was so busy with casework that I was a dead loss to them where teaching was

[2] I have described this problem in detail because I know it to be a vital concern of many counsellors at the present time. The variation of conditions of appointment and of salaries is considerable. A sub-committee of the executive of the Association for Student Counselling is working on a report concerning conditions of service for counsellors.

concerned, thus affecting the staff-student ratio. Before he left, Billy had a talk with the Vice-Chancellor, who in turn had a word with Dr. Binnie. One day, early in 1967, Hugh Binnie rang me up.

'Come and join us?'

'Yes,' I replied with no hesitation. Intuitively I knew the decision to be right. Later, before Billy died in 1972, he told me that he was perfectly contented about the move. In the final report (1967) I wrote:

> I was trained in a balanced team which included psychiatrists, psychologists, psychiatric social workers, and clerical staff. Despite Dr. Turner's invaluable support for the more severe cases I have felt very cut off during all these years, particularly where adequate medical coverage and understanding at the general practioner level were concerned, and I shall value the mutual aid and team work more than I can say.

This change came true, and I was very happy during the five years in a rapidly growing group which included Dr. Isobel Hunter-Brown, our consultant psychiatrist who is a psychoanalyst; an ever-increasing team of doctors, some of whom are psychiatrically trained and/or experienced in psychotherapy; a considerable nursing staff (for our old Institute of Education building has been converted into an in-patient health centre[3]); secretaries and receptionists. It was like old times, and good to pool problems at case conferences. For the first time my official designation was that of 'Psychological Counsellor'.

For the first time, too, after twenty-two years, in 1970 I felt able to apply for a term of study leave during the autumn term, to write a book. This was granted *if* I managed to find someone adequate to fill in for me. Experienced student counsellors are rare—and to get one for only one term almost an impossibility—but the miracle occurred. Alan Ingleby, after six years of counselling at a college of education and extensive marriage guidance experience, 'happened' to be free just at the right time. The

[3] Now called the Hugh Binnie Student Health Centre, in memory of Dr. Binnie.

chance to work with a medical team in a university was exactly what he wanted; so it all fitted in perfectly. Afterwards he went on to a permanent appointment as Counsellor at Hull University to carry on the service built there by Muriel Kay, and now is establishing a counselling service at the University of Glasgow.

Growth of the Area Student Health Service

The advantages of transfer were not all one way. It was good to be able to make a real contribution to the future administrative pattern designed with such energy and imagination by Hugh Binnie before his untimely death in 1972—the same year as Billy Tibble's. In a commemorative talk about Dr. Binnie's work on 'The Leicester Area Health Service' given to the British Student Health Conference at Keele University in July 1972,[4] Dr. J. L. Crighton, our present Director, said:

> What is special about the Leicester service is that it is an *area* student health service which serves not only the University but also the Leicester Polytechnic and the City of Leicester College of Education.[5]

Jimmy Crighton had been with us right through the period of expansion and reorganization, and he continued:

> In 1967 we were lucky enough to inherit a going psychological advisory service. For twelve years, Dr. Mary Swainson had been acting as Counsellor and Psychotherapist to the University's graduate School of Education, and during that time she had been available as therapist to students at the City of Leicester College of Education and at the teacher training department of the College of Art (now part of the Polytechnic). In this sense, there already existed the germ of a unified service, and when in 1967 Mary Swainson

[4] Published as 'The Leicester Development', *Proceedings of the British Student Health Association*, 1972. Quoted by kind permission of Dr. Crighton.
[5] By 1972 the College of Education had just completed a period of expansion in which, as well as having two outposts, it absorbed the School of Speech Therapy, the College of Domestic Science, and the College for the Training of Youth Leaders. Now (1976) in its turn it is merging with the Leicester Polytechnic.

became a member of the health service team, still retaining her connection with the colleges, it began to seem a logical development that students in the other colleges should benefit from all the facilities of the Student Health Service. Certainly the good-will which Mary Swainson had built up with the college staff and students alike through her ready availability and the skill of her therapy was a major factor in smoothing the course of the merger with the College of Education when it followed.

This merger took place in 1968, and that with the rapidly expanding Polytechnic in 1970. In 1971 the Polytechnic also appointed its own student counsellor, Jean Clark, who works in close association with the university team, and now is already expanding her staff. In 1972, in my sixty-fifth year, I retired. Michael Jacobs from Sussex University was appointed, also on lecturer grade, in my place. Billy Tibble's, Hugh Binnie's, and my dreams are coming true, and I feel well content with the improved facilities in mental health for now over 7,000 students in Leicester.

* * *

During the five years with the Student Health Service, three specific aspects of the work were much in my mind: the need for a residential centre; my impression of that generation of undergraduates; and (chiefly) the increasing co-operation with tutors.

The need for a residential centre

This problem came from the past. In the 1967 report I wrote:

> There is a need for a residential centre, staffed by a trained and understanding warden and his wife (acting as parent figures), to take for shorter or longer periods those students or ex-students whose homes are of no use to them and who need special background support during a course of psychological treatment. To give examples:
>
> (1) *Present students.* Some of the more hysterical types tend to 'act out', upsetting other students in Hall, or their

landladies in lodgings. The wardens and lodgings officers cannot be expected to put up with too much of this, and in most cases the students are not sufficiently ill to be sent to mental hospitals.

(2) *Students who have had to leave college* for a year, or who have been sent down, perhaps in mid-treatment. These may go downhill rapidly in lonely bed-sitters with no one who cares any longer about them. Some of them have had to be sent to residential centres—at someone's expense.

I can produce quite a number of case-histories : people who have taken up far too much of my time in sheer problems of living—time which should have been spent in psychological work. I am very grateful here to all the tutors and their wives who have helped me voluntarily with such cases, sometimes even 'adopting' a student for the time being in their own homes. At one stage I tried the experiment of periods of 'residential care' in my own home, but this was not altogether wise. It is a crucial need.

In 1969, to give the team some idea of the problem, I wrote a highly confidential document : 'Some Problems of Management', including statistics of the time spent on such cases in general, and giving particulars of five very long-term and demanding cases (anonymously of course) which had been responsible for restricting my vacations. Although we now had our residential health centre, where acute cases could be held for a while during intensive therapy (one student remarked how good it was that 'you can get depressed in complete seclusion') this did not quite meet the specific need. We wanted something like a Richmond Fellowship hostel where there is containment, support, and understanding, yet a steady launching into independent work and life.

Impressions of undergraduates

I started to take undergraduates again at the time of the post-Robbins expansion, and was shocked at the difference from my experience of such students before 1955. I have no statistical evidence, no proper sampling, on which to base this impression, but judging from those who came my way I formed the considered opinion that many should not have been in a university at all, and I advised one or two to seek an alternative career without wasting more public funds.[6] In my 1968–9 report for Dr. Binnie I wrote:

> Although I am very used to the problems of student teachers and social workers and others doing professional courses, most of whom have some sense of vocation, after two years of exposure to the full range of undergraduates, I am struck by the number among those referred who are ill because they have made the wrong vocational choice, or who go to university for the wrong (?) motives, enduring their three years as a grind, taking little if any share in university life, travelling home for any recreation they allow themselves. This year, out of nineteen undergraduates sent to me, three I feel ought never to have been here at all, and five others are finding it an almost intolerable strain. That is eight out of nineteen! Typical remarks are:
>> 'My Classics mistress said, "Oh well, you might as well go; it's only for three years, and there's more money for the rest of your life afterwards." '
>> 'It was accepted at school that everyone went to university. If you didn't fill in the U.C.C.A. form you had to see the headmaster.'
> What with parental, school, social, and moral pressures, a good many of these conflicts are repressed, showing up as psychosomatic symptoms, and the students find much difficulty (yet great relief) in listening to what the psyche is trying to communicate *via* the body.

A good many who picked up in their second year were found to have been suffering from utter confusion in their first year owing to lack of educational guidance; they did not know how to study. Even allowing that the difficulty might lie in the quality of the student or in the sixth-form teaching, this point leads directly to the need for close contact with the tutors.

[6] It is quite likely that this problem was the result of the sudden swing towards expansion, and that with the present equally sudden swing towards contraction it may not operate—but other problems will! When will the variations of educational policy settle to a middle way based on longer-term foresight?

Co-operation with the tutors

At the time of the move to the Health Service, it seemed important to try to build a bridge between the educational and medical approaches. To quote the 1967 report again :

The great thing in running the Service from the School of Education, as I see it, is that we were concerned primarily with the *prophylactic and educational* as well as the remedial personality work, and this as an integral part of teacher training; I very much hope that this outlook will not be lost. Several tutors, in both the School and the College of Education, have expressed concern at the change, realizing the importance of preventive work which attempts to 'stop the rot before it sets in'. They feel that the students may not refer themselves so readily for confidential personal problems which they wish dealt with outside the academic framework of their courses (such as coming to terms with being an adopted child, coping with a drunken and in-adequate father, dealing with a mother who is in and out of a mental hospital) if they associate such referral with the label of 'illness'.

The new ruling is that all referrals shall be made only through a medical practitioner. Tutors and students who have used our Service in the past will need to become accustomed to the idea that it is quite in order to approach our team of doctors for *all* problems which interfere with their studies and their well-being, whether these manifest psychosomatically or in anxiety or behaviour troubles. If they are in need of psychological counselling, they will be passed on to us.

It has been suggested that most personality and character problems should be dealt with by the students' personal (or moral) tutors; that in the past some tutors may have shelved their responsibilities by passing these on to us. To this I would reply that I think there are two levels here, and that the tutors' art may lie in discriminating between them. In the brochure it was stated : 'The Service is not meant to overlap with any tutorial system, but is intended for those students who have some nervous trouble or some personality problem which may be hampering them in their work or in their college life, causing unnecessary suffering and anxiety.' There have been a few cases where I have sent a student back, confining myself to consulting with the tutor about the kind of tutorial help which I felt he could well give the student himself, but these cases have been rare, and in one I was very wrong. The vast majority of character problems selected by tutors for referral have been symptoms of deeper disturbance usually originating in early childhood and were certainly of the kind which needed the trained skills, confidential conditions, and length of time which tutors cannot be expected to provide.

A large number of presenting problems such as severe inability to concentrate, compulsive conflict with authority, incapacity to relate to their fellows, or (most important to student teachers) to children and to the child in themselves —all these may indicate underlying personality blockages and disorders as frequently as do the skin troubles, vomiting, headaches and fainting displayed by other types of students. I have found that those tutors who have attended the experimental training course, or who have had similar psychological experiences (e.g. the Tavistock courses in inter-personal and inter-group relations), or—so many— who have the necessary flair by nature anyway, do not make errors in selection for referral. Hence I would stress the value of continuing such courses, especially with groups of tutors interested in learning and practising mental health attitudes sufficiently to discriminate wisely. This would be a real economy because such tutors would then be able themselves to take groups of students for informal personal discussion, which might well serve to prevent matters reaching a stage of neurosis or severe depression; alternatively they would be able to spot such cases in the important early phases. One tutor (a warden) has suggested that there is a need for someone to take a group of students, selected from various halls of residence, who find difficulty in adjusting during their first year; the realization that there are others who feel the same and the sharing of common problems would, in itself, be prophylactic. Another tutor has asked me to quote Jung's attitude that the findings of analytical psychology are not only for the sick but for all.

Actually, the doctors themselves were taking many prophylactic student groups, e.g. for examination phobia, spotting well beforehand, by means of a questionnaire, those who were likely to be affected.[7] (There was also an attempt at a homesickness group for those first-years who could not bear even the first week or two, and ran straight home, but clearly it was difficult to catch these in time!) They also took remedial therapy groups with good effect. For myself, although I had taken many semi-educational, semi-therapeutic groups with the normal run of students, I found that in actual casework one-to-one counselling saved time, mainly because of the limited duration of so many courses and of frequently late referral. But this was purely a personal preference.

To return to tutors: I had been experimenting for some years with tutor groups. In the report of 1963–4 it was noted that 'the main growing point lies in advisory work with tutors', and in the following year, in response to a request, we formed a small group for nine sessions, primarily to discuss ways of teaching the insights of depth psychology to the whole range of students in the education courses. Obviously, all these were tutors responsible for professional training (including also one senior P.S.W. engaged in training others for psychiatric social work), but they came from a variety of backgrounds, and the sharing of different experiences was valuable. In 1966–7 a larger group, running for ten meetings, included some university teachers. After I moved to the Health Service, a very good group in 1969–70 continued for nineteen meetings, followed by another in 1971–2 for twelve meetings. In all these we started by discussing student problems 'out there', but soon brought them 'home', ending by working on our own problems in dealing with students. By this time several of the doctors had also been taking tutor groups, and we compared notes. I would like to make it very clear that the exchange was a two-way one; we learned from the tutors as

7 J. Crighton and D. Jehu: 'Treatment of Examination Anxiety by Systematic Desensitization or Psychotherapy in Groups', *Journal of Behav. Res. and Therapy*, 1969, Vol. 7, pp. 245–8.

much as they learned from us—and all individually from one another. In fact I personally felt very much in the middle, being an educationist yet practising therapy; I particularly valued the medical knowledge. The whole exchange was very creative.

In 1969, following Dr. Nicolas Malleson's example, Hugh Binnie organized a course of lectures for tutors on 'The Management of Student Problems'. It was significant that those who attended were mainly from professionally oriented colleges, relatively few from the university. But the course served as a seedbed for groups, which more university tutors attended. The lectures were given partly by visiting lecturers, partly by ourselves. Chapter 10 is adapted from the talk I was asked to give to these tutors. Chapter 11 is on the same theme, but I have included it because of the entirely different presentation when given to a body of counsellors.

CHAPTER 10

The Tutor's Point of View

[A paper given to tutors in 1969]

In this talk I am speaking mainly out of my own past experience, first of having been a tutor (in and out of residence, academic and professional) in universities and a college of education, and secondly as a result of courses run at Leicester for tutors in student counselling.

Problems as the students see them

From a recent investigation in the rapidly expanding colleges of education[1] come these comments by students in reply to a questionnaire on the tutorial relationship :

Some were positive in tone, e.g. :
Fifty per cent of the staff are never too busy to listen. They are *available*.
Many were qualified :
It depends on individual tutors whether or not you feel welcome to discuss problems or just feel you are being a menace and holding up the tutor's time.
But a much higher proportion were unfavourable. Tutors were felt to be 'remote'; it was said that there was a lack of opportunity to meet personal tutors and that the conditions were 'too formal'.
There is a Hall Warden to go to with problems, but it is not successful as she does not know who you are. You

[1] J. H. Tiley: *The Adjustment of College of Education Students to Problems of College Life and Teaching Practice.* Unpub. thesis for M.Ed. (Leicester), 1968, pp. 371–2.

first have to identify yourself, then pour out your problems to a stranger. This is the result of large numbers and rather apathetic wardens.

Several said that they would prefer to have a trained adviser as a member of the staff.

University students' views are illustrated in Bryan Wilson's contribution to a recent survey[2]:

> But even when the tutorial system is in operation it is often under strain. There are doubtless many conscientious tutors, but students I have known well often provide gloomy reports of their tutorials: 'He comes late every week'; 'He seems to be just waiting to get through the hour'; 'He isn't interested in us'. The moral tutor is even less meaningful than the academic tutor. Some see their students once a term when they summon them to an interview. They make no pretence of getting to know their students. The 'Any problems?' approach is common; or the questions: 'How's the grant? How's the digs? How's the girl?' are a matey technique which imposes superficial *bonhomie* on to a situation where it serves only to guarantee that the student will say he has no problems, or none which, in this context, he is prepared to discuss with his tutor. It is an approach which does much to salve the conscience of the tutor without doing much to solve the problems of the student.

Here, then, is our challenge. Yet I would suggest that these opinion-finding surveys need to be examined with some critical detachment. Do we not need to 'listen with the inner ear' to hear what the students are really saying? Although at their face value there is much truth, yet there are also many levels of understanding, many psychological overtones. In these overt demands and criticisms they complain that tutors are too busy to care, whilst at the same time they often reject tutors (we all know that just now many university students say they do not want

[2] Marjorie Reeves (Ed.): *Eighteen Plus*, Faber, 1965, Chapter 3: 'The Needs of the Students', p. 74.

tutors, especially in hall). This attitude appears to be ambivalent. Perhaps if we look more deeply than the *wants*, to see the *needs*, we may realize that *they need to express ambivalence*.

Such a need is not easy for a tutor to take; so let us look now at the problems of relating, as the tutors see them. The following comments are all actual remarks of tutors in discussion groups.

Problems as the tutors see them

The first problem raised is almost invariably that of *accessibility*:

How do you make the initial contact? At coffee parties there is always the difficulty of getting the students to talk; they don't seem to *have* any interests.

How do you connect personally?

How do you make the bridge between the social and personal levels?

Some tutors understandably feel diffident about probing:

How far can one intrude into a student's private life, e.g. girl-friends, the marriage problem, or the home background where the trouble so often lies, even if we know it is holding up the work?

Such tutors may fall over backwards from over-consideration. Others say:

To what degree have students a *right* to find one accessible?

And (a very subtle and perceptive question):

If one offers accessibility and then they still don't come, is one then really accessible? And what does this imply?

Here the tutor may possibly be too self-critical. Even official counsellors may well wait for weeks or even months in setting up a new service until the word goes round that 'You can talk to *him*'.

So here again, in looking at these remarks, just as we did with the students' comments, we have to ask, 'What are the tutors really saying, and what are *their* basic needs?' Most of us find difficulty in professional relationships because we have to function in the field of tension between inner and outer demands; we try to be true both to our own nature and to what the job which we have undertaken expects of us. There are indeed very real external problems which depend on the nature of the institution and the role which the tutor feels he is asked to play.

The social structure of university or college and the role of the tutor

Sociologists often criticize psychologists, perhaps rightly, for underestimating the effects of the social framework in activating images—even stereotypes. To the students, the institution will take the place of home and family, and they will react accordingly.

Most of those students who are problems to us suffer from prolonged and delayed adolescence. In this group, highly selected for intelligence and for academic achievement, there is frequently a wide intra-psychic gap between the forced intellect and the immature emotions, causing inner tension. The problem is exacerbated in the cases where younger siblings, possibly more inwardly balanced, have already obtained jobs and established themselves in the adult world, albeit at a lower economic level. Some of our students have never been through the normal teenage rebellion at home, and so may need to do it now, on us, within the institution. A few—the most sick, I find—have not even come as far as the break-away stage. So, what happens?

In so far as the institution is authoritarian, they will react to it as to an authoritarian parent, either complying or rebelling, the latter overtly or by negativism.

In so far as the institution is wisely permissive, encouraging the assumption of personal responsibility, they will either feel frightened and lost, longing for the firmer framework of school, or, if sufficiently mature, will feel free to grow, find themselves and create. Yet, even in a free and mature institution, it is difficult to achieve spontaneity in relationship between staff and students. For example, one college devoted most of a staff meeting to discussing the mutual use between staff and students of Christian names. This may sound a trivial point, but its significance is not trivial. Name is identity, and students are searching for their identity, just as tutors are searching for their role in the whole educational process: 'What is the role *that suits me*? If I can find it, then I can resolve the tension between inner and outer needs; I can be myself and also be what is needed, with spontaneity.' (How difficult!)

How do we feel about relating to the so-called 'human' aspect? Is it important to us that those students who have not yet done so can find the kind of set-up in which they can work through adolescence and grow towards maturity? Are we responsible for their emotional education as well as for their studies, or not? How do we see our roles here?

One factor to be considered, when working on our attitude, is the growing importance of horizontal relationships. At the student stage, vertical relationships (i.e. between parent and child figures, teacher and taught) become progressively less important than the relationships of the peer group in the maturing process. In learning to relate to equals—sibling patterns, group patterns, opposite-sex patterns (involving the issue of single-sex or mixed colleges and halls)—they are practising interdependence rather than one-way dependence on parent figures. In the first year away from home, it is noticeable how the group (especially the 'preliminary group' in a college of education) takes the place of the home. One dependent first-year man found that regular coffee with a group of *several* girls, at their hostel, was a life-line until he could stand on his own feet. Many tutors and wardens comment how good students are with each other in crises. Personally, I am always struck by the number of students who use fellow-students as personal 'counsellors', saying that 'they understand'.[3] Young tutors also have a place here, being 'close enough'.

So perhaps our part is to work with, make use of, and if necessary alter the pattern of the social structures of the institution in which we work.

The role of the tutor in the institution

The main difficulty of which tutors complain is that the institution requires them to play two, or even three, roles at one and the same time: teacher, moral tutor, and perhaps hall tutor as well. In so far as these roles involve showing different faces, lack of trust may result. If students know that tutors are

[3] In 1973–4, five years after this paper was written, 'Nightline' came into full operation in our area. This is a student-run telephone service for students in difficulty.

responsible for marking their examination papers, they may well project on to them images of powerful authority figures in whom it is dangerous to confide; at worst they see such tutors as condemning tyrants who 'mark down' unless their own theories are 'dished up'! Even in the less traumatic 'continuous assessment' pattern of colleges of education, they still realize that they are being watched and assessed 'from above'.

(1) *Academic tutors.* From this particular angle, academic tutors have the most difficult task. Suppose a tutor works in a department in which the subject matter has nothing to do with human personality. He may well feel that his colleagues think of students only as brains and would regard it as odd—possibly even 'a bit sick'—to consider personalities. I think we must accept that many academic tutors are frankly not interested in the human aspect, and that the students sense it. 'Oh, they are not bothered with you *as a person* in that department.' In such circumstances, the rare tutor who is 'bothered' will be much valued, and the students recognize at once that 'He is human'; 'He'll listen'; or 'You can talk to him'.

The word 'listen' is significant. Counselling has sometimes been defined as 'creative listening', and perhaps it is harder for the academic tutor than for others to reverse the normal lecturing role in this way. Yet so often what a student needs is just to be able to *tell* an older person. Sometimes a tutor has said to me, 'I wouldn't know what to *say* to the student,' and I have replied, 'Do you need to say anything?' One of the happiest traits of a wise tutor is to be able to hold, contain, and let things be, rather than do too much probing, analysing, and giving advice. Students have often said, 'Oh well, he *knows*; he didn't say anything, but I felt received,' and they have gone away lighter in spirit.

On the other hand, if 'he knows' what will he do with the knowledge? One student said, 'He's the sort of man I *could* talk to, but I can't because he teaches me.' This matter of confidentiality is crucial.

(2) *Moral or personal tutors.* Therefore we find the establishment of moral or personal tutors to deal with the more confidential aspects. Should their tutorial groups, then, consist only of students whom they do not teach? Obviously, there is the

advantage that this tutor is not assessing the work; on the other hand is he too far removed from the area of study to understand? In former days in the University School of Education we found it an advantage to combine the role of personal tutor with subject tutor. This was because we were dealing, in a one-year post-graduate course, with another break-from-home period. After three intensive years in an academic department, the student feels sure of himself in respect of his subject and his recently achieved degree; at least he has succeeded *there*. Then he is required to plunge into a very large school with different subject matter and attitudes which challenge him on his emotional and social, instead of intellectual, sides. Moreover, he has to mix in many groups with other students from all departments and even from other universities. The subject group, led by a tutor who is a specialist in his own degree subject, feels to him like 'home'; there are common values and language. However, there is clearly a difference between the position of personal tutors in the academic field and in professional courses.

(3) *Tutors of professional courses.* At first sight, tutors of professional courses have a much easier task from the human angle, and this for three reasons :

(a) Because they teach the very subject matter of personality in their courses.

(b) They are deeply concerned with training the personalities of their students as an integral part of the work.

(c) They are indeed training the students to work practically in the field of personality, with children, young people, or (in social work and often in speech therapy) with disturbed or handicapped people of all ages.

The great advantage, then, is that initially the thorny personal problems can be introduced and looked at *at one remove*, and this takes care of most natural resistance. Thus the whole course can be run with a double reference; everything we discuss in the subject matter, and everything that forms part of the actual structure of the course, are really a part of the personality education of the students. Usually most of this process is implicit, or made explicit to a certain degree only towards the end.

[*I then outlined some of the methods described in Chapter 4.*]

These methods need very careful, balanced handling or else the process may become too intensive, too involved. Students may come to feel that every attitude or action is being watched, assessed, analysed, and even perhaps condemned. But that is the abuse of the method, and not necessary.

Tutors of professional courses have one main conflict of loyalties which academic tutors need not face. They are responsible for assessing personality as well as intellectual attainment. Suppose that a tutor discovers in a student some personality defect, such as compulsive stealing or excessive drinking, which might cause severe trouble in future professional life. If this is displayed openly, there is no conflict for the tutor. (In the example of one student, who drank so persistently at nights that he failed to turn up in the mornings at his school during teaching practice, sanctions could be used: 'You will go to Mary Swainson for help, or ELSE . . .!' *Not* the best setting for counselling, but he did come through finally.) The conflict arises when the student confides in the tutor something of the kind which otherwise would have remained undetected. In view of the promise of confidentiality—yet also of duty to the profession and above all to the children whom the student will teach—where does the tutor's loyalty lie? He can advise the student very strongly to seek skilled help, but what if the student refuses? A good deal depends on the severity and permanence of the problem. In an extreme and potentially dangerous case, some tutors have given fair warning: 'I have advised you to consult X, or, if you prefer it, some doctor at home or elsewhere; if not, you will understand that in my position I *must* inform the Principal —but it would be so much better if you did so yourself.' (Such a case is very rare.)

In my former dual role as counsellor and tutor, I was often asked to give advice about homosexuality, which is not *necessarily* a 'defect' so much as a personality orientation (see p. 204). In the more fluid cases, where the pattern *is* a psychological defect owing to a block in development, psychotherapy can very often help the students to re-orient themselves to their innately dominant heterosexual pattern. But in the instance of the firm homosexuals (some of whom came voluntarily for vocational advice), my main criterion was whether they were oriented to younger boys, on the one hand, or to men of their own age or older, on the other. The former group I advised very strongly not to choose teaching or youth work as a career. I did all I could to help them to adjust their life-pattern responsibly, but I never betrayed their confidence. With the latter group, I always remembered the advice of a wise psychiatrist, who used to say to them : 'We are all bisexual to some degree, physically and emotionally. You teach (or nurse, or do social work) largely from your feminine side. Accept it; use it; value it; sublimate it. Then there will be no *extra* conflict which is what causes so much of the trouble.'

(4) *Hall wardens, resident tutors, and lodgings officers.* In some ways, these—especially the wardens—have the hardest time, being 'on duty', as it were, day and night. And even though they may not teach the students in their halls, yet they often experience a division of loyalty, as is shown by the following problems which they have raised for discussion :

> Responsibility to university or college regulations, although the warden does not himself agree with them. He feels split; he cannot be himself spontaneously in his relation-ships and the students know it.
>
> Responsibility not only to the students who are disturbed but to all the others—'normal' students, staff, domestics—who live in the hall. Wardens often complain of the strain under which a student group is placed by one disturbed case, especially a hysterical girl. On the other hand, some wardens see this as part of the process of group education.
>
> When should they leave things alone, turning a blind eye? When take decisive action? When refer responsibility to the doctors?
>
> Where can they draw the line concerning confidentiality?

All these are major issues, frequently raised, especially the last. Torn by conflict, some become over-identified and feel guilty when crises in hall occur; others 'opt out' and are then accused by students of apathy, when perhaps their real feelings are those of fear and avoidance. I have the greatest admiration for wardens, most of whom seem to walk the middle way miraculously.

Perhaps their chief challenge is that of timing. It is easy for the official counsellor who has a regular hour per week for his client, but a warden or resident tutor or lodgings officer may have to be up half the night dealing with an examination panic or suicide attempt. It is so important to deal with the crisis when it arises; then the other students also have trust that 'he is there when needed', not fussy, but truly accessible.

Whatever roles tutors are expected to play, however, the counselling which we all do takes place at different depths and in different ways according to inclination, ability, and training.

Levels of counselling

In training courses, tutors have always asked for a working model, so here is a hypothetical framework for discussion :

(1) Tutorial Level : (a) Educational Guidance
(2) Tutorial Level : (b) Personal Guidance
(3) Trained Counsellor Level
(4) Psychiatric Level

(5) Level of a Living Philosophy

I would suggest that the only way in which we can be true to ourselves is to find the level on which we feel at home, and then work there, referring uncongenial problems elsewhere. The framework is qualitative and does not indicate any order of merit. Moreover, the fifth category has been placed alongside, since anyone who has searched and found at least some degree of his own working philosophy may well have the know-how to help others to find theirs. Let us take each level from the surface inwards—from the obvious to the fundamental—which is the way we work in counselling anyway. At any point, you may feel : 'This is, or is not, for me.'

(1) *Tutorial level: (a) educational guidance.* A useful 'way in' is to start with the 'presenting problem' which, in a college or university, is often inability to work. Students complain that they cannot concentrate, are overwhelmed with too many essays, or they may show signs of compulsive perfectionism. Here there is much to be said for individual or group tutorials in the first

year on techniques of study, involving such themes as getting to know one's own rhythm and working with it; selective reading; planning of essays; and use of libraries and equipment. All these are specific to the departments concerned and can be done by most tutors. I have found that group discussion at this level is of particular advantage, because students fresh from school realize that others have similar problems; they feel less isolated, and by pooling help one another. (In teacher training, all these skills have particular relevance because of their double reference.) If however, the trouble persists, there may be underlying emotional blocks.

(2) *Tutorial level: personal guidance.* Why cannot the students bring themselves to work?

Is the trouble typical first-year difficulty in settling into a freer and more stimulating environment? Are they homesick, never having lived away from home before? Or is there a need to have a fling in order to balance up after the great pressure of A levels? (Imbalance between intellectual and emotional needs is a frequent source of psychological disturbance, and nature may be trying to redress the balance.) Some students have complained that hall was too noisy to work in, but on investigation it was found that they would not shut the door on their friends because the need for social life and experience was stronger than the need to study.

Is the difficulty one of internalizing discipline? Many find self-discipline very hard to acquire. Up to the sixth-form level others had made them work; they felt it was the responsibility of the school 'to see that we got through'. Or at home, 'Father stood over me', and the student may complain bitterly that tutors do not seem to care in the way that teachers or parents did; one or two have even begged tutors to stand over them and see that their work is done. Granted that many school teachers exert too much pressure; do we perhaps go far too suddenly to the other extreme? Is there a place for some guidance in order that the student may effect the transition? How do we teach students to internalize discipline?

As a psychological counsellor, I find that much of my time which should be used for deeper problems is taken up at this level because students either cannot or will not go to tutors about it. For example, a science student had written no essays for years, but she could not bring herself to ask for help. Taking the Combined Studies course, she found herself faced with a series of essays in sociology. She floundered, worked through many nights copying out her attempts five times! The neurotic troubles for which she was finally referred to me were secondary and totally unnecessary.

Or do the students need more drastic vocational re-direction? Should they have come to university or to college in the first place? If not, the sooner they are re-directed, the better.

Financial worries and other practical matters often inhibit work output. Student welfare committees can be of great help here. Students may well feel ashamed, and be more likely to confide in their peers than in tutors.

At a deeper level—and a wise tutor can handle these—are the personal problems concerning love affairs or home troubles causing anxiety and preventing concentration. Here one has to go more slowly and carefully, and timing is crucial. Generally speaking, the earlier a problem is tackled, the better, since quite a long period of re-orientation and re-experiencing are often necessary. On the other hand, forcing confidence does harm; if one can spot the moment when the student is ready to talk by just 'being there', much time and unhappiness may be saved. I find, for instance, that there is a great deal of ignorance about the *feeling* aspect of sex. In view of the wide knowledge of techniques, and the social pressures concerning experience-status, the human feelings, especially of the woman, tend to be lost sight of altogether. I would suggest that, if the students want, as some do, to consult an older and experienced person, this could well come within the province of the personal tutor, with special reference to meeting as whole persons. The same applies to students who are 'living it up', experimenting with drink and drugs and with the danger of pregnancies. Is there, perhaps, a place for informal discussion of such matters, with or without a tutor, all in a normal way, and not considered as an 'illness'?

If all these ways have been tried, and the student still has obviously deeper problems, then referral can be made, through the team of doctors, to the trained psychological counsellor.

(3) *The trained counsellor level.* These are the students who come to me : people who cannot find out by ordinary talk with a tutor what is the trouble, because the causes lie buried in the unconscious; or sometimes what they think is the trouble is really masking a deeper issue that cannot yet be faced. It is very important that tutors should be able to recognize the signs so as to know when to refer, or when there is no need to refer.

Some of the following patterns of behaviour are useful indications, but they are not *necessarily* yet actual psychological illnesses; they may be more in the nature of a block in growing up, or an imbalance in life-style. Moreover, one can rarely label a symptom or behaviour-trait and say, 'This means that', because, given, for example, the same bad home conditions, different individuals will show the effects in different ways, according to personality type. Thus, some sail through and are all the stronger. Of those who show damage, extraverts tend to display it outwardly in behaviour—even amounting to delinquency—whilst introverts tend to internalize the problem, registering it in minor neurosis and withdrawal. To give some examples :

> *Extraverts* include hysterics, delinquents and paranoids.
>> *Hysterics* tend to 'act out', mobilizing a whole team of 'helpers'. They cause a nuisance in hall. They tend to be over-dependent, always leaning on others, with tears and tantrums. Their behaviour is usually directed at some other person, and they will often play up one tutor against another.
>> *Delinquents* are often hitting out at society. Unconsciously, they feel, 'You've hurt me; I'll make you suffer!' Stealing from unconscious motives is very common, but must be distinguished from straightforward conscious stealing. Violence may well come into this category.
>> *Paranoids* need unconsciously to see themselves as 'good' and others as 'bad'. They are, therefore, the most difficult to help. If there is a severe pattern of persecution they should always be referred to a doctor.
> *Introverts* on the whole are much easier to help, because

they will usually work on themselves. Nearly always they show considerable *anxiety*, which may take many forms :

Sleeplessness, nightmares, sleep-walking and -talking. Absent-mindedness to an abnormal degree, total lack of concentration. Phobias of various kinds, e.g. compulsion to go out of lectures, or to sit in the corner of a coffee bar.

Physical habits such as nail-biting, picking skin to make sores, hitting walls with fist or head, any abnormal trait of self-punishment. Obsessional patterns : a very common trait with students is perfectionism : must get an A or nothing !

The so-called 'inferiority complex'; shyness, social isolation, cannot mix, draws chair back in groups, can't speak in seminars without agonizing tension. General withdrawal from life and escape into fantasy. Tutors complain they cannot 'get through' to the student.

Some people repress the conflict so completely that the body has to take it over, and so we find *psychosomatic symptoms*. It is always necessary for a doctor to see such cases because there may be a physical cause. But if the student is physically sound, we have to ask : 'What is the body trying to tell us?' There is a kind of 'organ jargon' by which physical symptoms symbolize the emotional trouble that is repressed. Thus, a painful back may well mean that a person carries too great a load in his unconscious mind. Or there may be what we call a 'secondary gain' from the symptom, such as eye trouble, or hand tremor which prevents a student sitting for his examinations. What we do is to endeavour to bring the original conflict back from the body into the feelings. This is far more painful emotionally, but at least it can then be faced and worked on consciously.

Such behaviour patterns and symptoms are on the slight or moderate psycho-neurotic levels and can be dealt with by a trained psychological counsellor or psychotherapist. But the more severe degrees of neurosis, and the psychoses—serious depression with suicidal tendencies, the bizarre behaviour or extreme withdrawal of the schizoid or schizophrenic states—these come into

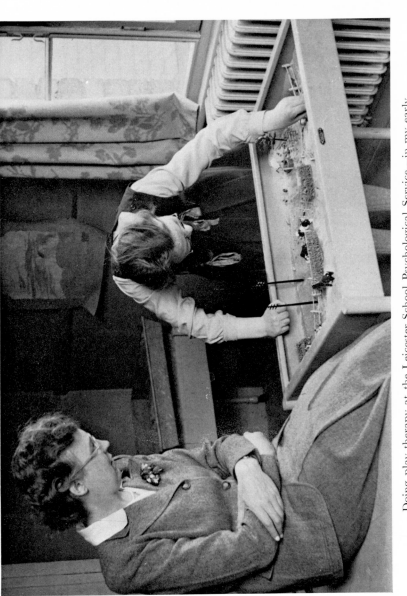

Doing play therapy at the Leicester School Psychological Service—in my early forties.

(Reproduced by kind permission of the Leicestershire Education Committee)

Listening at a counselling session

the fourth category : the psychiatric level, and should always be referred straight to a doctor as soon as possible.[4]

(5) *The level of a living philosophy.* In all this work, we are trying to get to the root of the problem : what is the disturbed student's psyche really trying to say, really reacting to, really needing? All this promiscuity, drug-taking, or whatever : what is it all *for*? So often, psychological illness—especially psychosis—is a flight away from personal commitment to the world : a flight not to be condemned but rather understood. Indeed, I would dare to suggest that often the best counsellors are those who have had a good deal of trouble themselves, *yet have come right through*.

In this table of levels, I have placed this aspect of counselling beside all the others because, although it is the most fundamental, it is needed at all stages, and for the healthy as well as the sick. Moreover, especially in universities and colleges of education, it is the foundation upon which true higher education is (or, in my opinion, should be) based. It is, therefore, not a speciality in the sense that psychiatry is. Any tutors, who have lived, thought out, and are prepared to discuss, deeper issues *alongside* their students, can share in such counselling, although naturally some will be wiser, more experienced, more skilled than others.

In some recent research in colleges of education,[5] Muriel Kay found that underlying all the problems are five basic questions. The work on these cannot be done purely by thought, but by feeling and by living experience. Writing from her own experience as a tutor, she says :

> Concisely summarized, it could be said that students in difficulty were ultimately seeking answers to the following questions :
> Who am I?
> Why am I here?
> Who are my significant others?

4 In this course for tutors, lectures were given by doctors on spotting the signs of psychoses and of drug-taking.

5 Dr. M. M. Kay: *Personality and Adjustment Problems of Students in Training for Teaching: A Contribution to Developmental Psychology.* Unpub. thesis for Ph.D. (Leicester), 1968, p. 134.

How do I relate to them and to the cosmos?
What are my fundamental and enduring values?

You will remember that Jung tells us that the problem for most of his patients was that of finding a meaning in life, and that we are less likely to take a neurotic attitude to life-experience if we can find it significant and purposeful.[6]

Here then, is a challenge for all teachers in centres of higher education. Psychological disturbance has become a problem for remedial medicine because the meaninglessness of life has now reached a point at which the psyche becomes ill. So we cannot refer all responsibility to the doctors; here is something that faces us all, *in so far as we are persons*. For the fundamental problem and taboo of today is no longer sex but death—or rather the duality life/death—because if we cannot die we cannot deeply live. The young, partially realizing this, are exploring the next dimension of consciousness by various methods. For some, at the outset, this takes the form of drugs, but for many, drugs are merely a phase. Beyond is the new direction, the exploration of 'inner space'.

Most of us do not profess philosophy as a teaching subject. But I would submit that, although we cannot be responsible *for* young adults, we are responsible *to* them, *to be what we are*, with them, somewhere along the way to the discovery of meaning. Otherwise, why live? Why want to help others? Why want to help oneself? The test is often the way in which we talk with a potential suicide.

The personal aspect

Fundamentally, therefore, it all comes back to the personal aspect. Quite simply, what shines through all techniques is the openness to be ourselves, and this works. It does not mean trying to be 'perfect'—far from it! Often I find that one helps people more by admitting a good deal of emotional immaturity in oneself, accepting it, not minding it, and even still liking oneself.

Take, for instance, our reaction to the problem of authority. Students will project on to us all sorts of figures, good and bad,

---

[6] C. G. Jung: *Modern Man in Search of a Soul*, Kegan Paul, 1936, Chapter 11.

feeble and useless. Of course we do not sail through this process unscathed; it is horrible to be alternately sought after and rejected; it is not easy to stand for some figure in their own psyches, and to let them kick it.

Of course we want students to like us, just as school teachers want to be liked by the children. Of course we are afraid to jeopardize our popularity; hence, when young, we often try 'to be a student with the students' which, though understandable, is not true, and therefore is not what is basically needed. Of course we sometimes get over-anxious and spot neuroses everywhere. Or, alternatively, we may have a resistance against 'these psychologists', and suggest, as one tutor did, that a sailing holiday would cure a near-suicide.

A useful way to find out how we feel is to think of individual students. Just as a school teacher finds that some children get under his skin more than others do, so do we react to students. Which kind of student do we find easy to relate to? Which difficult? Why?

Further training

At this point, tutors often ask what further training is available in order to discuss and gain insight into such reactions. Unfortunately, very little is yet organized, though there is great need.[7] But there is nothing to prevent tutors meeting in informal groups—in hall or in the department—to pool problems. Especially useful are such meetings where people from different disciplines, e.g. social work or education, share experience and training. For, when we put our problems, ideas, and achievements into the pool, we find that we are no longer so alone in the work. We do not have to learn any imposed doctrine, but rather each person, in the group situation, can find himself and his own way of working. In this way, through participation in a fluid *gestalt*, which soon becomes of greater significance than the sum of its parts, we discover that, for each individual, life has gained in meaning.

[7] This was in the 1960s. See note 5 on p. 92 for further developments.

CHAPTER 11

Counsellors and Tutors

[*In contrast to the preceding paper (prepared for tutors), this one was presented specifically to counsellors, at a conference for those practising counselling in higher education held at Keele University in July 1970. Requested as a brief introduction to the conference, it was designed to stimulate discussion; hence in places it is deliberately provocative, and some statements are possibly exaggerated. Examples quoted come from other colleges I have known, as well as those at Leicester. In the ensuing discussion it became clear that the issues raised were common to nearly everyone—in some form or other.*]

Counselling the students seems to me to be the easiest part of our work. But we are given very little guidance about our relationship with our colleagues. And do we know what our function is in the *specific* educational establishment in which we work? Or do we learn to play this by ear?

Do you find, as I do after twenty-two years' experience of several colleges and university departments, that, quite apart from the deeper personal neuroses stemming from childhood, students from a specific educational set-up will tend to bring similar problems, year after year? For example, from certain tutors in a college of education may come a long line of potential drop-outs. In a university, we may find that certain traits are common to the Maths department; Philosophy students show specific difficulties owing to the nature of the subject; in one or two Science departments I have found it is 'not done' for the staff to have personal relationships with the students; if a member of staff is interested in personality, his colleagues may think him 'sissy'. (So what does a 'moral' tutor do?) At the other extreme, in some Sociology and Psychology departments, students (and some staff) tend to know all the answers with their heads. A few tutors may even attempt counselling without proper training (as we would conceive training), possibly becoming involved with their own pupils, possibly failing to spot an incipient psychosis. Yet very many tutors, as we know, are naturally gifted in human relations; they do wonderful work and are most co-operative with us. So, where does tutoring end and 'expert' counselling begin? I have tried to draw the line in the paper 'The Tutor's Point of View'[1], but this is not easy; I would suggest that it is not so much a line as a zone.

On the administrative side, in a new university or college we may find a 'ragged' set-up, where doctors, chaplains, tutors, wardens, and others are all working separately. And then the students demand that a 'proper' counselling service shall be set up as well. My impression is that, at least in universities, students are extremely critical of the tutorial system in so far as it is personal. The appointment of 'moral' tutors is open to question. Many young lecturers are working out their own personal problems on the students, who in some cases may be the more mature.

Perhaps all this is to be accepted as the nature of the specific community? If so, how does it affect us, as counsellors, in our rather new and experimental position? Most of us who are pioneering in human relationships in a community find, I imagine, that there comes a point at which we can go no further with our cases until the new attitudes are shared by the rest of the staff. We feel a need for a kind of 'therapeutic community', otherwise the students (or in a school the children) may become split between opposing attitudes. How do we achieve this? Should we offer to counsel the staff? Or is this presumptuous?

At one extreme, some of us, perhaps over-enthusiastically, may try to 'reform' or 'therapize' the staff! A slow job, and one which may cause understandable resentment, hampering co-operation; anyway, there is always built-in resistance because of the very nature of the work. And what right have we to attempt such a thing? 'For the sake of the students'?

[1] See Chapter 10, p. 124. This paper was available at the conference as a supplementary hand-out.

At the other extreme, we may 'opt out', doing our work quietly, well away from the rest of the college (e.g. in another building, or at home, as I do). We may choose to swim around in our own little duck-pond, except for the few members of staff who are ready to co-operate anyway. Here we may err on the side of not participating enough.

Most of us try to aim at some middle way. But if we do feel called upon to spend time and energy with tutors: how? Here are some suggestions:

(1) *Through informal working together and fraternizing.* This is the most usual way. Gradually we build up good relations with colleagues by sharing, by creative listening to their points of view, by learning from them. Perhaps the best way? Slow but sure? However, there are two problems:

(a) *Confidentiality.* Of course the most natural way to meet is over a case. Here is a dilemma. In normal fraternizing in the senior common room, a friendly tutor comes up with the usual spontaneous remark, 'How is John going along?' If one is cool, reserved, and off-putting over detail, as to some extent one must be, tutors may well complain of 'No feedback', or 'We don't hear enough about our students'. (Note 'our'.)

Again, if, in a small college, clients see the counsellor going into the senior common room, or especially into an academic assessment meeting, understandably they are filled with suspicion. Moreover, especially in a deeper case, to see their personal counsellor out of context can be a shock. Hysterics, on the other hand, often use the situation to enjoy the degree of concern which, they imagine, is going on about them, involving as many parent-figures as possible! It is not easy to find the middle way through all this.

(b) *Time.* Fraternizing and building up contacts with tutors takes time. How much of one's working day should be spent in this way? It's not a process which can be hurried, yet it is *so* important. But we can't record it as 'hours of work' in our annual reports!

(2) *We can offer our services more formally,* either clinically or

educationally, or a mixture of both, according to our own training and background.

(a) *Clinically*. Those counsellors who are trained as
clinical psychologists have specific skills to offer in testing
and ascertainment, assessment and evaluation. Those trained
as psychotherapists can offer to take members of staff for
formal psychotherapy (and all trained counsellors can take
staff as clients at the counselling level). This way is often
valuable for building up a core of more self-aware people
with insight, in the community. But two main difficulties
arise :

(i) *Time* (again). Older people usually make longer
cases. Are we justified in using hours, for which we
are paid, for staff? (In the past, I used to take a good
many; now they are referred elsewhere, often to a
private psychotherapist.) After all, they can pay, and
should do so—or shouldn't they, as members of the
community?

(ii) *Dual relationship*. Especially in a small college, it
can be a very tricky position when one has to meet a
colleague sometimes as his therapist, sometimes in the
environment of daily college work. Some of my greatest
mistakes have come from attempting such a dual
relationship.

(b) *Educationally*. If we are asked to give lectures to
students, or to take discussion groups, such courses can be
a good initial break-through, largely because they are in an
idiom which tutors understand and respect. When we have
to frame our basic assumptions, aims, and values in clear
concepts, tutors have the opportunity to grasp with their
minds what to them, otherwise, is often a puzzling—even
esoteric—'expertise'. [*I then described our experiment with
a series of lectures on 'The Management of Student
Problems'.*] Such a formal course was fine for basic theory,
on the intellectual level. But subsequently the keen core of
the group asked for more 'whole learning'. They wanted the
opportunity for personal discussion and pooling of problems,

and so we provided a further year of work in small groups. If, in this way, we act in response to demand, this takes us to:

(c) *The blending of educational and clinical approaches in a discussion group verging on a psychodynamic group.* (This is an untidy heading, and purposely so, because such groups cannot be labelled according to any rigid pattern.) This year we have been experimenting with such groups. Has it been worth our time? One and a half hour sessions, weekly, for a whole year, with eight or so people? I think so, but of course I'm prejudiced. From running many such groups in the past, I find that these self-selected tutors are potentially the leaven in the loaf of an institution; and such quiet work with a few can be one of the best ways of helping the *organic* growth of a therapeutic community.

Every group, I find, is different. The one this year (i.e. 1969–70) was the first which I have taken consisting entirely of academic subject-tutors. Compared with professional tutors, they needed a much longer time to get going, and we only began to operate dynamically about half-way through. Here is the picture:

Meetings 1 and 2 : Mainly introductory.

Meetings 3 to 7 : Discussion of problems in college, and of difficult students 'out there'. Tremendous spate of talk, liberating anxiety.

Meeting 8 : Aggressive explosion. They felt they had exhausted their own resources and were getting no help. I was 'not doing enough'.

Meetings 9 and 10 : Interpretation and insights. The whole pattern shifted to a deeper level, and we worked on what we all felt and believed.

Meetings 11 to 13 : Work on our own attitudes to authority, roles, wholeness. (These discussions were not intellectual but quite deeply personal.)

Meetings 14 to 17 : The group was smaller, usually with four or five present. This was due partly to the demands of the summer term, partly to some being unable to take the deeper personal implications. The small group really got down to tutors' own problems and attitudes.

Meeting 18: Post-mortem: work on death, mourning, and resurrection.

Meeting 19: The deepest yet: right down to basic values—what we understood by good and evil.

I never had a group quite like this one before. You have to trust the process and allow each group to develop naturally. As you know, it is wise to deal with separation and 'mourning' a little *before* the final break. I say 'death *and resurrection*' because next year the keen core of this and another group are linking to be taken further on more medical aspects by Dr. Crighton.

A question: in such semi-educational, semi-clinical groups, what role does the leader take? That of the ordinary leader of a discussion group? Or is he a relatively silent 'consultant' or 'observer', perhaps giving occasional interpretations or comments on group behaviour? Or does he share, coming in wholly as a person—as a full member of the group? I feel, myself, that a fluid shift of role is necessary, from time to time, according to what the members need, or can take. This shift may be seen as inconsistent, and indeed it is; but we use everything that happens, and as long as the inconsistency itself is brought into full awareness, it can highlight the whole question of roles. And for the trainers of teachers this topic of roles is of primary importance. Everything which goes on can be understood, not only in a double, but a treble reference: the role which we take with the tutors may be reflected in the role which they take with the students, and the students with the children; so the more conscious we are of what we are doing, the better.

Such fluidity and lack of a defined framework can be more difficult in practice than when running a clear-cut clinical group, education group, or those based on distinct background-theory such as the Bion, Berne, or Encounter-group systems. But personally, I see a certain degree of fluid adaptability as an essential practice for us, in so far as the future of counselling itself seems to lie in the *integration* of the disciplines of psychology, sociology, education and medicine.

CHAPTER 12

Quantities and Qualities

The informal conference at Keele, at which the paper in the last chapter was given, had been by invitation of Audrey Newsome,[1] one of the chief pioneers in the field, and now Vice-Chairman of the British Association for Counselling. In the following year, July 1971, a larger group met at Cambridge by invitation of Jean Ferguson, then in charge of the Cambridge Medical Counselling Service. Here Patricia Milner,[2] Counsellor at University College London, spoke to us about the new Association for Student Counselling, founded in November 1970, of which she is Chairman. I joined at once, but a year or two after retirement felt I should resign; however, I was most grateful to be made one of the two first honorary members. The Association already has a membership of well over 300.

What a change from the position twenty-five—or even ten—years ago! In the seventies, counselling is mushrooming, and this gives me immense happiness.

At the end of this chapter, just for the record, are tables of our own small statistics; but in all the joy of expansion we need also to think about quality. This is a very personal matter, varying with values held. Perhaps my own individual contribution can best be made by recording a brief farewell paper I wrote in the summer of 1972.[3]

* * *

[1] Author of *Student Counselling in Practice*, Univ. of London Press, 1973.
[2] Author of *Counselling in Education*, Dent, 1974.
[3] Reproduced from the Newsletter of the A.S.C., December 1972, by kind permission of the editor.

QUALITIES OF A COUNSELLOR

It was the end of a staff conference during my last term in student counselling, for I was about to retire.

'Tell me quickly in one sentence,' said one of our team just as we were rushing off, 'what would you say from your years of experience are the essential qualities of a counsellor?'

In a snap test such as this, what surfaces? It flashed through my mind that each can contribute only what he is, as a result of what he has needed to learn himself by means of the gruelling work of counselling. I wondered what others would say, but characteristically I closed my eyes, called (as always) for a 'hunch', and then found myself replying: 'Commitment and acceptance.' Certainly, these were the two main lessons which I have had to learn and practise, but whether they are the essential qualities for counselling in general, who can say? Anyway, I offer them as a basis for discussion.

Afterwards, in writing, I tried to allow the essence of my twenty-four years of casework with students to crystallize into concepts.

Commitment

What had I implied by 'commitment'? The whole truth seemed to mean commitment to the work, not only at the 'job' level, but at every level of being; yet to what extent was this possible? In my early years I had received a salutary shock when trying to act like a text-book therapist, finding that the near-psychotic types, like children (for I was trained in play therapy), saw right through mere words, acts, and 'correct' techniques. Carl Rogers' book *On Becoming a Person* was very helpful at this stage. So, as I grew older, I became increasingly wary of thinking in terms of the acting and interpretation of roles. With experience, I found that most of the work had taken place at a level of relationship deeper than that of mere ego-interchange, however carefully the session might be structured. The effect of such insight on my own ego was releasing, making me more detached, relatively carefree—yet far more humble. In saying this, I do not, of course, deny that thorough training is both necessary and valuable, but later one sees that standard 'clues' need very careful understanding or else interpretation can become imposed and arbitrary, whilst written—or even taped—records of sessions used as examples are inadequate, for they can never communicate the subtle empathy.

'Right empathy' is often quoted as one of the essentials in good counselling. If, however, we are working as far as possible from the whole of ourselves, what if we cannot feel the 'right' thing all through? On a conscious level of course, we cannot expect to 'empathize rightly' with every patient, because, even after long and deep analysis, and/or much experience of living, we cannot 'feel into' all the different types and individuals and their experiences in one life-time! Gradually I grew to accept this and to realize that it really didn't matter. Even if I still had a hang-up about a certain problem, so that the right empathy from my personality was blocked, yet true empathy *was there*— beyond the ego—if I could stand aside and let it be. For example, once in the early days I felt it impossible to love someone. The inner answer was: Why did I imagine that I should? Accept the fact; drop the effort; it's irrelevant. The thing to see is that the person *is loved*—and by something greater than oneself. Then one becomes aware of the unique value and significance of each individual beyond the unacceptable personality. In this way, we work together at a para-personal level where subsists a degree of detached harmony that is entirely different in quality from the attraction and repulsion of personality collusion and involve- ment—different even from the standard therapeutic relationship with its carefully structured rules and need for role interpretation. It is at this level that there is basic commitment.

Acceptance

All this implies what I call 'trusting the process'. Just as a doctor trusts the healing power of nature, so we find that we can safely trust what Jung calls the Self—the total psyche—and also collectively all the greater Selves in the group relationship; their fuller degree of consciousness knows infinitely more about it than does either my ego or the other egos. (We may speak of these Selves as being 'unconscious', but I think this is because we are blinded by their greater light.) For example, I have repeatedly been struck by the way in which timing is dealt with; 'something' seems to know exactly how much calendar-time is available (always a problem in student counselling) and takes the work at the level necessary or possible *at this stage* in the client's life, surfacing just before the end, often with no conscious interference on my part, and even sometimes (and invariably wisely) against my conscious wish. And this includes the acceptance that, in some cases, nothing can be done just now, and it is better to refuse a case and let it go, despite pressure from tutors, one's own fears as to what may happen, desire to help, or involvement with one's own prestige.

For *timing* is an important corollary of accepting the process. At first we may tend to think : here is the only opportunity that this young teacher in training may get for free therapy; consider the children he will teach ! He must be 'done properly' now— or never ! In the past I have tried to do too much before the client's ego was strong or mature enough to take it. But facilities are more widespread now; there's the rest of his life; he will probably find further help when he is ready. All we can do now is to start the process going—ploughing, weeding, sowing the seeds—and they will grow throughout the years to come (I have found much evidence of this fact). There is a time to work and a time to leave things alone; a time to grow and a time to consolidate; so much depends on the phase, the readiness, and the degree of commitment of the client's total psyche to the work. And *always*, I feel, his free will must be respected.

Depth of work is another corollary, closely akin to timing. I have learned with young people never to go more deeply than is absolutely necessary at the time, tempting though it may be with an enthusiastic introvert, and much as my colleagues may accuse me of letting students go too soon, or of 'cutting corners'. (I would make an exception here in the case of those who have already broken right down; one must, of course, start where they are.) But, generally speaking, my work in child guidance has taught me that, even though ego-boundaries may yet be thin, the younger the person the stronger are the forces of life working towards health, and the less rigid the neurotic pattern which is building up. People in middle and later life often seem to lack the necessary vitality to break through the entrenched defences and to grow afresh from their long-buried true selves. But with the young, if we can help to remove the blocks, nature and growth will do the rest. Trust the power of the life-force which works towards healing and wholeness: the *vis mediatrix naturae*.

Acceptance of oneself—of all that one is, inadequacies and all —is perhaps one of the hardest aspects, but I have found that empathy with the client does not work fully unless one also has empathy for oneself: the warm, tolerant humour which laughs when the exhausted personality curses the ring at the doorbell, and which sees imperfections as natural and even as irrelevant if we can put them aside, or—still better—use them in the work with detachment. A watchword which I have learned to respect and value is: 'Whatever happens, use it!' So, another corollary is to work always on the counter-transference, even (if appropriate) discussing it with the client. 'What am I doing? Why do I feel I need to say this to you? Why [*as my analyst once said to me*] do I feel angry with you?' Whether the problem lies mainly in the client or in oneself does not matter; looking at spontaneous feelings brings us up against reality, and is a valuable exercise in 'sitting loose' to personalities, giving deeper perspective. And one of the best ways to free the client from over-identification with his own personality is to take an objective look at our own, resolving the counter-transference by acceptance, tolerance, humour, and without guilt. For he will sense that we care enough to be able to use ourselves in this way.

However much one has been analysed, however far one studies techniques, the personality is always inadequate as an instrument. Does it matter? At first we may feel bad about it; we may try too hard to 'do the right thing', which may well precipitate harmful unconscious tensions and reactions. I felt this way, until one of my analysts made a lot of mistakes, showing himself fallible, yet he obviously *cared* in Eliot's sense of 'To care and not to care'. This attitude of his taught me and helped me more than all his efforts.

Acceptance of the life-situation can be still more difficult. How far can we keep perspective, see through the whole pattern in which the student is enmeshed, so that it too, can be accepted and used in its totality? So often we feel we should 'play God', put things right, change the conditions (and of course there is often a justifiable case for so doing). But how much of this compulsion to 'make it better' is a reflection of our own inability to tolerate the student's suffering, being unable to bear it ourselves? Here is a soul, struggling and learning painful lessons in a difficult context; are we to try to stop the learning, relieve the suffering and frustration by interference? Or do we help the student to look beyond appearances to what is really the challenge? I have often been struck by a client's appreciation (afterwards) of having been *allowed* to suffer, to *be* depressed, to take his own time in the wilderness until the essential learning has been achieved. Often one can do nothing but just be there— a companion on the way. And I have found, in these deeper cases, that the less I have interfered or tried to do, the sooner the true transformation takes place.

So, we work on our own counter-transference to the life-situation as well as to the client. And this involves our philosophy of life : something which is often ignored but which, to me, is basic to the whole process of counselling.

A living philopsophy makes us real, something against which the student can kick, bounce, find himself. (So many who have inadequate personalities have found relationships to be like thin air, or 'feather pillows' as one student called it; it is difficult to form a firm ego through relating to those who are but partly living.) We are taught that we must not attempt to influence our clients with regard to their philosophy, and of course I agree that in psychotherapy one does not use the time to teach one's own beliefs about life and death, though the student may well wish to use the time to find his own. But there is a good deal of self-deception here; even though we may fall over backwards in non-directive counselling, to throw the client back on to himself so as to mobilize his own inner resources, this in itself implies our belief that he has inner resources to invoke. (When I was doing what I thought was self-effacing, non-directive discussion with a tutors' group, they pointed out to me that I was showing my philosophy in action!) So I feel it is best to be open and honest and to realize that students will either 'catch' or react against our attitudes to life, however unverbalized or implicit. Personally, if I am giving any suggestion, I believe in giving it openly, stating what I am doing, since this shows far more respect for the other person's integrity than does suggestion done so subtly that the counsellor is unaware of giving it—a position which can result in a harmful 'double bind'. Yet as we counsellors, too, struggle painfully to achieve ever greater awareness, even this is an inevitable and hence acceptable occurrence, provided that we can use it; so that we learn to throw black and white, dark and light, all that we are, into the pool, committing and accepting it all.

*　　　*　　　*

Some statistics

Here are two tables summarizing for reference the development of the Service until my retirement. In any comparison of these figures with those of people appointed purely for counselling, it should be remembered that I did a great deal of teaching and other work, as has been described.

Notes on Table I

This table starts in 1951–2, as I did not keep the relevant data before that year.

It never occurred to me to count appointments made but not kept, as I believe, some do. When this was brought to my notice in 1971–2, I looked up my appointment book to find that the total number of hours booked would have been 538 instead of the 456 actually kept and recorded. This is a consideration since preparing for a client who does not turn up takes time. I always gave a full hour to each client.

Notes on Table II

This Table concerns the number of *new* cases referred in each year. The total case-load (given in Table I) was actually much heavier owing to some clients attending from former years.

The colleges are listed in order of entry. In accordance with the policy of amalgamation of smaller units, in the late 1960s the School of Speech Therapy, the College of Domestic Science, and the National College for the Training of Youth Leaders became departments of the City of Leicester College of Education, being named respectively the Department of Speech Pathology and Therapeutics, the Department of Home Economics, and the Department of Community and Youth Work.

TABLE I
Case-load and Hours Spent on Counselling

Year	Case-load	Number of hours	Average number of hours per client	Comments
1951–2	29	117	4.0	
1952–3	36	170	4.7	
1953–4	38	304	8.0	Several long-term cases
1954–5	40	388	9.7	Several long-term cases
1955–6	23	229	10.0	Transfer to Institute. My illness. Only serious cases taken latterly
1956–7	42	307	7.3	
1957–8	57	408	7.2	
1958–9	55	385	7.0	
1959–60	56	386	6.9	
1960–1	60	418	7.0	
1961–2	59	427	7.2	
1962–3	66	432	6.5	Rapid increase of student population
1963–4	79	418	5.3	Plea for an assistant
1964–5	111	682	6.1	Mr. Grainger appointed September 1964
1965–6	114	686	6.0	
1966–7	105	718	6.8	Transfer to Health Service September 1967
1967–8	102	746	7.3	Mr. Grainger left August 1968
1968–9	74	431	5.8	
1969–70	70	414	5.9	
1970–1	77	419	5.4	Sabbatical term autumn 1970. Mr. Ingleby did 102 hours (included)
1971–2	81	456	5.6	
Average number of hours per client over 21 years			6.6	

TABLE II

Number of Distribution of New Cases Notified 1948 to 1972

| Year | Students | | | | | | Staff or Staff Connections | Teachers in Service | People outside the Service | Total |
	University	College of Education	School of Speech Therapy	College of Art School of Teacher Training	College of Domestic Science	National College for the Training of Youth Leaders				
1948–9	9									9
1949–50	12						3		2	17
1950–1	14	3					3		3	20
1951–2	20	2							1	24
1952–3	23	2					3		2	30
1953–4	17	2	2				2		5	28
1954–5	15	7		2	2		1	2	4	33
1955–6	7	3					1	1		12
1956–7	12	9	4	1			6	1	5	38

1957–8	44	5	4	4			1	6	5	19
1958–9	48	8	7	1		1	3	7	9	12
1959–60	38	6	7	2		1			7	15
1960–1	44	4	4	4			1	2	11	18
1961–2	44	11	2	4			1		13	13
1962–3	49	8	3	6	1			4	10	17
1963–4	57	14	7	5	1			3	15	12
1964–5	82	16	8	3	5		1	11	21	17
1965–6	72	11	5	4	4			2	26	20
1966–7	68	5	3	9	4			1	19	27
1967–8	75	8		3	3			2	16	43
1968–9	56	5		2	4		1	1	16	27
1969–70	45			1					15	29
1970–1	59	3		2		1	15		11	27
1971–2	49	1		6			9		6	27
Totals	1,041	127	54	75	22	5	35	45	226	452

The College of Art School of Teacher Training was a member of our Institute of Education. In 1970, the whole Polytechnic (which by then included the College of Art) joined the Area Student Health Service, hence the sudden rise in numbers (which I have placed in the same column) in that year.

In-service teachers were dropped when I left the School of Education to join the Student Health Service in 1967.

The category of 'People outside' may seem rather large in numbers, but the majority of cases were seen only for one session, or at the most very few. They tended to be close relatives of the clients; people closely associated with the work but not strictly eligible; control clients for the trainees; or enquirers who came for advice and whom I needed to see at least once before re-directing them to suitable help elsewhere. This category somewhat reduces the average number of hours per client shown in Table I.

Some useful addresses

Please do NOT write to me for information or recommendation of recent books in the rapidly expanding field of mental health and counselling in education. I have now retired from *this* field, but the following addresses should cover all needs:

(1) *Associations*

(a) *Mental health* (general)

MIND (National Association for Mental Health), 22 Harley Street, London W1N 2ED. (MIND works to relieve the suffering caused by mental illness and mental handicap, covering all aspects. It is a valuable clearing house of information, and publishes many useful and inexpensive specific books and pamphlets.)

(b) *Counselling* (general)

The British Association for Counselling (B.A.C.), 26 Bedford Square, London WC1B 3HU. (Founded in 1971, the B.A.C. deals with all aspects of counselling, and issues some valuable up-to-date publications.)

The International Round Table for the Advancement of

Counselling (I.R.T.A.C.). Write to the Secretary, Dr. Derek Hope, Brunel University, Uxbridge, Middlesex UB8 3PH. (I.R.T.A.C. has organized seven conferences since 1966 in various European countries including England. Membership is open to anyone actively engaged in counselling.)

(c) *Counselling* (specific)

The Association for Student Counselling (A.S.C.). Hon. Secretary, Cassie Cooper, Harrow College of Technology and Art, Northwick Park, Harrow HA1 3TP. (A.S.C. is the professional association for those practising counselling in higher education.)

The National Association of Counsellors in Education (N.A.C.E.), Hon. Secretary, A. M. Jones, 4 Cuerdon Drive, Thelwall, Warrington, Lancs. (N.A.C.E. is the professional association for those working in the field of secondary education.)

(2) *Books*

(a) *The Alan Rook Library*, 3 Gower Place, London WC1E 6BN. (This is the special library of the British Student Health Association, but it is open to the general public, and it includes extensive source-material on counselling.)

(b) For school counsellors, see also: Dennis Reader, 'The Role of the Personal Guidance Counsellor in the Secondary School: A Selective Bibliography of Items Published in Great Britain and the United States 1965–72', *Educational Libraries Bulletin,* Vol. 17, Pt. 1, Spring 1974, University of London Institute of Education Library.

Part III: Transition

Introductory Note

Most counsellors and psychotherapists feel naturally drawn to some particularly congenial aspect of their work. As a Jungian, my own interest lay chiefly in the potential contribution and specific problems of introverted intuitives in our relatively extraverted and materialistic society.

But first, what does the term 'introverted intuitives' convey, and is such a description valid and useful? In a recent article[1] the Jungian psychiatrist Anthony Storr suggests that the value of Jung's construct of 'attitude types' and 'function types' is declining. He writes:

> In the popular mind, Jung is probably best remembered for his 'Psychological Types', his introduction of the terms 'extravert' and 'introvert'. In spite of the appropriation of this dichotomy by the experimentalist H. J. Eysenck it seems doubtful whether this particular categorization will survive.
>
> It seems certain that Jung's further subdivision of types into 'thinking', 'feeling', 'sensation', and 'intuition' has already had its day. But it was from his study of psychological types that one of Jung's important insights came which I think will remain valid. Realizing that everyone is a mixture of both introvert and extravert, Jung conceived the notion that neurosis was a matter of one-sidedness, and that health consisted in a balance between extraversion and introversion, reason and emotion, and so on. Therefore, neurotic symptoms were not merely misconceived patterns of thought and behaviour which originated in childhood,

[1] 'The Significance of Jung', *Times Literary Supplement*, July 25th 1975.

as Freud supposed; but compensatory attempts of the psyche to remedy its own lack of balance. This point of view is not only fruitful in clinical practice, but fits in well with physiological and cybernetic views of the organism as a self-regulating entity.

Dr. Storr's last few sentences about balance form the basic assumptions on which all my casework has been based. And moreover, I have found that the typology, if not too rigidly applied, is of great value *as a working hypothesis* in therapy. The very fact that the polarity 'introversion/extraversion' *has* passed into popular usage indicates that it gives verbal expression to a widespread experience.

Subjectively, I have found the model useful because in my own life I felt a need to reconcile the opposite attitude types of my parents, best understood in this way. It was my mother who contributed the remark of the old lady quoted on p. 160, while my inward-looking father was described by Freddy Chapman in his diary: 'Poor gentle Swainson says he dreads his parish councils more than anything.'[2] How much of their problem was due to lack of balance in temperament; how much was actually sickness? Anyway, I was concerned to validate the position of the healthy introvert in our unbalanced society, and so in 1961 I wrote the paper which constitutes Chapter 13.

Regarding Chapter 14: of the four Jungian function types, intuition seemed to me to be the most ignored—even derided—function, except by creative writers, artists in any medium, inspired scientists, mystics and young children. Certainly in schools and colleges the function has not received the recognition, education and training that have been given to sensation, thinking, and (to some extent) feeling. Yet the intuitive function can be one of our most direct ways of perceiving and knowing, provided that we exercise discrimination and bring it into working harmony with the other three. (No wonder that there has been such a swing of the pendulum in recent times towards the practice of meditation.)

If any aspect of the psyche is ignored, or derided, it is likely

[2] Ralph Barker: *One Man's Jungle: A Biography of F. Spencer Chapman D.S.O.*, Chatto and Windus, 1975, p. 54.

to become repressed and sick. And seventeen years ago I was much concerned with those natural intuitives who found the opposite function (sensation), as expressed in Western life, so difficult that they tended to 'opt out'. It struck me that these were mainly people who combined, as strong potentials in their personalities, the two aspects rejected by a highly competitive, outgoing society: introversion and intuition. They felt there was no place for them. Here again the question arises: to what extent were they sick, or was society sick? Much later, I was struck by what Dr. Esterson said on TV in June 1974.[3] He stressed that we should start with the assumption that most people are sane unless proved otherwise; that we should *listen* to what they say, and then deal with their family background and social milieu.

And—to go further—what about the deeper 'milieu' of which some of these people are so keenly aware? How well I know from my own life the feeling of being separated from it by incarnation, so beautifully expressed by the poet Kathleen Raine in the first volume of her autobiography, *Farewell Happy Fields*.[4]

> To be exiled from Eden is our greatest sorrow, and some forget, or try to forget, because to remember is too painful, to re-create too difficult. Those who choose the vision of perfection choose to experience the pain of deprivation as the lesser evil; or perhaps there is no choice. 'You are one of those who are not allowed to forget,' Cecil Collins once said to me. And ultimately the many are maintained by those images of a lost perfection held before them by the rememberers. Such, as I understand it, is the whole and sole purpose of the arts and the justification of those who refuse to accept as our norm those unrealities the world calls real.

To attempt to explain away such vision in terms of 'retreat to the womb' just won't do. Long ago—back in 1959—I had written a paper intended for a symposium on 'God, Sex and Society' which P. W. Martin was organizing on those 'initiations'

---

[3] This was from memory of the talk. For written confirmation, see R. D. Laing and A. Esterson: *Sanity, Madness and the Family*, Penguin, 1970.

[4] Hamish Hamilton, 1973, p. 79.

or 'rites of passage' which our young folk needed in order to play
their full part in society. In the end, my contribution had to be
quite different, in order to fit in with those of the others.[5] So I
did nothing with 'Initiation into Earth' until 1972, when I sent
it out to the Gildas Readers' Group (described in Chapter 16).
Judging by the response, so many older people reported having
had similar experiences when young, fearing they must be
'abnormal', and (still more important) told me of young people
they knew who were in a similar position but who failed to find
help, that I thought this paper should have a place here.

[5] 'The Experiential Approach', *Education for Teaching*, November 1959.

CHAPTER 13

Introversion and Extraversion in Health and Disease

[*This paper was read to the Association of Psychotherapists in 1961 as part of a course of seminars designed to introduce Freudian theory to the Jungians and Jungian theory to the Freudian members of the Association. It was one of the five on Jungian theory.*]

I shall start with a brief working definition so that we can ask questions about it. According to Jung, people whose values lie chiefly in themselves and in their own subjective processes are *introverts*. Those who give the object outside themselves the predominant value are *extraverts*.

These are the questions I want to ask :

First, is the extravert attitude the healthy and normal one, and introversion merely a prelude to disease? Or can we accept that *both* attitudes are quite normal and healthy, but that *both* can be diseased if they are extreme?

If we take the latter view, as I do, can we then describe how they appear? In health, what are the qualities by which we recognize the normal introvert and extravert? And does the degree of introversion and extraversion vary at different stages of life *within the range of normality*? In disease, what are the syndromes by which we diagnose each type? Do extraverts and introverts go in for different patterns of mental illness, and what have Jung and Eysenck to say about this?

Next comes the question of therapy. Here we have to ask, what are the dynamics of the psyche in respect of the two attitudes according to Jungian theory? We are then in a position to ask what are the tasks and challenges that confront each type in order to become whole. And, lastly, what is the nature of that healing process?

Is introversion as normal and as healthy as extraversion?

I expect you know that excellent documentary film *Shyness*? It shows three apparently withdrawn children : two are neurotic, but the third is a perfectly healthy little introvert who likes to play alone, yet is easy and friendly with anyone who values his world. At the end, the commentator says, 'There is nothing wrong with Robert; there never was.'

In the past, introversion has been confused with neuroticism. Why is this? Is it because of the predominantly extraverted tone of our Western society so that introversion can hardly be accepted as 'normal' in our culture? (This makes me wonder whether extraverts were considered abnormal in the East before Western ideas came in.) Or is it because Freudians have spoken of introversion *in terms of pathology*? (Eysenck has pointed out that most American questionnaires are based on this Freudian view, and so are bound to give a neurotic slant to their findings about introversion.) In 1920, Freud did identify introversion with *incipient* neuroticism, but Jung, in 1923, wrote, 'It is a mistake to believe that introversion is more or less the same as neurosis. As concepts the two have not the slightest connection with each other.'

I take the Jungian view, and shall now present descriptions of the two attitudes, first in health, then in disease, four in all. These are first-hand sayings and writings of people whom I know personally, so that in each case we can 'feel into' the examples with empathy, as well as observe them objectively; and then we can crystallize our concepts and definitions. But I must make the proviso that these four divisions are very arbitrary; they are abstractions in order to provide clarity for this paper; for we are mostly a mixture of introversion and extraversion, sickness and health.

The introvert in health

'Of course I talk to myself,' said the Professor, with a smile. 'Who ever else is there to talk to?'

The next quotation is rather long, but I use it because it illustrates all the qualities. The subject is Nancy, a young woman of thirty, introverted and with developed feeling. Watch for the emphasis on the value of the *subject*. Her ego, perhaps, is still rather vulnerable, yet she has a positive relation with the object in her own introverted way. In making a relationship she flows out with the essential vision of the creative artist, yet the process of experiencing, of forming and valuing, takes place within herself. She wrote :

Introversion in me implies not so much a disregard of external things, but independence of them. Mostly I am not interested in the outer world. I only ask that it leave me alone.

However, when there is no external pressure, a luminous quality from my own mind flows out and envelops objects which normally I should ignore. For example, a stretch of grimy railway fencing acquires a touching individuality that stamps it ever after as different from its kind.

I don't think there are different *kinds* of truth or worlds, but that there are different levels of perception, like using a microscope after ordinary vision. I don't mean that there is no objective reality, but that it acquires its real value for me when I look at it.

'My mind to me a kingdom is.' I do not go into the world like the extravert; I draw the world into myself. Passively, like a pool, I reflect objects, and also, like a magnet, re-organize them according to my own nature. I give the object a new pattern, not the one the extravert sees. We introverts are not lost in appearances; we have a kind of X-ray vision which pierces to the *essence* of what we see. In my case this seeing has a visionary quality but it is also *felt*. The inner world is just as real as the outer world— one realizes why Joan of Arc obeyed her voices. *It is the vision which is unifying.* All is. All is good in its place.

Here then, is a clear example of introversion as defined by Jung. It is conception—the idea—the feeling—that is more real to Nancy than the object in its own right. Indeed, there may well be a time-lag in registering experience, since introverts tend to live, not in the moment of happening so much as in chewing the cud afterwards, otherwise their experience may not be assimilated. Thus Neumann speaks of introversion as 'self-incubating heat—the creative force with whose help everything is made'. This comes out very clearly in Nancy's case, I think.

To summarize: in healthy, normal introversion, the relation between subject and object is made positively, yet in the intro-vert's own particular way, the light being in the eye that beholds, and the source of the creative force existing within. In health, the introvert is not caught up compulsively in his inner world, nor does he run away from the outer world; he keeps *his own kind* of creative balance.

The extravert in health

Significantly, perhaps, I had more difficulty in getting self-descriptions from extraverts! Anyway, here are two. It is interest-ing to see the need for the *object* in their lives. As Jung says, for them the object exists in its own right, whereas their own subject sometimes even appears as a disturbing accessory to objective events. Watch for the way in which they live in the here and now; the present is their reality. Bereft of the stimulus of outer objects, at the moment, the extravert may find it difficult to be awake and aware. Note also that, being *healthy* extraverts, both are balancing up, developing also their other sides.

The first is an old lady of eighty-four living in a home for old people. An extravert all her life, she has grown and changed very much in the last ten years and is becoming interested in understanding herself. She writes:

As an extravert I used to live in the present, very much so, and as long as things went as I wanted, then nothing else mattered. I still require an *other* to collaborate with me as to my feelings. For instance, yesterday Miss G. was on my line of thought re loneliness when among others and I was *glad* to be able to talk with her. But lately I am now neither one nor the other and am waiting to know which I shall be. *I do not know myself.*

The second example is a man in middle age—a doctor—who has both sides well developed but he writes from his extravert side :

> There is no doubt that 'living in objects or objectively' expresses the feel of my life. Attending to what is around me is how I go about things : what people look like, what they do, what they say, how they respond to what I say and do. The presence of other conscious beings is my support during the major part of my time. My satisfaction comes to me from either doing something *for* people or doing something *to* them, according to whether my better or worse self is holding the field. My great love of solitude does not contradict this. To be alone releases me from the demands, real or apparent, of other people, not so much to investigate myself as to respond to everything animate and inanimate, but not human, by which I am surrounded. But this would not be sufficient as an end in itself. After this period of refreshment, I wish to communicate what I have observed to my human companions.

It is clear, I think, from these examples that the extravert, in health, *has his own kind of balance*. Although his natural pattern is to relate constructively to the outer world, yet he is not compulsively caught up in it, nor is he afraid to look at himself as yet another of his objects, dealing with his personality and loving himself, perhaps, *as* his neighbour : no less, no more.

The stages of life

So much for both types in health. Before going on to disease, we should note that rhythmic swings towards either pole are quite to be expected at various stages of life within the range of normality—so say the findings of developmental psychology.

We all know the general phases :

> The relative introversion (if we can call it that) of very early childhood when the ego is emerging and building up.
>
> The extraversion of middle childhood : collective living and the gang stage.

161

The introversion of adolescence when growing the personality anew. The extraversion of early and middle adulthood (job, family, adjustment to society).

And, finally, introversion again in later middle age, particularly about the time of the change of life, when there is the need to grow one's own soul and find the meaning of life, first for oneself and then, perhaps, for others.

[*I was fifty-three when I wrote this, but now, purely from my own experience, I would suggest another relatively extravert phase in the later fifties and sixties, when the inner findings of 'the change' can be expressed in the outer world. I wonder what comes next?*]

Of course, an essential qualification is that introverts and extraverts will react differently during these *general* phases. For instance, I have had many extraverted students (mostly men) who have never remembered being conscious of themselves at all during adolescence. 'This psychology is a lot of hooey', they said. On the other side, to quote Nancy again (and note the discrepancy between her advanced inner perceptiveness and her backwardness in outer functioning):

A month before I was two—when I could neither walk or talk—I was conscious of my identity. I remember being bored with the photographer's antics to make me laugh. I remained solemn just to spite him and because I thought he was a fool.

She goes on to say that even in the middle childhood stage she preferred to play alone and was always happily independent.

Do we accept these general phases and swing easily with them? Is it a difficulty that our social *mores* do not favour introversion, so that we may feel wrong in letting the extravert values go? Gerhard Adler comments on the difference between Eastern and Western culture in understanding the value of the introverted attitude. Laing, in *The Divided Self*, shows only too clearly that schizoid and schizophrenic people behave very differently according to the kind of understanding which we bring to them. I would suggest then, that a good deal of sickness is due to the

162

social neurosis or imbalance that does not accept the real values of the inner world, nor truly understand them.

Disease

I have defined health in terms of being what you are without compulsion, relating to the opposite in your own positive way, and allowing for the natural rhythmic swings of the libido, or life-force, from phase to phase. What about disease?

Jung sees the psyche as a self-regulating whole. 'Every individual,' he says, 'possesses both mechanisms, extraversion as well as introversion, and only the relative predominance of one or the other determines the type.' Disease he would see as a lack of balance, lack of a healthy rhythmic alternation and flow of libido between the two attitudes.

In disease, then, we find a compulsive, pathological extreme of either attitude in the *conscious* mind and behaviour. This means that the opposite and complementary attitude has been relegated to the unconscious. 'Down there' it will automatically assume primitive, negative, and probably terrifying form, driving the ego from behind, as it were.

Now, the unconscious will always try to compensate for any extreme conscious attitude, and so the person suffers appalling tension. (At least, this is true, I would say, as far as the *neurotic* is concerned. The *psychotic* may have given up the struggle completely in submergence or retreat.)

The extravert in disease

Let us see how this state feels in the experience of the neurotic sufferers, taking an extravert first this time: a woman, Margaret, aged fifty (note the age—change of life when some introversion is becoming a necessity). Margaret had a wonderful record of public service, but she came to me for help because of severe depression and panics. Here are two 'blow-offs' which she wrote to me. Notice first her fear of the inner world; she cannot relax into it; she ignores her dreams, yet seeks for 'magic' from outside to save her. And even her main value of object-relationship, to which she clings frantically, is becoming diseased; instead of relating creatively to outer activities and people, she is becoming terribly dependent on them. (She collected mother and father figures galore.)

(1) When I am with (my therapist) I feel I can relax and talk freely. There is a feeling of being safe and secure. I feel less isolated.

When I am not with (my therapist) I seem to develop all sorts of unpleasant symptoms: depression, a curtain descending, dizziness, *unless* I engage my mind in things which don't allow me to think of myself. I *must* be busily occupied with something to keep depression at bay, yet it's tiring to be always on the go. Often, however, after hours of deep sleep, sometimes with dreams vaguely remembered, I awaken with a sense of heaviness. When I'm not conscious of ME I behave and feel normal, but it's an effort to keep myself occupied. I get so tired and wonder how long I can keep going. Then I think of some of the things (my therapist) has talked over with me, and try when depressed, not to feel depressed at being depressed.

(2) (Worse.) I feel ghastly. Tenseness, especially round the back of my head, a feeling of sickness and panic. Efforts at acceptance don't work now. Can I keep going? Is there no relief? I feel despairing—I *must* be able to continue to do my job. I want a magic formula to relieve me. I can't bear having to wait—I can't last out—can I last the term—can I last another day? I *do* seem to be able to lose myself in teaching, meetings and routine work, but I'm terribly tired . . . have to make terrific efforts. I'm sick with worry because this thing seems to have trapped me. There's no escape and I'm nearly crazy—there's utter blackness—I'm trapped.

Here, then, is the sick extravert. As Baynes says in his *Mythology of the Soul*, she ignores the claims of the inner world, and projects these claims outwards in the form of excessive and irrational demands upon the object. So, Baynes sees the challenge to the sick extravert to be that of coming to terms with his *desirousness*. Only when the inevitable disillusionment forces the extravert back upon himself, says Baynes, does he encounter the claims of his neglected subject. Thus Margaret made inordinate demands on her parent figures, her therapist, and her job to hold her together. Only when she relaxed and accepted her symptoms, finding that what she needed was inside rather than outside, relinquishing these compulsive demands, did the tension lessen, and she found a measure of peace.

The introvert in disease

Here we find the opposite. When the conscious attitude is too introverted, then the objects of the outer world, through neglect and projection, will assume a terrifying power, invading and threatening to disrupt the precious being. Here is the diary of a woman of fifty-two (introverted intuitive with developed thinking), so that, in view of her inferior sensation and feeling functions, her dreaded outer objects are practical things and human relationships :

> My main trouble is that of facing these dangerous outer things. Saucepans scream to be cleaned, grates to be done. I have to force myself all through the day to telephone, to contact people, imagining they will be angry with me. I would always rather write than ring up, then I can vet the letters many times, putting everything clearly so that I am completely justified! Letters coming in at me through the letter-box are a potential menace; who wants to bother me now? Why won't they leave me to live my own life? I have no weapons against their claims; people have the power to prevent me being myself. But when I withdraw into my own room, then I can open up and breathe and *be*. I'm never frightened of being alone, or of the inner world; I know my way about and have mastery there.

This one is on the edge, not severely neurotic. She keeps her sense of humour and is healthy on her introvert side. But in more severe cases not only is the ego unable to face outer invasions, but it loses grip of its own inner realities, and begins to break up. For, although both introverts and extraverts can be schizoid, according to Baynes, 'the effects of dissociation are liable to cause more far-reaching disturbance in the introvert because of the latter's greater reliance upon unification. The prime necessity for the introvert is the integration of the self upon a reliable foundation.'

Pamela, a student teacher of nineteen, was beginning to break up, mainly into two bits. Her obvious symptoms were fear of teaching practice and of supervisors in the outer world. In therapy she was insulated and isolated, very schizoid. After several sessions of almost complete silence, she burst out, 'I hate people. I hate school. I hate college. I hate everything. All I want is to get away from people and be quiet.' She sat with her head in her hands, saying she felt she was going mad. Faced with the examiners coming to assess her teaching, she nearly failed to turn up. *I can't bear people looking at me any more.* But she did turn up, passed, and recovered.

Now Pamela had a great gift for inner vision, but parallel with her near-breakdown in the outer world came a change in her inner world, which became peopled with terrifying images instead of being a source of strength and illumination. As she recovered, however, the inner world became more positive and creative until at present she lives a very full life in both worlds. But if she lets them get too out of touch with each other, the outer world becomes dark and threatening, the inner world a place of escape and fantasy.

Beyond this stage is the complete vanishing of the object in schizophrenia, with an equivalent lack of reality in the inner world, too. What should be the source of vision and creation and power becomes mere illusion—either power of an inflated kind within the ego, or else all the power is seen outside.

So it is no wonder that Baynes sees the prime challenge to the introvert to be that of coming to terms with the *problem of power and superiority*. I shall have more to say about this when we come to healing.

Patterns of illness

From the descriptions, it looks as if introverts and extraverts are liable to different *kinds* of neuroses and psychoses. Both Jung and Eysenck have something to say here.

As we know, Jung's initial contribution to the field of psychological types was stimulated by his interest in the comparison between hysteria and *dementia praecox* (as schizophrenia was then called). It was from this study that he deduced the principles of extraversion and introversion as two contrary movements of the libido, and then he widened these concepts from the pathological field to include all mankind.

To Jung, the hysteric belongs to the extraverted type. Look at the exaggerated emotional responses and the centrifugal flow of his libido. To the introverted category, on the other hand, belong those types which Jung then called 'psychasthenic'. This is an old term, now replaced, according to Eysenck, by the term 'dysthymic'; but anyway it includes anxiety types, reactive depressives and obsessionals. These dysthymics are characterized by their withdrawal, their apathy towards environment, and the centripetal, inward-flowing direction of their libido.

Eysenck worked on this topic, both in original experiments and by collating evidence. His results, published in 1947 and 1953, agree completely with Jung as far as neurotics are concerned. In measuring personality, he found that the dysthymic group showed introverted traits, and the hysterical group extraverted traits, so that the two dichotomies dysthymia/hysteria and introversion/extraversion are closely related. But when it came to psychotics Eysenck's attempts to correlate the introversion-extraversion scale with the schizoid-cycloid scale met with no significant result.

[*I then described Eysenck's subsequent publication of 1957, 'The Dynamics of Anxiety and Hysteria', a contribution from the field of experimental psychology offered to psychiatrists and psychotherapists as a basis for treatment of the two neurotic types, especially where re-conditioning and learning-theory therapy are employed. Being somewhat technical, it is omitted here.*]

In fairness to Eysenck, we must realize that he is concerned in his research *only* to establish whether extraversion/introversion is a reliable and valid axis in personality measurement, and to study its correlation with other axes. Nevertheless, Jungians might well feel the need to look more deeply. Is healing—making whole—achieved only by de-conditioning and re-conditioning through 'socialization'? To some extent, perhaps, but what of the deep centre in man, the SELF (in the Jungian sense) which seems to know so much more wisely than the ego, or other egos, how to redress the balance that it has been called the Prime Mover in psychotherapy? And so we come to ask:

What is the nature of the healing process?

In Jungian theory, this SELF—this deep centre of the whole being—will heal the psyche if we allow and follow the natural flow of libido between the opposites in the search for equilibrium, following it sometimes into the darkness of the symptom, since the disease is the beginning of the cure.

This process of balancing, of integration of all parts around the centre, of 'centreing down' (as the Quakers call it), Neumann calls *Centroversion*. It is not an average between introversion and extraversion on a linear scale of measurement. If we must use an image, it is more like the point of a triangle—the 'holy mountain'—the third principle existing in another dimension from that of the two opposites, and thus giving perspective; just as the resolution of any pair of opposites is not achieved by a compromise but by a comprehending synthesis on a higher level. This process, Neumann says, works in us all through life, but usually we are conscious of its working only in the second half of life. Eventually, through centroversion, an individual may come to transcend his own personality and to live from the deep centre beyond the ego, beyond his introversion and extraversion.

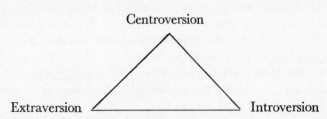

A clear explanation of the change comes from Dr. Arthur Guirdham, who ends his work on *A Theory of Disease* by saying[1]:

> The individual who lives by the dictates of the You which is Not You, which we had perhaps better refer to frankly

[1] p. 200 in the 1957 edition.

as the soul, is also enabled to live fully and healthily. It should be emphasized that such an existence is not what is implied by the term introversion ... Even if they lead cloistered and contemplative lives it is not justifiable to refer to them as introverts, since they do not live in their own thoughts and feelings. How can they do so when they have disclaimed possession of them in order to dwell in God or the Absolute? Furthermore, many people so dedicated are busy about their daily affairs and leading what appears to be an ordinary social existence, but with this difference, that, whereas before they confronted their daily tasks as a challenge to their personalities, they now offer themselves to the same occupations as instruments of the Infinite. Such a state of enlightenment may seem to be a form of self-externalization but it is essentially beyond what is understood by extraversion.

What are the tasks and challenges in health and disease?

Let us ask how the healing process works in practice. For those who are already pretty well balanced between the two attitudes, the work is surely easier. And we must not forget that an individual may have some of his functions introverted and some extraverted—which can aid balancing.

But for those in health who are markedly one or the other, and for those in sickness who have gone to extremes, I see the process in three stages:

First, find out who you *are* and *be* it, whether you are mainly introverted or extraverted. Establish firmly the rock of your own true value.

Then work on the process of balancing up, for now you are sufficiently strong and sure to allow the unknown and therefore feared opposite to approach, and to make a relation with it.

Finally, through much to-ing and fro-ing along the axis between the opposites, the higher synthesis of controversion is made.

To make it practical, let us take it from the point of view of each type:

(1) *The introvert* needs first to redeem his own inner world from the bolt-hole of fantasy to a real source of power and

169

illumination, and to value it, even if society does not. Before he
can relate to others from his real self, he has to go up into his
holy mountain to pray, and to see how to unify his inner family
—the scattered bits of his psyche. So, we find that, to start with,
introversion is necessary, but introversion of a creative kind. Thus
Baynes, describing the work of salvage in a schizophrenic, says,
'The only cure of an inverted autonomous system is through
purposive introversion.'

In this way, the individual comes to experience his inner being
as valid. One young man said to me, 'The only thing I'm sure of
is that I AM, and that is where I start.' A woman felt a profound
sense of peace and rightness with life when she said, 'I *know* that
for this I was born; for this came I into the world.' Pamela's
inner world became alight with life, beauty and creative experience, helpful figures replacing the former terrible images. (Here
we can see a link with Kleinian theory—the concept of 'inter-
nalised good objects'.) And so the introvert comes to experience
his inner world as a source of love. He knows, without inflation,
that, good or bad, he and others *are loved*, and, still more, he
and others *can love*; he knows the immensely creative power of
love and of creative imagination, and that he must learn to use
and not abuse them. And so he comes to terms with the challenge of *power*—which Baynes says is his particular test.

In educating the introvert to the wise use of his inner power,
it is not widely enough known that *he needs creative work* in
order to become more extraverted. (And here is the problem of
the artist in our society!) For instance, if a child is full of fantasy,
we encourage him to write stories or draw pictures and bring
the imagery right through into life. In this way, an introvert
comes to the second stage, that of relating to the object *through
his own developed creativity*, learning gradually to build in love
instead of to 'cope' in fear. (I have found that the unconscious
produces interesting images of this transition. In the case of
thinking-type introverts with inferior feeling, at first the power
may appear to be all outside them, manifesting as huge waves
or rough seas drowning their little islands, but as the work proceeds, the outer threats subside, and the power comes gushing up
from an inner spring in the centre of the island—a spring of
living water.)

(2) *The extravert*, on the other hand, needs first to learn to live in *real* relationship to people and to things, not in the dependence of the hysteric or the selfishness of the psychopath. As Baynes says, *his* real test is to come to terms with his claims, his desirousness. In the initial stage, this desirousnes is a valid need of his very existence, for without the other person he cannot *be*. 'How do I know who I am unless you tell me? I am not me unless you value me; you are necessary to my sense of reality.' This has been called the Tinker Bell pattern : 'In order to exist someone must believe in my existence.' But slowly, through loving others, he can learn to find and love and value himself, facing that frightening hollow inside, ceasing to look without for what he needs from within. Eventually, through his own way of relationship, he will find the same treasure as the introvert finds, *but he will approach it from the other side.*

For instance, in religion extraverts tend to stress the transcendent aspect of love, seeing God as over against them, as 'Wholly Other'. There are definitely two approaches here theologically, since the introvert, not necessarily inflated, is far more aware of love acting through him, and so emphasizes the aspect of immanence.

I will end by quoting from an extravert mystic who, I feel, has achieved the final synthesis, in that he sees love not so much as 'Wholly Other' but rather as 'Between Man and Man'. Yet he still approaches from his own supreme value—that of relationship. And this is Martin Buber, writing in *I and Thou* :

'Feelings dwell in man : but man dwells in his love. That is no metaphor, but the actual truth. Love does not cling to the *I* in such a way as to have the *Thou* only for its "content", its object; but love is *between I and Thou*.'

Books referred to in the text
Jung, C. G. : *Psychological Types*, Kegan Paul, 1944. (Now Vol. 6 in *Collected Works*.)
Eysenck, H. J. : *Dimensions of Personality*, Routledge, 1947. *The Structure of Human Personality*, Methuen, 1953. (3rd ed. 1970.)
Neumann, Erich : *The Origins and History of Consciousness*, Bollingen Series XLII, Pantheon, New York, 1954.

Adler, Gerhard: *Studies in Analytical Psychology*, Routledge, 1948. (Hodder, 1966.)

Laing, R. D.: *The Divided Self*, Tavistock Press, 1960. (Penguin, 1970.)

Baynes, H. G.: *Mythology of the Soul*, Routledge, 1955.

Guirdham, Arthur: *A Theory of Disease*, Allen and Unwin, 1957. (Spearman, 1973.)

Buber, Martin: *I and Thou*, T. Clark, 1945. (3rd ed. 1971.)
Between Man and Man, Kegan Paul, 1947. (Fontana, 1961.)

CHAPTER 14

Introverted Intuitives and Initiation

Introductory note: 1972 (when issued to the Readers' Group)
This paper, written originally in 1959, is—in my opinion—even
more significant today. Since the 1950s, we have passed on from
the 'angry young men' and the 'beat' generation to the many
varieties of 'hippies' and those who are seeking a simpler and
more directly meaningful way of living. We are still working
through the (often drastic and sometimes fatal) learning-
experience of drug-taking; psychedelic drugs (at last) are being
seen as inadequate and false methods compared with meditation,
yoga, or true 'encounter' ways of approaching the inner realities
of relationship.

In the case of students, I find that the movement is paralleled
intellectually by current interest in existential psychology, particularly the works of R. D. Laing, and in Eastern sources (such as
Zen): all this is in order to explain, and perhaps validate, some
of their own inner experiences. Often they are afraid to speak of
these experiences in a culture which may even label them
'schizoid'.

At a meeting of counsellors recently, I heard an excellent paper
on the clinical 'schizoid' type: on depersonalization, derealization, and all the associated traits such as lack of ability to make
warm human relationships without feeling swallowed up on the
one hand or totally rejected on the other. But convenient terms
such as 'depersonalization' and 'derealization' beg the questions:
'What is personality?' and 'Do we all perceive the same aspect of
reality?' Further, 'Do we sometimes mistake "impersonal" for
"depersonalized"?' Here, may I submit that many of these not-
so-much sick but *different* people are able to express impersonal
love and to contribute creatively in their own way, although not

necessarily in accepted 'socialized' conventions. *All* traits cannot be explained away in terms of illness, though of course some can. True, as counsellors, we have studied the early genesis in infancy of schizoid patterns, but I would submit further that perhaps the basic problem which may create, sustain, and fail to heal such patterns is the value-system of our society, which is limited and foreign to such people.

Adolescents and those of student age often bring as their 'presenting symptom' a great confusion as to what life is all about. Too often, we therapists, doctors, and counsellors explain this away as the 'normal adolescent identity crisis' (which it usually *also* is), or, in more severe cases, as a neurotic defence or intellectual 'front' denying the deeper emotional failure to relate (also partially true). But I suggest that some of us may well be escaping, by way of clinical categorizing of patterns of mal-adjustment to social 'norms', from these very basic issues of meaning in life.[1] Some psychiatrists and psychotherapists are now prepared to take into account a further dimension in the psychodynamic pattern.[2] Dr. Arthur Guirdham, a psychiatrist of wide experience, feels that much of the disease from which we suffer is due to the repression of the gifts of clairvoyance and far memory, and of our faculty for the perception of presences from more subtle worlds. He has suggested that many so-called symptoms of disease are felt when the patient is drawing close to a world more real than our own. In a talk given to the annual conference of the Radionic Association, he said, 'What we have practised up to date is psychology and psychiatry with no psyche, an approach which regards man as having no soul, or at least as not having a soul which is in connection with the spirit or the universal consciousness.'[3]

However, in 1959 I was only groping towards these issues, and it seemed wiser to express the paper in the (then) more accept-able idiom of Jungian terminology.

*　　*　　*

[1] See Viktor Frankl: *Man's Search for Meaning*, Beacon Press, Boston, 1962. (Hodder, 1963.)

[2] See Joan Grant and Denys Kelsey: *Many Lifetimes*, Gollancz, 1969. Gina Germinara: *Many Mansions*, Spearman, 1970. Arthur Guirdham: *A Foot in Both Worlds*, Spearman, 1974.

[3] *Radionic Quarterly*, Vol. 17, 1971, p. 22.

INITIATION INTO EARTH   [*1959*]

A considerable number of students referred to our Psychological Service are misfits of a certain type. They form a 'problem group' which has, potentially, a unique contribution to make to our present-day world, and hence it is vital that their gifts should be valued and their educational needs understood. I propose first to describe the way in which they appear, both to others and to themselves; then to attempt to explain their special difficulties, and suggest ways of approaching them. Owing to the confidential nature of the material, the cases have been slightly 'scrambled', but all remarks noted are true.

As others see them

Tutors complain of their apathy and withdrawal from commitment to life. The students are 'not there'. 'Where *is* she?' is a frequent question. Performance in work tends to be uneven and spasmodic, varying in quality according to mood or interest, or to the personality of the lecturer; in some cases, indeed, it is uniformly poor, as if the students were not concerned with the course at all. Yet they are not lacking in ability. 'I feel there is a good deal *there* if one could only get *at* it!' cries the baffled and exasperated tutor. Such students may appear clueless in a practical context, or show little, if any, sense of direction in life. When urged to work harder, they do not seem to care. Arguments concerning their future careers and responsibilities fall on stony ground; efforts to get them involved in (to others) absorbing external interests and causes are fruitless; anger and threats of being failed or sent down only drive them further away until they retreat altogether. The more anxious may become neurotic, running away into illness, depression, nightmares, and sleep-walking. The less anxious play around irresponsibly, doing what they enjoy doing, avoiding uncongenial work. Tutors long for the type of keen student who throws himself wholeheartedly into an outer interest and its discipline, but these people, they complain, do not give of themselves to life; they are apparently self-absorbed, and—beneath the protective apathy—highly on the defensive. Defence patterns vary with individuals. Joyce had a bright, attractive presence; she dressed beautifully and seemed

175

to care only for boy-friends. She deceived tutors and fellow-students alike into thinking she was a superficial good-time girl. In reality, this pattern rendered tribute unto Caesar in the form of accepted social currency, but underneath she was far more concerned to keep inviolate her secret self which sought the 'things that are God's'. Pamela adopted a cheeky, little-girl attitude, trailing her coat to get teased, which attitude hid many other things. Janet told such a tissue of lies that no one knew where she stood, least of all herself. Pat, a Social Science student with an excellent brain, used it so effectively that her tutors praised her justifiably as the best student of her year, but eventually she had to face what they—and later she—knew must be tackled some time: her inadequacy in rapport with her clients in the practical placements. For this is where the trouble shows; not only do tutors complain that they cannot get through to the students, but also that the students cannot get through to the clients, or to the children they teach. Between their inner being and the outer world these people set up a barrier—distorting-glass, brick wall, ice cliff, misty cloud, or thorny hedge, according to individual temperament.

As they see themselves

In the freedom of counselling sessions, these students will gradually explore life and themselves; one soon sees that beneath the apathy and the other defences is a profound unsureness about being-in-life—an unsureness of which, unlike their more down-to-earth fellows, they are only too acutely aware. Sometimes they will begin by an intellectual rationalization of their defences. Pat plunged into a discussion of metaphysical values in purely abstract form, demanding that I should provide a moral philosophy for living. However, after a few sessions she realized that she was afraid to take up social work because she could not deal with emotional problems either in her clients or in herself. 'I think,' she said, 'I had better get myself sorted out before I explore all this.'

Many start with a kind of despair. 'What is life for anyway?' 'If I could find a meaning, *then* I could throw myself into it.' Young men are not even angry; they complain that they do not see why they should fight or work in a decaying world, doomed

176

to destruction, and they may take up music or painting in the search for values that they cannot find elsewhere. If these students are asked the diagnostic snap question: 'What would you do if you were quite free from all external pressures?' nearly all want a chance to be quiet, in order to think and feel. (Universities used to cater for this need; less so now.) Pauline replied, 'I would go alone into the country to *think*.' Joan complained, 'You have people with you all the time, even at night. You can't get away.' A favourite choice is reading. 'I would lie in bed all day and read.' 'If I were left alone,' said Anne, 'I would go to Italy and lie in the sun and just *be*.' Her dreams and paintings showed her alone, high up on a windy hill, safe with nature from the painful exposure of her vulnerable personality to the human world. She felt hounded, invaded, and she reacted by withdrawal. But, after sitting for five minutes in complete silence, she said, 'I haven't felt so still inside for ages.'

'If you give of yourself, of what you are, you will not get it back,' Anne had found. Although these people lead an intense inner life, they dare not allow it to show in their college work. Instead, they 'give the tutors what they want' (or rather, judging by former school marks, what they imagine is wanted). They submit essays consisting of bare bones, while filling their personal diaries with passion, poetry and philosophy. Elizabeth said that it was too dangerous to show what you really are to a tutor; you would be ridiculed. Yet when she did summon up enough courage to bring her real self into an essay on English literature, the tutor valued it and gave her a good grade. She then saw that she had projected lack of understanding where it did not exist, and began to dare to trust.

Even to fellow students, except perhaps to one close friend, they do not speak of their rich inner life, for they judge others by the prevailing 'student image'. I had an interesting experience when two girls of this type were thrown together in the same school on their final teaching practice; both were coming for counselling, but neither knew that the other came. Each complained to me bitterly that she was alone in a world of uncomprehending Philistines, and, although they became quite friendly, neither found the other at any depth.

Where the intuitive function is innately strong, they feel acutely separate and 'different', believing that the world does not want them as they are; and so they are unable to accept themselves or to build a confident and resilient ego. For instance, in methods of learning (which in formal education are largely geared to thinking and sensation) they feel obviously inferior—yet often secretly superior—to the steady 'plodders'. With their volatile minds, they jump to conclusions, and their essays tend to be thin. Because their insight can see the end from the beginning, they do not see the point of writing long arguments based on factual evidence except to please tutors. Joyce said, 'I never felt valued at school because the mistresses wanted facts, and you had to get it all from books.' Only in French and English literature, which she loved, were her real gifts of imagination and insight recognized. She had no idea that anyone else felt as she did, and hence thought she was abnormal. One brilliant Science student told me, just before finals, that he had to depend on a strange autonomous 'gremlin' which might work perfectly for him but might not work at all. With no training in learning to co-operate with this gremlin, he found it unreliable. His tutors had referred him (at the last minute) because he should get a first but might fail, for he could not study in the normal way.

Some of these people are wide awake on inner levels and have valid psychic or even mystical experiences. Maureen was clairvoyant and clairaudient, but her fellow-students ridiculed her gift until she felt she must be mad. She became severely disturbed and was referred for sleep-walking. Recently her father had died, and her friends said, 'Forget him; you will never see him again.' But she often saw and spoke with him. A few reliable books on clear-sight helped her to realize that she was not going crazy but, provided that she regarded her gift sensibly, was very fortunate. Such people have an acutely sensitive nervous system, being unable to protect themselves against the cruder vibrations of noise and city life, but gradually they have to learn to adapt. To them, incarnation seems like a foreign prison in which they are exiles. At the beginning of her treatment, Phyllis dreamed constantly of escaping from a concentration camp (as indeed she was—failing in her studies). Later, however, when she had accepted outer conditions to a certain extent, she dreamed that the concentration camp was quite nice; she didn't mind it. She needed first to find her way to her own truth, and then she could accept material life, however dark. When sleep-walking, she dreamed that she had a bunch of keys in her hand. She was walking down a long hall, full of doors, trying all the keys, but none would fit. This inner picture was paralleled in the outer world by her search for her own spiritual path; she showed some fear of leaving the security of the collective when she admitted that she would rather meditate alone during a Sunday walk than attend a church of which she was a member. When, however, she had the courage to follow her own intuition without fear of social condemnation, she felt much stronger. Then, through finding her own value, she was able to relate in a more real way to others. During her first year in teaching she wrote that she was engaged to be married, and was very happy teaching in a slum area. She had come a good deal of the way through into commitment to life.

Because of this feeling of being at home in the inner world, most of these students are profoundly religious, though nearly always in an unorthodox way, based on personal experience. From the point of view of the outer world they are classed as 'late maturers', and feel the stigma of the label 'immature' in a society in which so-called 'maturity' in dealing with the outer world is so highly valued; yet from the point of view of imaginative and spiritual experience they can well be *early* maturers— this part of them being old and wise before the rest of the personality. They tend to tackle the question of their personal philosophy at an age when many of their fellows are either like children in this field, or simply not interested. They explore, trying out various religions and sects, finding their way steadily to their own Source. Thus, by nineteen, Rachel had tried and discarded several churches and was now facing the ultimate question: 'What is my life for?' It is characteristic that she wanted to see ahead before living. Whereas a more extraverted sensation type will plunge headlong into life, as it were by touch, these tender souls, frightened of living, test the water first with one toe. Rachel could not bear the idea of learning how to live by letting life happen to her; she took the line, '*If* I can know what life is for, *then* I can get on and live it.'

Why are they as they are?

According to Jung's model of psychological types, such people fall clearly into the class of introverted intuitives, with either thinking (as in Pat's, Pauline's and Rachel's cases) or feeling (as in the others) as their secondary function, but *all have sensation as their inferior function*. So we can understand that consciously they find great difficulty in 'coming down to earth', although, in compensation, at a less conscious level they are often fascinated by animals, gardening, 'life'. Pauline's essays were constantly on the theme of life. At a deeper level they are often very tangled up with problems of sex, and physical and practical matters generally.

According to Jung, the first half of life is the period of establishing a strong ego in relation to the outer world. But, just because of their inferior extraversion and sensation, this is exactly the most difficult task for these people. Jolande Jacobi writes:[4]

> This adjustment to external reality, that is the task of the first half of life, is usually easier to the extraverted than to the introverted, who are by nature more inclined to a life determined by inner experience and images ... The introvert is already, by his own nature, attracted to this 'way into the interior', but ... this way, apart from a few special cases, demands a well-established ego that the introvert, owing to his own insecurity and anxiety over concrete realities, can only with difficulty achieve.

It has been said by a wise educator that introverted intuitives are slower to be 'born' into the world than are other people, much of the psyche still remaining in the dream world; but that, given time, in the end they may be able to bring through more than those who are 'born' early. He felt that the problem in teacher training was that of timing; students of this nature were not really ready for teaching between the ages of eighteen and twenty-one; they should be given at least another five years to 'come through'. (But, of course, administratively such policy is quite impracticable.) Being only 'half-born', they have only

---

[4] 'The Process of Individuation', *Journal of Analytical Psychology*, July 1958, p. 100.

partial—often merely embryonic—ego development when this is measured by our Western standards, which demand tough and highly competitive egos for survival. Like the little children they are in a worldly sense, they escape readily into fantasy, poetry and myth because they still need to spend a great deal of their day in the realm of mythological time in order that they may be able to relate to the demands of concrete passing time at all. Always nostalgic for the light they still can see, it would be easier for rapid ego-strengthening if they were well boxed down into the body, knowing nothing beyond. But they are not.

Give me the darkness of the flesh, or the full light of the spirit.
How shall I endure this prison, whose walls open and close,
Or maintain this silence wherein thy music sounds continually?[5]

The students' difficulties of contact with children in school can be accounted for because so much of themselves is still an unborn child. Before they can become sufficiently adult and detached to deal objectively with children, they have to allow their own child-self to come out of Eden, to be born, weaned, educated, and initiated into the everyday world. In many ways these students still show 'infantile' traits : marked attachment to mother and father images is a frequent pattern, and if discouraged, they tend easily to 'run back into the womb'.

Yet these are the very people who, *when* they have achieved balance and strong egos, will be able to mediate much-needed spiritual values to the community, because they still have access to the inner world. They seem to understand the language of symbols and dreams by instinct; they can communicate directly in this idiom if others can listen; they are the potential visionaries, seers, mystics, and prophets of the race. But if we misunderstand, drive, or neglect them, as we have done in the past, they will become the neurotics, ne'er-do-wells, drug-takers, and general drop-outs from society. One particular form of escape must be watched carefully because it gives a false impression of maturity. Owing to the congenial nature and comparative ease of inner work, an occasional gifted introvert may attempt to start the task of the second half of life—the realization of the SELF—

[5] Charles Morgan: *Sparkenbroke*, Macmillan, 1946, p. 153.

before the ego is fully formed. But 'There is no escape,' says Jacobi, 'from the necessity of developing the necessary conscious forces and the consistency of the ego. It is *only then* that he can undertake the hazards of the second stage of the process of individuation.' It follows that methods of initiation must consider above all else the formation of strong and resilient egos.

What kind of initiation is required?

To become whole and rounded, we all need initiation into every aspect of being, into each of the four elements with all that they symbolize, into heaven and into earth. In mythological terms, of the two daughters in the fairy tale—the father's daughter and the mother's daughter—these intuitives are children of the unmanifest Sky-Father, and their great test lies in learning to relate to the manifest Earth-Mother in all her forms.

But the form of the archetypal Mother in our present Western society fails to provide enough incentive for the earthing of their energies; no wonder many travel to India in search of ashrams. What positive value has our over-urbanized culture to offer so as to constellate the idealism—the spiritual fire—in a 'quest' that is felt to be worth while?

Again, the 'Father' principle in them is as yet only potential, not sufficiently incarnated. At one level, this may be associated with the general misunderstanding of Freudian psychology by parents, and the *abuse* of otherwise good 'free activity' and 'permissive' methods by certain teachers (mistaking freedom for licence or chaos), at the time when these young people were children; at the same time [*this was written in 1959*] this generation suffered the difficulties of war-time conditions, evacuation and separation from their families, constant change of home and school, and the absence of the father whose function it is *to mediate reality*. Thus, the very people who are naturally most likely to find the discipline of living most difficult, have not, in many cases, been helped sufficiently to internalize security and self-discipline as a firm framework for coping with life. Some young men waste our time playing with 'the psychological problem that somehow I can't make myself do anything I don't want to do'. In most cases this is not a neurotic problem; one sees by the absence of enough tension in the limp body and feeble personality that the trouble goes back to the lack of firm, consistent training when the character was fluid, in childhood. In the relatively fatherless society of war-time, there was insufficient practice in accepting the 'work-demand' of a relatively uncongenial task, and, what is more difficult, in accepting it willingly and without resentment. To learn self-discipline for the first time at eighteen is very hard. Both 'push' and 'pull' are necessary. How can tutors help?

The push

Those tutors who favour 'pushing' may be called members of the 'outward bound' school of thought. Either strong sensation types with no 'nerves' to speak of, or else highly sensitive people who have driven themselves into over-compensation, they tend to get angry and irritated, speaking of a 'gutless generation', 'soft' and 'nesh'. (To what extent, I wonder, is such irritation a reflection of the fact that these students may represent their own rejected 'shadows', and that really they are annoyed at being unable to deal with their own undeveloped function, which is equally sensitive and 'nesh'?) Be that as it may, the remedy suggested is shock in order to stimulate the biological capacity for survival by adaptation. 'Rub their noses in real hardship! Face them with primitive needs; let them come up against life in the raw!' For some of the complacent and flabby types who have no neurosis, this treatment works effectively, always provided that they have enough strength to take it, and that the tutor is not so much involved in his own irritation that he cannot deliver the treatment reasonably objectively. Otherwise the student may complain, 'X has a grudge against me', and fail to tackle his own problem.

I think most of us would agree, however, that such methods need discrimination, since the 'unweaned' cannot take them yet, and may go down in helpless despair, withdrawing altogether. To these students, 'robust' treatment, with crude 'jollying along', or 'getting at' them by rough, even if friendly, teasing, feels like sheer cruelty; they bottle up considerable resentment which they are unable to release in healthy aggression. They *want* to come out and risk change, but cannot do so if the impact results in a crippling degree of anxiety. Further, can we also recognize definite stages in emergence, so that treatment can be graded to the stage reached? As in bringing up little children, the security and attraction of love is blended with encouragement to explore and gain skills. In the case of a very frightened and withdrawn student, at first an encouraging and gentle 'pull' is needed, with great patience to wait for the necessary time for growth. Only later, when the ego is sufficiently strongly rooted, when symptoms of fear and escape have given place to self-pity and sulks, can a little toughening be used with advantage, and here the tutor's deliberate challenge is of great value in bringing out the latent aggressive strength in the student. By fighting the 'parent figure' he gains access to his own repressed life-force for the struggle of existence. (I am reminded of animal mothers who care gently at first for their immature offspring, but later train them by mock fights, claws shielded in paddy paws, to tackle, first the mother herself, and then, in the real world, claws unsheathed, their legitimate prey.)

By this time, some tutors may well ask, 'Are colleges expected to be hospitals or nursery schools for immature students?' I think we should all be thankful if some of this initiation could be completed before the students came to college at all. We could wish for a year, at least, between school and college, away from the shelter of home, where the young people were self-supporting financially, working in industry, or with children, or—best of all —abroad. Several French Honours graduates of the too-sheltered type have told me how the undergraduate year in France provided the experience they needed. A job in Spain or Italy, in a hotel, as courier, or even *au pair*; a year in V.S.O. (Voluntary Service Overseas); all these have worked wonders.

The pull

'How can we help them to find the *incentive* to live fully, or indeed (in some cases) to live at all?' This question is often asked of counsellors by parents and tutors. Is it wise to see first how nature deals with this problem? As Jung has shown, one can make contact with the undeveloped part of oneself only through the mechanism of unconscious projection, by which the part that is 'unborn' is *first* seen outside, and only then can it be taken back into the psyche to strengthen and round out the conscious personality. This is the way the life-force flows out into the world *naturally*.

To the intuitive individual himself, it appears as if that un-earthly light, which used to be locked away in the dream-world, suddenly illumines some object in the outer world, be it a person, thing, cause, or some value such as beauty. Once this guiding star is seen outside, the individual recognizes it as 'for him' (for much of it is his own lost soul, or *anima*) and he pursues it with all the strength that is in him. Like a star reflected deeply in a pool, its purpose seems to be to draw him to dive into the depths of the waters of life. Of course, in diving, he finds that the water is cold, and his vision of the star is shattered into fragments. Since it is always the reflected glory that he seeks, and not its temporary vehicle, he is subject to a series of bitter disillusions. Especially is this the case with human relationships where, to change the metaphor, each vessel appears at first to be alight with the Grail, only to be seen later as dark and empty clay. These people find difficulty in accepting the imperfect, impermanent, and partial, because they see only too well what might be; they have not yet let go of the timeless world. Only with developed thought and feeling will they be able to love and understand human beings and other vehicles of the light *for their own sakes*; only with increasing maturity will they be able to relate to the real nature of 'the other', seeing him neither as clothed in the magic of their own projected soul, nor—at the other extreme—as a hollow shell, but rather as a creature in his own right, with his own inner glory, albeit of a different kind. And here they learn what is possibly the hardest lesson for these unweaned, untested sky-children—that of humility; for spiritual pride, or even a kind of lonely arrogance, is their besetting sin, and they may easily become 'intuitive snobs'. They will grow to learn that the holy light shines equally through all kinds of people; through the clear integrity of critical thinkers; through the warm radiance of those who feel; and even (how difficult!) through the tiniest sordid details of transient physical living, which can be as direct a way back to the Source as the highest flights of meditation. Indeed, they come to perceive through experience that all is One. (But usually this insight comes only later in life.)

Unconscious projection, then, serves a purpose in that it draws the life-force out spontaneously, starting the process of involvement going. So perhaps our first need with an apparently 'lifeless' student is to find out where the life—the libido—is : where the projections are. Then we can accept them and go along with them; we can help the flow of energy to widen out and fulfil itself, relating to the world more realistically. The important thing is never to drive it back from any supposedly 'unworthy' or 'infantile' object by condemnation. (However, this is not so easy when the temporary object of the projection is oneself !)

One of the most important features of the initiation process is that of showing the young people where they can fit constructively into the adult world—the valued role that they can play in their own way. Introverted intuitives need to feel that their strong function is recognized and that they are expected to 'be' it, just as cooks cook and artists paint; balancing up comes later. They need to be told they are not 'different' in the sense of being crazy, odd, or Laing's 'ghost in the weed garden'; different only in the sense that each of us is unique and we all have our contribution to make. How can this be done? By personal talks with an understanding friend for the very shy? In groups for the not-so-shy? Experiments have been tried with groups comprising students of different function types where, by a process of self-discovery and discovery of others, they find that thinkers in an intellectually snobbish world are not necessarily 'better', but that all have an equal part to play. It is particularly difficult to draw out the special contribution from intuitives in such groups, because they are understandably reserved about revealing their private worlds, and the tutor may well feel tentative, too. Writing may be an easier medium. In some recent groups where the initiation processes into God, Sex, and Society were discussed, people seemed much freer in talking about sex and society than about God. Do we need to establish more of the atmosphere of the Far East where subjects such as dreams, visions, other-world experiences and death are spoken of naturally, and with delight, and are not felt to be slightly indecent and taboo?

Finally, these intuitives need to bring their insights into full physical expression. Can we give them the opportunity for painting, pottery, sculpture, music, dance, movement, drama, gardening—all of which bring spirit into earth? Through the medium of such activities, they will come to recognize others. First kindred spirits: 'There are other people like me after all, I am not alone.' Then those who are opposites, yet friendly: 'The world is not such a frightening place after all; I do not feel invaded; it can be full of interest and joy.' And so even the defensive arrogance drops naturally away.

As a wise tutor said, 'They need the know-how.' We should not—we cannot—give this to them ready-made, but we can help them to acquire skills of relating and living without telling them how they should relate and live. Possibly this is the main function of us counsellors towards them, for they have their own Source and only need to learn to trust it. If we do not fail them, in their own time they will not fail future generations in giving to life freely of what they truly are.

Part IV: Further Dimensions in Counselling

CHAPTER 15

The Inner Side of Preparation: the Dark Tunnel

Although the problems outlined in the last chapter still remain valid for many, what a change has taken place during the last quarter of the century! When I first started counselling, one hardly dared to define psychology as the science of the human psyche or 'soul'. Still more, until very recently, was the term 'spirit' ridiculed and debased in our materialist culture. But now (as in ancient times, though more consciously and universally, on a higher ring of the spiral) the spirit is becoming recognized as the causal, creative *reality* underlying and permeating all physical, emotional, and mental life. Many young people (old souls in new bodies) are innately aware of it, their 'difficult' behaviour sometimes—though not always—arising as a reaction against the lack of understanding from parents, teachers, churches, and society in general. Having found that drugs give only a transient, limited, distorted and dangerous experience of the reality they feel to be there, they now search for it through group relationships, sex and love, art and symbolism, music and meditation, all on varying levels and in different modes. And at long last they are finding meaningful literature, a few broadcasts, courses, societies, and centres in which the new life can be lived 'right down through'. In this way, like yeast in a loaf, little groups springing up everywhere are providing space for the *pneuma*—the wind of the spirit—to aerate society.

I have told how the first forty years of my life prepared me for the counselling work of the next twenty-five. Now, after retirement, I can see the whole period of sixty-five years in terms of experience and training for a yet further phase. Old forms and assumptions of counselling will no longer satisfy many young people today. So much radical change is happening to prepare us, during the critical last quarter of this century, for what many feel to be the 'new age', that counselling needs a new dimension. (Of course I realize that I am only one among very many people now pioneering in this field, each in his own idiom, some very fine examples working from within the new-born churches, but my specific contribution can be only to give what I am, here and now.)

Although of an earlier generation, I can use my own experience as an example. Until very recently, my two 'lives'—spiritual and material—had to run side by side, but failed to find a context in which they could be integrated outwardly. It was a relief when Lawrence Hyde once spoke to me of what he called 'the schizophrenia of our time'. He explained that the schism was something that had to be lived with until the time was right. If the problem of leading a dual life could be accepted in full awareness, it did no harm to the personality; one simply learned to function by the light of the inner acting into the outer, and to keep quiet (except for a very few friends) about it. So, throughout my working life I did not speak about my inner life to my immediate colleagues, except a little to Hugh Binnie shortly before he died. Billy Tibble always teased me about being a 'mystic'—another 'bad word'! Only a few friends and clients knew overtly, but of course a certain quality was bound to filter through, however implicitly, into my therapeutic work. It was a great encouragement when the Quaker, Dr. Alfred Torrie, who was 'good father' to our Association of Psychotherapists in its early days, told some of us openly that he was in a condition of prayer throughout most sessions with his patients.

I have never been at all gifted in clairvoyance, clairaudience, precognition, or any of the other psychic powers (except for a fairly average degree of normal telepathy), although I am quite interested to read about the findings of parapsychology. My own inner knowing came more as self-evident intuitive insight into the nature of things, first largely through nature-mysticism, later through the deeper aspects of Jungian analysis combined with carefully trained meditation and spiritual experience. These insights usually took the form of recognition; for example I never had to learn how to meditate. My own way came naturally, as a practice long known, though I certainly needed the outer opportunity and discipline to exercise it regularly. Later I was drawn to find those particular books which helped me to codify each stage in inner knowing as I reached it. A book would 'feel right' for a time and then be discarded when outgrown. (Many have had this form of guidance.) Further, there were some books which, though good, did not register as the particular path for me, yet I scanned them because later they might well be the path for others, and therefore useful to recommend.

The period of feeling and intuition

As a child and in my teens I was brought up in Christian teaching as formulated by the Church of England and preached by my father. But I learned far more of the immanence of the spirit from nature which, to me then, was shot through with the magic of the subtle worlds. When I was sixteen at Gardenhurst we were prepared for confirmation by the local parson. In my 'thought book' (to God) I wrote. 'Mr. P. tells things very nicely but I would rather have the song of the wind.' There follows a communion with wind, sea, trees, hills, and the moon, through which I learned something of my present life as seen in the light of a different dimension of time (though I did not put it in those words!) I could begin to accept the 'beauty of struggle and endurance', even (this refers to my mother's marital problems with which I was deeply concerned) 'in living a life of misery for seventeen years'. I concluded, 'And so God taught me through the things he created; he tried to teach me of his wondrous love, but I am such a stupid little fool that I cannot understand it at all, it is so very hard to understand.'

Such communion came through feeling-awareness; it could not (at that age) be conceptualized intellectually. The most congenial medium for me—and for so many teenagers of my type— was verse, allowing scope for that imagery which transcends literalism. Just as some people draw or paint so as to learn from the reflected image which their hand portrays, so I used to let the verse express itself in order that I might find out what the real 'I' thought and knew. (Similarly, I am writing an autobiography partly to see the emergence of a pattern.) I have called this chapter 'The Dark Tunnel' because in early life I was so confused; there seemed to be no outer light; one had to find one's own light or else be lost.

In this way, puzzling one day when I was fifteen about the nature of the orthodox concept of heaven, I asked myself, 'Is it a wonderland?'

> Or is it just a world of thought
>> Not anywhere, but everywhere,
> A world of peace, not on this earth,
>> Yet here?

*　　*　　*

> So heaven perhaps is all around,
>> Not in our sight, but yet we know
> That they can see us, whom we loved
>> Not long ago.

Science was not taught at Gardenhurst, and anyway I doubt whether school physics in the early twenties would have provided an adequate conceptual framework for understanding the theory of interpenetrating fields of different frequencies of vibration and of consciousness. So I had to express this dimly-perceived idea in the very simple words of poetic insight and paradox, which were all I had. Anyway, the image of a 'thought world' seemed to fit my inner 'knowing' more truly than did the orthodox, somewhat concrete, heaven of contemporary religion. (It is important to remember that we had no radio or television, and that free discussions on such subjects have appeared only recently on their programmes.)

The particular set of verses from which these two are taken I wrote for a bereaved school friend. Often, if people were in trouble, they would say, 'Write a poem for me'. So I did. I could turn them out easily enough—such as they were—not good poetry but they seemed to fulfil the need, and I enjoyed doing them.

At the same time, some of us were quite practical. (Here was the germ of the future experimental approach, though at the time we did not see it in this way.) What we did was to test out literally two of Christ's sayings:

If ye have faith as a grain of mustard seed . . . nothing shall be impossible unto you.[1]

If two of you shall agree on earth as touching anything that they shall ask, it shall be done for them of my Father which is in heaven. For where two or three are gathered together in my name there am I in the midst of them.[2]

Accordingly, two or three of us did get together and believe completely, with the result that school friends in trouble would ask, 'Do a miracle for me', just as naturally as one might order a pound of butter. We did our best, though we did not think of the work as miraculous; rather we took it for granted as one of the laws of nature which Christ had been concerned to explain. Requests were usually about the small things which loom so large at boarding school : exams, music lessons and other ordeals; finding lost objects, minor health problems, worries about family at home, personal relationships; but this work was the seed of my future interest in healing, and with very few exceptions it was effective. The ethics of the matter concerned us no more than if we had pressed a switch to make a light; we had not reached the intellectual and critical stage. At our age we still personalized God in a somewhat human way. We believed there was this God-power and that we had been told how to use it. At the same time we learned that it was 'not done' to speak of it as a reality. Our very able English mistress, Miss C., had definite views on this. I recorded :

Today, in answer to 'Explain "Man proposes, God disposes" ', Elizabeth said, 'Man tries to do something but if God does not wish him to do it he will never be able to do it.' Miss C. said, 'Don't be so pious, Elizabeth, say rather, "If man tries to do something he will be hindered from doing it by *adverse circumstances*." ' Why should your power be called adverse circumstances?

I was always deeply concerned with the power of thought. Again at fifteen :

[1] Matthew : XVII, v. 20.
[2] Matthew : XVIII, vs 19 and 20.

Children are taught, as soon as they can understand, the wordly way to think. If a baby was never taught *how* to think would it not always think and know about heaven? But as they get older, they forget.

(It was not until two years later, at seventeen, that I was to find, rejoice in, and agonize over, Wordsworth's Ode: *Intimations of Immortality*; by that time indeed I was mourning that 'there hath past away a glory from the earth'.)

Sometimes I am so afraid of my thoughts that I think I shall go mad. I can quite understand what mad people feel like. Miss C. says I have a very morbid mind and should not encourage it. I suppose as usual my mind is different from normal people's, but why should theirs be considered right and mine wrong? You gave everyone gifts to use, why should I not use my morbidness if it is morbidness? I think my whole life is spent thinking about things I cannot understand, wondering and asking why.

When Miss R. (Churn—the music mistress) had frightened one girl nearly out of her wits, I asked God for help in writing a poem for her. I went on:

Do show me how we can help people and be some good in the world. What use are brains and imagination if you are 'so devoid of common sense and so babyish' like me? Perhaps some day you will find a special work for me, something peculiar that I am fit for. I suppose Miss C. would call this morbid. Let her!

At the age of eighteen, at Redland, awareness of some form of reincarnation began to emerge, again through the use of verse, and again as a feeling of recognition:

When have we known it all before?
Where have we heard that haunting tune?

Then came the impact of something deeper than mere human

reincarnation. On meeting a friend, a deep part of me was aware that I had known her essence, in and out of varying forms, throughout involution and evolution, though of course such concepts were as yet foreign to me. This idea, pounding away in its urge for expression, was one of the most difficult themes to capture that I have ever experienced; indeed I remember lying prone on the floor when writing it (this position always helped!) I wrote a verse for each stage. It started :

> Long, long ago when the world was new
> Man was a thought, as yet unmade.

Then we condensed, through different colours, right down to the furthest point of crystallization in mineral (jewel) form, and up again until the 'swift and awful hour' of incarnation in a mortal frame :

> Now we know when the world is grey,
> Filled with the jar and din of strife,
> Filled with the rush and heat of the day,
> What is the price we pay for life.

Needless to say, I had not then heard of Rudolf Steiner or Theosophy, nor had I read any cosmology, or anything on reincarnation (except Wordsworth's Ode).

As I grew older, I became more fully conscious of the underlying unity of the subtle essence permeating all form. I saw earthly trees as life 'trapped in time and space' and 'longing for release' (considerable projection here!) In my first year of freedom at Exeter as 'Bunny', under the title of *Spring Song of a March Hare*, I wrote :

> Mad, the world says : let them say,
>   For we are part of a windy day;
> One with the earth and one with the sea,
>   Perfect, eternal identity.

I reproduce these extracts, without embarrassment, because they form a contemporary record, and because I know (having

met and corresponded with so many) that there are other perfectly ordinary people like myself who needed the vehicle of
verse to carry what they dimly felt and knew. Why are some of
us so ashamed of our youthful verse? Why is it ridiculed, why are
we told that we shall 'grow out of it'? As I see it, perfection of
form is not the vital factor during the verse-writing period of
school and early student age. Later this outlet is too often tragic-
ally lost in the pressure of money-making, except by those who
are genuine poets; and of course verse is only one vehicle; we
need to encourage all possible skills which facilitate the art of
'imagining true'. In so many cases we do not need to teach these
deeper perceptions from studying secondhand 'authorities'
(though it is wonderful to meet them by reading their findings);
only to open out a way, listen with humility, value, and share.[3]

Before I leave school days, there was one crucial happening,
while I was still at Gardenhurst, that must be recorded. Recently
I wrote it up in response to a request from the editor of *Light*
for actual personal experiences which had convinced readers of
life beyond the physical body.[4] It contained no euphoric or manic
quality; it was calm, clear, still, and aware.

When, I ask myself, have I been able to say, 'I do not
merely believe; I *know*'?

Only once. It was this experience which started me on
the way of learning to 'see through' material appearances;
to interpret them in terms of the fuller life. I was seventeen and at boarding school at the time of a severe 'flu
epidemic. When my temperature rose to 105° they moved
me to a separate room from the other 'flu victims, for I was
seriously ill. I remember the experience of delirium, whirling
round the room, calling for 60 cotton; it must not be 40,
it must be 60! I mention this because a part of me was

---

[3]   '... and "*to know*"
    Rather consists in opening out a way
    Whence the imprisoned splendour may escape,
    Than in effecting entry for a light
    Supposed to be without.'
                            Browning: *Paracelsus*.
[4] 'An Experience of Dying', *Light*, Spring 1972. Thanks are due to the
acting editor for permission to reproduce this contribution.

aware of my state as being confused, and this was completely different from what happened next. I then came out of my body, not only into clear consciousness, but into a more intense livingness than anything I had previously experienced. There was an awareness of expansion, of immense well-being and clarity, of joy and meaning. Several of us, typical adolescents, had often discussed matters of life and death, and I remember thinking, 'If *this* is death, how wonderful, how easy, how natural.'

Something seemed to say to me, 'This is very important; fix it.' So I looked down, finding myself lying still, horizontally, about six feet above my body on the bed. Below me, Matron was lighting the gas fire, piling blankets on me; the school doctor was sent for in the middle of the night. I was aware of a tremendous magnetic pull to go *on*, for I was far more alive and well than in my physical body; but, although everything in me wanted to go, I knew I must not do so—yet.

The next thing I knew was that I was back in my physical body, with a very sore throat, feeling awful. Going out had been wonderful : expansion, awareness, light, life. But coming back was the opposite, and very unpleasant, like being constricted and limited into something heavy, cold, dark, and painful. The next morning my parents arrived : my temperature was 99°—it was one of those crises—and I felt very weak.

By the age of seventeen, and brought up in an orthodox clergyman's household, I had never heard or read of dying described in this way, as a living experience. Later I did read descriptions similar to my own, and I realize now that I had not been actually aware of that 'cord' which many perceive as linking the two bodies. Since this experience, however, I have never been afraid of dying; to me the limitations of the three-dimensional world can be far more alarming. When suicidal patients seek death as a means of escape into oblivion, I often wonder what they will find; for death, as I nearly had it, is life to the nth degree. And so I have always sought to understand this box-like existence in the context of that wholly simple and obvious awareness of what living can really be.

The intellectual period

During early student days at Exeter, the feeling-intuitive stage reached its climax; I did a good deal of writing, both of verse and stories. At the same time a period of critical doubt was catching up on me. I had given up church-going; I made fun of the narrow views of the college Student Christian Union. The scientific discipline of university Geography made me question everything and argue ceaselessly—a horribly awkward and aggressive phase! My father, however, was most understanding, for he had been through what he called 'the usual ten years of chaos period' himself, mainly at Oxford. He took it as a healthy phase through which all thinkers must go, and this helped a great deal. It *did* last about ten years, roughly from eighteen to twenty-eight.

Of the three ultimate values: Beauty, Truth, and Goodness, my chosen conscious value has always been Truth. Every Remembrance Day at this time, as well as praying for the world, I used to pray: 'Let me *see*; let me *understand*.' Despite all the outer joyful activity of college life, the inner conflict reached a peak in my middle twenties, when I wrote:

> Dark and twisted
> Is the eternal
> Circle of thought;
> Round it we wander,
> Ignorant, faithless,
> Broken by human wit,
> Blinded by human form.
> How can we, hearing
> All voices calling
> Know which to follow?
>
> And yet to some Being
> From habit we pray,
> 'O God, make us free
> Of the circle of flesh,

Of the dark globe of earth,
Of the great ring of time!
O give us the power
To find and know Truth.

But silence replies,
And so we go on
Blindly and coldly
Dulling our senses;
Only the drugging world
Lulling our questions,
Bidding us work on
And on in the darkness;
Only a glow
Round the circle before us :
The dim light of courage.

The problem was sharpened by a friend on the university
staff whose chief values were music and nature, so that she
represented all I was losing. Although we were equals academically (indeed she took a first, while I had only an upper second,
in our first degrees), she had none of my mental restlessness. She
was gentle, beautiful, and feminine, radiating unquestioning
serenity; soon she married and left the academic world. Shake-
speare's phrase 'my gracious silence' always reminds me of her.
She mirrored a value that I needed to find in myself, and so—
because what she stood for was as yet latent in me—I saw her
as asleep. I asked :

Why do we torture mind and will
    With reasons why and how to live,
When nature simply says, 'Be still',
    All womanlike, intuitive?

For as in pools and mountain streams
    Unerring truth lies buried deep,
So goodness filters through her dreams
    And certainty is in her sleep.

But I could not put my hungry mind to sleep again. The time had come when I must try to synthesize these apparent opposites, and I knew that true synthesis was possible only at a higher level. Intuition must be trained by discrimination; intellect must cease to play the 'logical' games of adolescence, and become illumined by insight. This was a very long path, and it began through reading.

CHAPTER 16

The Inner Side of Preparation: Slowly Into the Light

It was Eve Lewis at Exeter who first led me to an interest in psychic research, but it was not until I went to Lincoln at twenty-six that I started to read systematically the evidence and theories behind so-called 'occult' knowledge. Beginning with Steiner, Ouspensky, Alice Bailey and Theosophy, the Christian mystics and the classical Eastern sources, I studied some of the many different idioms which reiterate the Ageless Wisdom. Steadily I built up my own library; books were cheaper in those days, and many obtainable secondhand. In this way, through reading, if not yet through outer contacts, I found companion-ship, intellectual validation, and deepening of my previous gropings. The doctrine of reincarnation made sense to me, men-tally as well as in feeling, though it seemed that the concept needed clarification and interpretation on the highest level that we can understand while still incarnate. It did not surprise me to learn that some form of reincarnation was accepted by most great religions of the world, and by Christians until the doctrine of the pre-existence of the soul was believed to have been anathematized by majority vote in the Fifth Ecumenical Council of A.D. 553.[1] But reading is only head-learning; the wisdom needs to be sifted, applied, and deeply felt.

Very slowly, over the years, I came to accept that our higher selves select our parents and our major life-tasks, so that at this level we *do* ask to be born. Difficult conditions and relationships

---

[1] For detailed qualification of these anathemas see Joseph Head and S. L. Cranston: *Reincarnation in World Thought*, Julian Press, New York, 1967.

can then be seen as a challenge and an opportunity to resolve the tangles of many lives. (What, for example, might 'I' have done to 'Churn' in some other place and time?) Further, I began to realize that we can tap—for use in the here and now—deeper wells of experience and wisdom than the few drops gained in one lifetime. A fresh perspective was thrown on the (apparent) disqualification which I mentioned on p. 44 about lacking marital and maternal experience. From the greater self (or perhaps from the group soul—we cannot yet know fully) I could 'cash in' on the experience of lives both male and female. This awareness gave me more confidence inwardly, but was not an argument that could be used outwardly! (In counselling work, later on, all these insights were to be fundamental in enabling clients to accept and tackle their problems positively. Especially valuable was the light thrown on homosexuality and trans-sexuality. After several lives as a woman, the first life in a male body may not always be easy—and vice versa. Not that the doctrine could be discussed overtly in most cases, but it helped my attitude in therapy.)

Through books I discovered the existence of groups and societies in the outer world where one could speak openly of these matters. Part of several vacations I spent in London, exploring, testing out everything from spiritualism to psychic science, finding some charlatanry, and a great deal that could be accounted for psychologically, but also much of obvious integrity. It was an excellent exercise in discrimination, and I learned through errors on both sides. Sometimes I was over-critical, so that I rejected a system of teaching because its idiom repelled me; at other times I was not critical enough.

One day when I was about thirty, I was browsing in a public library. Somehow my hand seemed led to touch an unknown book (many seekers have had this experience). It turned out to be the first publication of an esoteric group which, at long last, 'felt right' for me, at that time. I joined, gradually working my way into close contact with the inner teaching provided. I cannot be too appreciative of the sound training given by this group. It was pure and simple, yet profound, emphasizing the heart. This was good for me, helping to balance my over-active mind. (In fact in this setting my mind began to feel rather 'bad' as 'the slayer of the real' until I learned to use it at a higher level.) Spiritual healing was taught, and we learned to give it both by direct contact and at a distance. During the twenty years after the war ended I went to annual retreats where we were trained carefully in group meditation and spiritual experience, combined with both general teaching and personal guidance. Those intensive weeks helped me to survive all the difficult years at Leicester: one week 'in harbour' for re-fit, followed by fifty-one battling it out at sea. Yet now I was no longer alone; at any time I could contact group members, and some of my most long-standing friendships have come in this way. It was so good to meet in depth people who spoke the same language. And it was an especial bonus when, about the time of my father's death, my mother became an interested member, so that during the last twenty years of her life we could talk and resolve some of our difficulties at this level.

Although I have remained faithful to this group, quite early I was told (from the higher world) that 'We would not restrict you in any way', and *always* advised to follow my own inner light. It felt inwardly right to branch out, continuing to explore all possible schools and movements. Looking back now, I can see how useful these varied links have been to students and other clients and friends who were searching for their own paths. Towards the end of a course of counselling a student might say, 'Well, now I see more clearly, but what do I see?' In longer and deeper psychotherapy the answer usually comes from within, but at the counselling level how should a counsellor reply? Is it our job to go into metaphysics? A psychiatrist once advised me to 'give them a philosophy', but I doubt if anyone should or even can do that. What I have done is to turn them loose to browse in my own particular library, sharing my own searchings. Each student might then find a path congenial to himself, and this provides useful practice for him in selection, learning to be true to *his* inner light instead of just accepting advice.

So I ranged freely. One of the most stimulating early contacts came through a postal course *An Introduction to Spiritual Science*, offered by Lawrence Hyde. This was very sound and intellectually demanding. It led to many visits to him and his wife, Lorna, and later I reviewed his book *I Who Am* for

Education for Teaching. For a period (1958 to 1961) I attended and contributed to several conferences of the Centre for Spiritual and Religious Studies,[2] serving on a committee concerned with religious education. For four years, about this time, I went into Subud, then centred at Coombe Springs, under J. G. Bennett; it did not ever register as my particular path, but it had the great advantage of putting me in closer touch with my body—something I needed. Although resilient and basically healthy, I was never quite fit owing to constant nervous strain. Yet even physical weakness was used for increasing contacts and experience, for I received a great deal of healing, not only from my own main group but from many other sources—an education in itself. One of these was Ronald Beesley at White Lodge, Speldhurst, where, with some friends, I often went to stay, once taking Part I of his course in Spiritual Psychology. As is usual in learning any skill—in this case healing—it is part of the process to be a patient first. Ever since the 1950s I have had help from radionic or radiesthetic practitioners; I joined the Radionic Association as an associate member in their early days, and lectured at two of their annual conferences, in 1962 (on Jung) and 1966 (on Art Therapy). This Association forms a spearhead of pioneer work in linking the subtle bodies with the physical body through working on the electro-magnetic energy field which all life forms possess and share.[3] Through these and other contacts, I was gradually building up a wide range of friends and associates beyond—yet occasionally including—the academic world. As well as providing a richer and more varied life, these links stood me in good stead when, in my own turn, I came to be instrumental in disseminating the work of Gildas.

One of the most lasting relationships has been with the College of Psychic Studies[4] which is a gold-mine for all seekers, offering a wide programme, and housing a library (with postal service) of 11,000 volumes in this field. Lawrence Hyde, then editor of the

[2] Organizing Secretary: Miss A. E. Barnard, 4 Wimpole Mews, London W.1.

[3] For literature, write to the Secretary, Radionic Association, Field House, Peaslake, Guildford, Surrey, GU5 9SS. The Healing Research Trust, designed to promote and investigate new healing methods, can be contacted at the same address.

[4] 16 Queensberry Place, London SW7 2EB.

206

College's quarterly journal *Light*, in 1956 published a paper of mine *The Dark Sister* (on the principle of feminine creativity); subsequently in 1958 I was asked to give a couple of talks at the College to make a bridge between psychological and psychic aspects: 'The Psychologist, the Occultist, and the Mystic' and 'A Psychologist at Work'. In 1966 Paul Beard became President of the College. He and his wife Rosemary were old friends, and I came close again. In 1969 I gave a talk on 'The Gildas Scripts', followed in 1970 by 'Depth Psychology and the Inner Man'. From that time on, I became a regular contributor to *Light*,[5] and attended two residential conferences organized by the College in 1971 and 1975; the latter, at Winchester (one of those rare outstanding experiences), was on the subject of 'The Inward Journey'.

Inner Journeys and the Gildas Scripts

Right from the time of my childhood reading of *Pilgrim's Progress* and my father's preoccupation with Dante, inner journeys have always fascinated me. They form a vital link between the fields of psychology, psychic research, myth, and literature. Judging by the rapidly increasing number of books, lectures and conferences on the subject, they are experienced—or perhaps openly confessed—by more and more people at the present time. It so happens that several friends and clients of mine have 'been there', in some form, or to some degree; so for a long time 'journeys' became my chief—though at first secret—topic of research.

My main colleague in this work has been Ruth White: first student, later friend and co-author in two books. I have written a long introductory account on 'What are inner journeys?' in Ruth's account of her experiences,[6] so no description is needed here.

[5] Articles on the Gildas Teachings published in *Light* include: Mary Swainson: *The Gildas Scripts*, Winter 1969. Ruth White: *Gildas and Ruth: An Experience of Mediumship*, Winter 1970. Gildas: *The Changes and the Golden Age to Come*, Summer 1971. Gildas: *Wholeness and Healing*, Spring 1972. Gildas: *The Seamy Side of Aquarius*, Spring 1973. Mary Swainson: *Gildas and the Readers' Group*, Spring 1974. Mary Swainson: *Gildas on the Awakening of Areas*, Summer 1974. Mary Swainson: *Gildas and the Readers' Contributions*, Autumn 1974. Mary Swainson: *Gildas on the Changes: 1967 to 1972*, Autumn 1975.

[6] Ruth White and Mary Swainson: *Seven Inner Journeys*, Spearman, 1975.

Ruth and I had started our work in 1957. During the 1960s only a very few friends knew of it. Then, after Ruth and I had visited him privately, Sir George Trevelyan asked me to give a talk on our findings as a contribution to a week's course on 'The Allegorical Journey' in 1969 at Attingham Park, the Shropshire Adult College. This course led to friendship with the Wrekin Trust which Sir George founded after his retirement from Attingham.[7]

How did all this type of research, writing and lecturing fit in with my official job? It did not. I found it increasingly difficult to run the two aspects of my life together. It was one thing to contribute the odd article to a specialist journal which my colleagues would probably never see; it was quite another to dare to publish a book on teachings from the higher world, particularly since in autumn 1970 I had been granted my very first term of study leave in order to write. This was the time when I had a frank talk with Hugh Binnie. In the event, there was no problem; no strings were attached to the study leave. This time the conflict of loyalties was entirely within my own mind. But after the experience with Billy Tibble, I dreaded once again to be an embarrassment to colleagues who had been so good to me. Yet I knew that the teachings had to come out, and as soon as possible.[8] I compromised by deciding to retire at sixty-four and a half, a year before I needed to do so; and also by giving in my notice a whole year in advance, two months before *Gildas Communicates* was published in November 1971. Thus, in a sense, and with good heart because I was tired of casework and longing for time to write, I gave myself 'the sack'! And I was quite open about it. In the annual report of 1970–1 for Hugh Binnie, I wrote:

[7] The work of the Wrekin Trust may be seen as a kind of adult education of the spirit, offering courses all over the country, and encouraging the development of local groups for meditation, discussion and healing. Its aim is to disseminate the ageless wisdom in this difficult period of change, so as to increase awareness and to help the birth of the New Age. Write to the Secretary, Bowers House, Bowers Lane, Bridstow, Ross-on-Wye, Herefordshire HR9 6JX.

[8] Ruth White and Mary Swainson: *Gildas Communicates*, Spearman, 1971. (This is a more general book, giving the story and the teaching. *Seven Inner Journeys*, which was published after I retired, is more specific, but those for whom it was written, who have 'been there too', have been immensely appreciative that such experiences could be contained within the bounds of sanity.)

The research work on which I have been engaged for the past eleven years is on the borderline between depth psychology and psychic research. The bulk of the book is written for the general public, but Part III : *Evaluation* is a technical section intended for academics, chiefly those engaged in psychic research and parapsychology; this section may possibly interest some of my colleagues.

After retirement I felt glorious freedom to launch out. So many of us, in this and cognate fields, I notice, have felt that we must wait until retirement to give what we really want to contribute. We have more time, yet because of age the amount of energy begins to decline. In these days of redundancy, is earlier retirement a possible solution? Or will this type of work increasingly be recognized by universities and similar institutions as legitimate research?[9]

I spent my final year largely on my job, preparing to hand it over, refusing all outside lectures. But from August 1972 to early 1974 I lectured all over the country on the Gildas Scripts : to local branches or joint one-day conferences of the Churches' Fellowship for Psychical and Spiritual Studies; the Seekers at Addington Park; the Wrekin Trust; and several other groups. Although different aspects of the work were asked for, I prefaced them by a brief explanation, which by now is overdue here.[10]

THE GILDAS SCRIPTS [1969]

Among the increasing number of non-professional sensitives working privately nowadays for the New Age is Ruth. She is a young woman of thirty-one, married with one child, a full-time teacher in a primary school. Her communicator has given his name as Gildas, but he is not to be confused with the mediaeval historian or any known person of that name. Gildas is mainly concerned to help us to raise our level of awareness and so to adjust progressively to four-dimensional living.

---

[9] There are signs that it will be, especially on the scientific side. See pp. 245–6.

[10] This version is selected and adapted from 'The Gildas Scripts', *Light*, Winter 1969, by kind permission of the editor.

Since, in the spiritual field, the best criterion of assessment and discrimination is that of quality—'By their fruits ye shall know them'—here, as an introduction, is an example of his teaching on wholeness :

> When you see a vision, or learn a new truth, or perceive something new, or see something old with a new vision, pray for understanding and the ability to be able to fit this into the pattern of things and you will make a step towards the true vision and attainment of wholeness. Try to achieve insight into the implication . . . this is the thing which includes all things within it—the wholeness of truth, beauty, feeling, pain, sin, healing, goodness, evil—in fact everything you can think of. So much of your conversation touches on these things : the language of alchemy, the integration of black and white, darkness and light—the symbols of wholeness in different forms; and above that, if you can follow my meaning, comes as it were the wholeness *of* wholeness.

This would appear to be an exercise in stretching insight and imagination, in a *gestalt*-like series of increasing significance, to the fourth-dimensional level, working through the intuitive function. And Gildas shows a thoroughly scholarly attitude when he brings insight down through all the other functions—thinking, feeling, and action—in balance. Thus, in respose to some critics, he told us :

> Wholeness of *mind* is the quality by which the uncommitted will finally judge you. Pay constant attention to your thinking, and make your communications as precise, direct, and sincere as you are able. Avoid wide speculation, but keep an open mind. Be true to your knowledge of inner vision yet retain if you can some 'scientific' detachment. Be minute observers of detail, and do not be afraid to say to your critics not only 'I think' but 'I know', for there are certain things which you *do* know, therefore admit them without fear, but admit also those areas in which you cannot yet be certain. In short, cultivate integrity.

Preparation for the work

I work as a psychological counsellor for students at a provincial university and local colleges. When Ruth was referred at nineteen in her final year of teacher training, it was partly because she had been told by an oculist that she would eventually go blind, and understandably was somewhat depressed about this. At a deeper level, it emerged that she had certain gifts and perceptions which she could not understand nor share with her friends; these might have been interpreted as pathological by people ignorant of psychic and spiritual matters. So, very soon, I had her seen by a first-rate psychiatrist in London who reported that he could find no trace of psychosis.

There followed eleven years of personality work much of which was thorough psychological analysis, though latterly I became progressively less her therapist and more a friend and companion on the way. (Incidentally, her sight improved markedly quite early on, and she has had no more trouble since.) During the eleven-year period, Ruth experienced six gruelling (yet wonderful) 'journeys' in inner space, each deeper and more radical than the last. One—the fifth—she did entirely alone. These 'journeys' included work *on* her own personality and also work *beyond* her own personality; indeed who can draw boundaries and say : this is where I begin and you end? Although in the early stages we did not realize it, the experiences were purifying and strengthening her as a fitter instrument for the work to be. In Ruth's case, psychotherapy was ancillary, taking the personality to a certain point. After this point, direct teaching and spiritual exercise, both given by Gildas, took over; indeed, from the inner, he made full use of the outer psychotherapy, training his own sensitive throughout the period.

The beginning of the teachings

It was half-way through the journeys that Gildas ceased to be concerned solely with Ruth's preparation. At the end of the third journey I asked him whether he would be willing to give some information through Ruth which could be circulated to a small group of interested people; he agreed, provided that questions came first from us. Naturally, as a Jungian psychotherapist, I was particularly interested in the nature of the psyche and the relation between objective and subjective experience, although I realize that the higher one goes in awareness, the more closely they are seen to be one. Therefore, in view of the argument about the extent to which these communicators are separate entities or are a part of the sensitive's 'unconscious mind' (whatever that may mean) or, at the deepest level, are personified archetypal principles, the first question I ever asked Gildas was: 'Who are you from your point of view? Spiritualists would call you a "guide", Jungian psychologists the "animus" part of Ruth's psyche. How do you see yourself?' He replied:

> It is difficult to qualify ideas to express them in language. Perhaps the spiritualists are more correct than the Jungians, for I am indeed a separate entity in many respects. I do not exist solely as a part of Ruth. We are linked from ages past, the perfect partners, able to live apart yet incomplete without each other. We have lived lives apart, we have also incarnated together, and now I have achieved to a state where I can live separately and yet within Ruth. She sees me as a separate being, yet I never really leave her, for our spirits are so intermingled in the web of time and the pattern of life that we are never really apart.
>
> A truth, like a jewel, has many facets. These theories which are held by different schools are often part of the truth, yet not the whole of it, and, like a jewel, the true value and beauty are only seen when one holds the complete thing. Oh that men would achieve the humility to see this —how much valuable energy would be saved for other things! Therefore to some extent our relationship can be understood in any of these ways, but only when an attempt is made to accept the universal truth are you near the actuality.

Method of communication

There is no question of trance, nor of automatic writing. By a slight shift of level of consciousness, Ruth can function in the 'inner world', can see Gildas and talk with him. Asked to describe the subjective aspect of the process, she wrote:

I 'see' Gildas clearly enough, mainly with what I think of as my spiritual eyes, and I 'hear' him with my spiritual ears. He is tall and has a beautifully radiant and compassionate face. His eyes are a luminous pale brown colour (which he laughingly describes as yellow); the expression in them defies description.

When messages are being received from Gildas . . . I prepare myself by ten minutes or so of silent orientation. When he is ready, his words come into my mind in a steady flow like dictation, and I write them down. Sometimes he will say, 'Go back, that is not right', and direct me to correct some word or phrase . . . I do not take completely into my mind the full sense of what I have recorded until I read it or it is read out afterwards.

I have been told that this contact with Gildas will continue and develop throughout this life, and I believe that our work is inextricably linked. His allotted task on the 'other side' seems to be to teach and prepare for the coming changes as many people as he can reach on this side. The work to which I am committed seems to involve being his sensitive and recorder and helping to spread his words . . . Fortunately I am not in the position of having to earn my living by mediumship, but having the gift that I have, and fitting it into the life I lead, is by no means all joy. Almost unbearable conflicts arise between the demands of the inner and outer worlds. It is only a conviction that we are following the allotted path that enables these feelings to be overcome and the directives of Gildas to be obeyed. Then there comes the sudden patch of harmony, and the upsurge of joyous feelings of completeness which brighten the way ahead and make all the difficulties more than worth while.

Expansion of the work

I, too, have had to live a double life. We would have preferred to continue in obscurity with quiet research, but in 1967 —that critical year—Gildas urged us very strongly to make the work known as widely as possible, with discrimination. We therefore expanded our small group of readers with the result that the permanent mailing list is now [*1969*] nearly 300. This is entirely a postal group; there is no one centre territorially, although many readers have their own centres. Although we issue the material, we do not function as a teaching school. Further, we work towards our own redundancy, for it is symbolically significant that our centre is, as it were, empty—thus throwing the onus back on to the individual to find and commune with his own inner source. This is one of Gildas's most important principles.

[*The rest of the paper consisted of excerpts of Gildas's teachings.*]

*   *   *

The readers' group ran for six years, from 1967 to 1973, when Gildas himself suggested that we closed it down in order that we might have time for further growth ourselves, and that readers should find and use their own inner source. By this time we had over 700 on our mailing list, and the correspondence was overwhelming. Understandably, as a psychotherapist, I had many personal requests for psychological help which could be given only in a modified form through letters. The experience of 'counselling by post', covering all ages from adolescents to the elderly, from a self-selected and specific public, was quite different from university work. It taught me a great deal, but as it has little to do with ordinary student counselling, it must be left for another story.

Then I was asked to contribute a lecture for the Wrekin Trust, and a course of four seminars at the College of Psychic Studies, all on the subject of death. Death, rather than sex, I feel, is the taboo subject of the present day. Although important in my own thinking, and in that of many at our time of life, it does not come specifically within the scope of this book. Perhaps in another?[11]

More appropriate are the two lectures forming the final chapters which do apply to a large extent to students. They constellate all my ideas at the time on further dimensions in counselling.

11 The latest development is a talk on *Reincarnation Experiences in Counselling and Psychotherapy* given at another Wrekin Trust conference in August 1976, while this book was in the press.

CHAPTER 17

Scylla and Charybdis in New Age Learning

[At a very outstanding Wrekin Trust Summer School in August/ September 1972, as well as a talk on Gildas, I was asked to contribute to the main theme of the week: 'The Inward Odyssey'. (The members dramatized the story of Odysseus, which gave it an added dimension.) Characteristically, the episode of Scylla and Charybdis appealed to me. This was partly because the School was held in Northumbria which some of us had experienced as a country of sharp opposites, of extremes of the hard and the beautiful, of darkness and light; partly because so many readers were complaining of difficulty in negotiating the problem of the opposites; and also I wanted to apply the theme particularly to student counselling. So I chose the phase when the hero, Odysseus, must pass through the narrows between dangers which, being archetypal, are inevitable in his path of initiation.]

This challenge of the dangerous gate—or narrow straits—occurs in many legendary journeys. There is the parallel of the Wandering Rocks in the earlier story of Jason. Indeed, when the goddess Circe instructs Odysseus beforehand, she gives him a choice of routes: he can go either through the Wandering Rocks—which up till then only the *Argo* had survived—or the passage between Scylla and Charybdis. But he cannot avoid the test, and he chooses the second.

Once the challenge is accepted, how does the traveller negotiate the straits? Here is a personal contribution.

At first, with my usual arrogance, I thought: Here am I who have been brought up on the classical myths; this should be a nice easy lecture on the Middle Way. Just keep safely right down the centre of the channel and all will be well. I didn't even bother to re-read the text. *Hubris*. Pride due for a fall! I emphasize this, because even the Golden Mean can be abused and can show its negative aspect *if it comes at the wrong time*. And, when you are avoiding something, life shows you. My daily life began to show me that the middle of the channel was becoming not a true synthesis but a compromise—a sitting-on-the-fence —a way of opting out. I found myself escaping from responsibility. When asked for yet another commitment or judgement, I'd say, 'Oh well, I'll keep an open mind.' Useful phrase, that! It sounds tolerant and mature, and, of course, can be so, but just then it masked my own laziness, boredom, and (to be be fair) sheer exhaustion.

Now, as a psychologist, I've learned that when anything otherwise good goes bad on you, like this, it's time to contact the *source* again, in every sense of the word. So I did. I re-read the Odyssey. I realized that even the centre of the channel was far too near Charybdis. I found that, instead of being a nice easy dissertation on the Golden Mean, this was one of the hardest I've ever had to prepare. For the answer at *this* stage of the journey is quite different.

[*I then read the passage from the Odyssey[1] where Circe describes, on the one hand, the monster Scylla who will snatch men from every boat that passes through; and, on the other, the whirlpool Charybdis which swallows the whole ship.*] The goddess ends :

> 'You must hug Scylla's rock and with all speed drive your ship through, since it is far better that you should have to mourn the loss of six of your company than of your whole crew.'

So we see that, at *this* stage of the journey, the challenge is to accept risk, to 'live dangerously', to be willing to lose part rather than lose all. But Odysseus, that 'crafty man', over-full of

[1] Homer: *The Odyssey*, trans. E. V. Rieu, Penguin, 1964, pp. 190–1 (*et seq.*).

confidence and pride in his own ego-strength, tries to get by without suffering loss at all, and this by fighting :

> 'Could I not somehow steer clear of the terrors of Charybdis, yet tackle Scylla when she comes at my crew ?'
>
> But the goddess only cried out at me as an obstinate fool, always spoiling for a fight and welcoming trouble. 'So you are not prepared,' she said, 'to give in even to immortal gods? I tell you, Scylla was not born for death: the fiend will live for ever. She is a thing to shun, intractable, ferocious, and impossible to fight. For, if you waste time by the rock in putting on your armour, I am only afraid she may dart out once more, catch you again with all six heads, and snatch another half-dozen of your crew. So drive your ship past with all your might.'

Here again is a point to note : we are wasting time trying to resist Scylla, for she is archetypally indestructible—one of the essential tests on the journey—so it is no good trying to prevent her being *there*. We have to accept loss, let go, get beyond with all speed. However, Odysseus persists in arming himself with harness and a couple of long spears, though he follows Circe's advice to 'hug Scylla's rock'. [*I then read the terrible account of the passage, where Scylla catches and devours six of the best men.*] Odysseus mourns :

> In all I have gone through as I made my way across the seas, I have never had to witness a more pitiable sight than that.

And so, with loss, they win through to the Isle of the Sun God.

The symbolism
The symbolism is so rich that I think each of us will interpret the images in a different way. Any *valid* myth has many levels and forms of understanding—all of them true. These suggestions are only my own ideas, as a psychologist.

The hero I see as the Divine Spark in man. He comes into incarnation; he must be clothed in potentially fallible personality-material in order to experience the lessons of life and win through. Some see him as a superman. I suppose for us he does represent an idealized image, but I see him more as the universal hero, the archetype, in each one of us; he has to make mistakes, fail, go back, as we all do in order to learn and achieve. Certainly I do not see him *yet* as the 'Superior Man' of the *I Ching*. He may eventually become so, when the Divine Spark has worked through the personality for long enough.

And what is the special position of Odysseus *when at the narrows*? We know that the specific contribution of Greek consciousness was to evolve individual masculine thought; to enable the independent and differentiated ego to take responsibility in freedom. So, understandably, in the story Odysseus often goes to rather inflated extremes with his cleverness and self-confidence, but that is part of the learning process. Culturally, male ego-values had to emerge from the domination of the primal Great Mother archetype of earlier matriarchal cultures; so we find that the images which test Odysseus are those of the negative Mother. Why negative? Because, when an archetype is needed and timely, it appears good and positive, as does the mother-image in early childhood; but when she is outgrown, she turns her 'dark' face; thus teenagers who are impelled to break away tend to see their parents as 'bad'. She may even appear as a monster, as in the story. There is a need to over-state when one has to dare to face the Furies and pass on. Many people in psychotherapy actually experience these images of Scylla and Charybdis in their inner work; other negative mother-images also appear, such as the Spider, the Toad, the Crocodile, and the Entombing Rock. In the Odyssey she appears in two of her aspects, one on each side.

Charybdis is the rhythmic whirlpool, sucking down and spewing up. I see this as a more archaic form, as the unconscious, undifferentiated maternal mass out of which we all evolve : the Great Mother in her swallowing aspect of death, reducing individuals back into the mass; but also in her aspect of giving re-birth, tossing up fragments for another life. Other similar images which often occur in dreams are the primal marsh or quicksand, or a kind of cosmic compost-heap. Later in the story Odysseus has to meet her again.

Scylla I see as more differentiated. She is the octopus-like monster which encloses, possesses, devours. She often stands for the family, as in the play 'Dear Octopus'; or for our society in its enveloping, conditioning, brainwashing aspect.

What of the other symbols?

The armour and the spears could be understood as ego-defences, what Jung has called the *persona*, in its aggressive/defensive aspect in this case, protecting the vulnerable ego. But it's a waste of life to fight; the hero must cut losses and look ahead.

The crew could be understood either on the individual or the group level. They might stand for *alter egos*, other parts of the personality; how often it is the most cherished and powerful aspects of our personalities which have to be lost and surrendered as we go through the stripping process. Or, on a group level, the crew could represent those who are casualties in our society, apparently in order that the rest of us may live—the most terrible thought. Are they paying the price for us?

And finally, *the ship*, traditional symbol of the soul. Personalities may come and go, but the ship goes through. (And yet, as we shall see, in the second encounter with the narrows, Odysseus has to face the loss of all but the basic structure of his ship, and even that goes down into Charybdis.)

How can we apply these symbols in new age learning, in modern journeys and initiations? So many people are journeying now, as awareness increases, into exciting if dangerous adventures in range and mode of consciousness.

The basic rhythms of consciousness

It seems that there is a major cosmic rhythm, an outbreathing and an inbreathing, from unity to diversity and back again to unity. The important thing to keep in mind is that the final union is at a higher ring of the spiral of learning and evolution than the first; like the prodigal son we have to go forth in order to return, this time of our own free will.

The first unity is that undifferentiated state in which we are barely self-conscious; we are part of the whole, of the Great Mother : the state which the sociologist Levy-Bruhl called *participation mystique*. This is experienced by young children and by primitive peoples.

The second stage comes with the growth of awareness as a fully separate 'I': the individual sausage in its skin. We feel thrown out of Eden, isolated, exiled from our source. Here arises awareness of duality, conflict, need for choice and decision between apparent opposites, going right to the extreme of un-related, fragmented knowledge and the abuse of over-analytic differentiation.

Thirdly, we return to the experience of oneness again, but this time bringing the consciousness we have won; no longer is there the duality of 'either/or'; unity is perceived in the *transcendence* of duality or of fragmentation; we see that we can be both an individual and also part of a whole; we go beyond the opposites to 'all and everything'.

The great hero-journeys are concerned with all stages, but I suggest that the problem in our present world lies in getting from stage two to stage three. The separate ego has 'gone bad' on us, with its fear, aggression, grasping materialism. We are cut off from our source, and so we are now experiencing what Anna Morduch[2] calls the 'tremendous *thrust* towards unity' in the new age.

It is exactly here that the test of Scylla and Charybdis faces us. Do we see unity as an easy way out, try to avoid Scylla, and slip back into Charybdis? This pattern occurs in some people of all ages who rush to join the new community-groupings. 'Hurray,' they think, 'now I shall be looked after and can cease responsibility.' At one community, someone rang up: 'Can I join you, I want to get away from it all?' The secretary replied, 'If you feel like that, don't come, because we've got it all here, too!'

To bring these general principles down to earth, I want to illustrate from a specific field which I know: that of student counselling. Among students there is so great a search for in-creasing awareness, through drugs, meditation, and all ways of communication.

Application to student counselling

As far as chronological age is concerned, the application of the test is to the earlier phase of transition: from stage one to

[2] See book list at end of this chapter (p. 228).

stage two of consciousness. However, those who are searching most keenly may well be 'old souls' going on *at the same time* from stage two to stage three. This position needs very 'fine tuning' in discernment on the part of the counsellor, who needs to hold the balance between development of the ego and the finding of the greater Self (to use Jungian terms). How does this work out in practice?

Most people of student age are going through what is currently termed an 'identity crisis'; most of the referrals are in this category. The majority are between eighteen and twenty-two: late adolescence (often delayed because as students they are still relatively protected) and early adulthood. So the main task in development is that of finding themselves as individuals, as distinct from their conditioning by family, school and society. Nearly all who come to me, as counsellor, say, 'I don't know who I *am*'. Some haven't yet grown through the parental authority conflicts, but more important now seems to be the peer-group; one *must* be accepted by one's group of equals, sometimes to the extent of having sex and taking drugs because it is 'the in thing'. This is the *herd stage*, and here I venture to refer to an old but still valid book: *The Fear of Freedom*, by Erich Fromm. He makes the point that the herd, or undifferentiated peer-group, can still be a part of the *participation mystique*, although it is an essential stage in growing up. But the individual has to learn to find out who he is, to become a person, and *then* to share in a fully conscious group of individuals, not a herd; and this is what group work in colleges is all about. Otherwise, we get all the unconscious collusion, identification, and other dangers of Charybdis.

For it is often much easier to drop out, to die back into 'Mum' or into the collective, than to face the challenge of Scylla in becoming a person. Rilke, in his *Letters to a Young Poet*, shows how so many young people long to surrender themselves, or merge into a cause. This *can* be very genuine; again, fine discrimination is essential. But it may well be a premature surrender, an avoidance of having to assume responsibility for a separate ego; often it is so much easier to die than to live. *One has to become a person before being ready to surrender the personality.* And becoming a person can be painful, involving risk and loss, although it is infinitely greater fun, with all the joy of adventure and achievement.

I've spoken of students; what about the counsellors? The same tests apply to all those trying to guide others. We also have a Scylla and Charybdis strait, which lies in the field of *empathy*.

One of the essential qualifications of a counsellor is empathy: feeling into the other person, being *for* him, during his hour. But it must be the right empathy. If we ourselves have not yet escaped from the stage of *participation mystique* we get over-identified; we project our own need to help on to our patients without realizing it; we take over the patient's condition; we become negatively involved. If I find myself feeling hounded and invaded, swallowed up or devoured by these creatures on my doorstep, or if I feel over-anxious about them, I know I'm getting too far into Scylla or Charybdis. True empathy is imagining, directed realistically from one individual to another, yet with that kind of love that is non-attached. But non-attachment is particularly difficult in the field in which one is currently growing oneself, as so many of us are, into new ways of consciousness. And we may have preconceived ideas about the methods used.

Drugs and unwise forms of meditation

To define my terms: I'm talking of those drugs which expand consciousness, chiefly 'pot' and LSD. I'm *not* talking about the more dangerous, addictive hard drugs, although I agree that 'pot' can lead to hard drugs, as also that LSD can be dangerous in itself. And I am referring to meditation which is too quickly forced, not gradually learned and practised 'right down through'.

A fair number of students try drugs and pass on beyond that condition. It's part of their search for identity, for experience, for relationship, for the meaning of existence. They learn the assets and the limitations by experience, growing out of the phase—on the whole with few ill effects. But those who come to us—that is to the Student Health Service—are the ones who break down, terrified and disorientated through 'bad trips', or through too intensive forms of meditation without due safe-guards. Those who break down are mostly already immature, parent-fixated, and needing psychological help to regain balance and stability. Their ego-boundaries are not yet strong enough to face confrontation with unmediated archetypes, and so these take the form of horrors.

Thus John (aged twenty) had an experience in too intensive Transcendental Meditation[3] plus pot. He felt he was being reborn through the top of his head, and was urged by the leader to let go. With some this might have been a positive experience, but John was not ready to take it; he was frightened, came back, and sensibly asked us for help.

George (also twenty) took pot and LSD and got himself into an image of endlessly reflecting mirrors—a sort of existential infinity. Here he was in a state of complete isolation and alienation : he felt he was going mad. Terrified of chaos, he sought order compulsively; he was a bit of an obsessional. We worked, orthodoxly enough, on his mother-fixation and on his fear of becoming a separate person; in the idiom of psychology we *looked at* the mirrors, for, as Teilhard de Chardin says, 'Salvation lies in the very dangers that so terrify us.' George needed, not to go back to his childhood except for some remedial work, but to go *on*, and in the end he got over a good deal of his fear of responsibility and of being alone. Finally, he found his sense of order, but in a new mode of consciousness beyond the mirror sequence : an order that gave him the security of being himself and yet also being an essential part of the whole. Interestingly enough, he then felt drawn to read Teilhard, and quoted him to me as corroborating the new experience of order which he himself was discovering.

With both of these boys, I took the line that first you need a strong, balanced ego—a four-square personality—before you start experimenting in extension of consciousness. And, by the time they have been through a thorough course of psychotherapy, they usually find ways of making contact with the higher consciousness by means of psychological and spiritual exercises, including their own unique method of suitable meditation. Then, I find they leave drugs behind, naturally.

I see all these people who are searching for the higher awareness, albeit too violently or prematurely, as the adventurers, the ones who dare Scylla rather than falling back into Charybdis. I am infinitely more concerned about those who turn their backs

[3] This is not to criticize TM, which I know can do great good.

on life and go down into the whirlpool: the depressives, the alcoholics, the suicides; those who take overdoses for death and for opting out. I had one girl who tried four times; she is fine now, but at the time, when you have done all that you can, the only thing is to 'sit loose' and accept that it may be their path— even that.

With the Scylla types, however, I do not try to pull them back from facing Scylla. I try to get them through and away as soon as possible, so that they can make use of the experience.

Thus Richard, coming down from the heights of an LSD trip, saw an image of his parents, as it were at the wrong end of a telescope; they were very small, old and fallible, sitting up on high chairs so that he couldn't touch them. Now, an image like that, as in a dream, is extremely valuable, and we found it so in our work together.

Another student, Peter, went to one of these mass festivals and took LSD with a group which included his worst enemy. As they both rose from the bonds of personality into their more subtle selves, he realized the true nature of this man, and felt the most understanding and all-accepting love for him. He even reached a point of cosmic consciousness, experiencing unity with all life. Of course, the descent brought him back into the limited personality through which he saw only his enemy's limitations; naturally, the experience could not be sustained. But at least he remembered what it had been like; we could use it; it gave him a great incentive for self-work on his difficulties of relating, and his lack of tolerance.

Please do not imagine that I approve of these drugs; I don't. But when we get the people who have already taken them, I believe the attitude to take is to accept the experiences, which are a glimpse, albeit partial or deformed, and then show them other ways to attain higher awareness.

A good many students, of course, are not so serious in their motivation. They play around with drugs so as to keep in with the crowd. With these I often take the matter at a surface level and say, 'What, *still* in the drug scene? Surely that's "old hat" now?' But we also displace the problem to the deeper level of what they are really saying: they want acceptance, relationship.

Similarly with sex. Freud brings back so much to sex; but

Jung goes further and asks: what is sex a symbol *of*? Again—
the whole range, but in the case of those who are only playing
around, we try to understand what it is *for*: the need to relate,
to belong, to feel secure in the pair and in the group, to be
loved and accepted. And, above all perhaps, the need to
communicate.

Communication

This is the crucial problem, and here again we find three
stages of consciousness:

First, the baby, or the primitive, still not separate from mother,
communicating by that sort of empathy which is identification.
Such people, when they talk to you, say 'You know' in every
sentence instead of making the effort to put their feelings into
words. (I have to be dim and say, 'Sorry, I don't know; tell
me.') They get annoyed when you don't understand without
explanation; they tend to imagine that everyone feels as they
do, and are surprised if people feel differently.

In the next stage, that of learning to be a separate ego, isolated
in the diving-suit of incarnation, we have to accept communication through the skin, the mouth, the diving-suit. One has to
learn words, read books, paint pictures, make music, drama and
dance—study codes of all kinds. Here the ego can feel very cut
off unless he masters a code well; and even then he may find
that others do not share his particular semantic understanding.

Now we are coming up to the third stage: many feel that we
are going beyond codes to a more immediate *communion* rather
than communication. But how? Through enlightened telepathy,
insight, imagining? 'Think each in each, immediately wise,' as
Rupert Brooke wrote? The language of guitars, of encounter
groups, of sound and light, of meditation—all on a higher ring
of the spiral? But here, too, we meet the narrows, and must
always ask, 'Are we going forward or back? Or even both?'
How much is this relatively wordless communication a valid new
age form, or how much is it an escape from being 'incarnate
within the ring', as Graham Howe called it, for a day of life?
Very fine tuning is essential here.

There are many other aspects of new age learning: learning
to communicate, commune, and become one with *our own higher*

selves; all the problems of psychism and mediumship; but I shall leave these until later [*see Chapter 18*].

Conclusion: the Divine Essence

To summarize : in all these fields of new age learning, *if we are going on* towards the third phase of consciousness, we have to take the risk of loss and change, rather than disintegrating into primal chaos.

But what about all those who do not pass through; those for whom life is too terrifying and who get sucked down? What happens to them? The apathetic, the sleepers, drug addicts, suicides, completely sensual materialists, airy-fairy escapers, and many other personalities which (we must remember) may be parts of us (the explorers) too!

In the great myths, the symbol is often that of lotus-eating or wine-drinking—consciousness going back to the alimentary, vegetative state. And, heaven knows, don't we all experience some of this when we regress to comfort-eating and drinking—a sort of 'back to mum's breast'? Or smoking?

There is a less well-known part of the Odyssey, where, not Odysseus himself, but all his crew killed and ate the sacred cattle of the Sun God—a forbidden thing. And so they were all drowned in a storm. Odysseus, clinging to the keel and mast of his ship—all that was left—was swept back to the narrows, alone, and this time right into Charybdis. I quote[4] :

> All through the night I was swept along, and at sunrise found myself back at Scylla's rock and that appalling whirlpool. Charybdis was beginning to suck the salt water down. But as she did so, I was flung right up to the great fig-tree, on which I got a tight grip and clung like a bat. I stuck grimly on until such time as she should spew me up my mast and keel once more. At last the timbers reappeared; I flung my arms and legs down for a plunge, and with a splash fell in the water clear of the great logs, which I then bestrode and rowed along with my hands.

He then drifts for nine days and is washed up on the tenth on

[4] Homer: *op. cit.*, pp. 200-1.

Calypso's Isle, the 'central place of all the seas'—ageless, out of time (though given as seven years) until fetched by Hermes to build a new boat and sail home.

Here we have the image of the eternal still centre, and earlier that of the saving Great Tree, symbol of the indestructible essence of universal life beyond the ego. The Tree occurs in the inner experience of so many people 'on the path', and in many myths, from Norse to Indian. In the Bhagavad-Gita[5] Sri Krishna tells Arjuna, 'I am the holy fig tree', and later :

> There is a fig tree
> In ancient story,
> The giant Aswattha,
> The everlasting,
> Rooted in heaven,
> Its branches earthward . . .
>
> What its form is,
> Its end and beginning,
> Its very nature,
> Can never be known here.

This is the Atman, unborn, undying, birthless, deathless, change-less, to which, when all else is lost, the hero clings.

So, by this final, terrible yet wonderful climax of the story, I understand that even if all the personality dies, even if the soul itself has to go into the melting pot with all but its basic core destroyed, yet the divine essence remains. The hero is given another chance to remake his soul and find his way home.

Gildas, who also uses the tree image in his teaching on whole-ness of being (*Gildas Communicates*, p. 21), has given this recent message, with which I shall end :

> There will be many who are not ready to go forward, so many will be taken and many left. If they are not ready,

---

[5] Trans. by Swami Prabhavananda and Christopher Isherwood, Phoenix House, 1960, pp. 115 and 146–7.

then this experience will be part of their evolution; they will be watched over and guided until they are ready to enter into the new consciousness. Do not forget that the light in all its power and strength is tempered with infinite compassion, and not one of those who are left will be forgotten.

The Allegorical Journey: some relevant reading
(This book list is classified and annotated so that each reader may select a congenial idiom.)

(1) Some classical texts
(Dates not given since reprints are frequent.)

Homer: *The Odyssey*, trans. E. V. Rieu, Penguin Classics.

Apollonius of Rhodes: *The Voyage of Argo*, trans. E. V. Rieu, Penguin Classics.

Apuleius: *The Golden Ass*, trans. Robert Graves, Penguin Classics. (Chapters VII to IX: 'Cupid and Psyche'.)

Dante: *The Divine Comedy*, trans. Dorothy Sayers, Penguin Classics. (Three vols.: *Hell, Purgatory, Paradise*.)

Bunyan, John: *The Pilgrim's Progress*, Penguin English Library.

Swedenborg, Emanuel: *Heaven and Hell*, Swedenborg Society Press.

(2) Some modern books on interpretation of journeys
(a) General

Schnapper, Edith: *The Inward Odyssey: The Concept of 'The Way' in the Great Religions of the World*, Allen and Unwin, 1965. (This book places the journey in a very wide context. There is a chapter on 'The Tree of Victory'.)

Matthews, Honor: *The Hard Journey: The Myth of Man's Rebirth*, Chatto and Windus, 1968. (The traditional hero journey to the underworld and the return, mainly in the context of classical literature and its re-emergence in modern times in the novels and plays of certain existentialists, and of Kafka, Beckett and Brecht.)

Morduch, Anna: *The Sovereign Adventure: The Grail of Mankind*, James Clark, 1970. (Her idiom is that of the

quest for the Grail, the symbol of integration, with particular reference to the youth of today.)

(b) *In the Jungian idiom*
(Most of the works of Jung provide essential source-material,
but the following books distil his teaching. The first two
deal with general principles.)
Neumann, Erich : *The Origins and History of Consciousness*, Bollingen Series XLII, Pantheon Books, 1954. (See
especially Part I B : 'The Hero Myth'.)
Harding, Esther : *Psychic Energy: Its Source and Goal*,
Bollingen Series X, Pantheon Books, 1950. (See especially
Part II : 'The Transformation of Psychic Energy'.)
Harding, Esther : *Journey into Self*, Vision Press, 1958. (A
study of *Pilgrim's Progress* in terms of the archetypal
journey.)
Neumann, Erich : *Amor and Psyche*, Routledge, (o.p.) (An
interpretation of the text of Apuleius : the classical proto-
type of the feminine variant of the journey.)

(3) *Some personal accounts*
Jung, C. G. : *Memories, Dreams, Reflections*, Collins and Routledge and Kegan Paul, 1963. (His autobiography, recorded
and edited by Aniela Jaffé. See especially Chapter VI
onwards.)
Blacker, Thetis : *A Pilgrimage of Dreams*, Turnstone Books,
1973. (A journey experienced through dreams. Introduction
by Kathleen Raine.)
Richelieu, Peter : *A Soul's Journey*, Turnstone Books, 1972.
(This is in the mode of out-of-the-body experiences.)
Gage, Anne : *The One Work: A Journey towards the Self*,
Vincent Stuart, 1961. (An outer journey to the great religious
centres of the Far East to find teaching. This book should be
read together with her paper on the subsequent inner aspect :
'The One Work', *Light*, Summer 1975.)
White, Ruth and Swainson, Mary : *Seven Inner Journeys*,
Spearman, 1975. (See Chapter 16 of the present book for
explanation.)

CHAPTER 18

Psychotherapy and the Extension of Awareness

[*At the next Wrekin Trust Summer School at Moor Park College, Farnham, in August 1973, I knew that a few of my colleagues from the Association of Psychotherapists would be present, together with several clergy, counsellors and others engaged in the 'helping' professions. So this talk was specifically adapted by me for them.*]

Nearly all my working life has been spent on the dangerous pioneering edge of psychological counselling, and never more so than now. So I am not offering any of the *answers*. But I want to explore some of the special *needs* of the present time, and I'll start with a story about a child.

My friend Ruth White teaches infants. In her class of five-year-olds is a boy from a very disturbed home—quite a problem child. Yet people, including other children, recognize that there is something special about him. Nothing from his home could possibly explain his remarks, nor anything from the lesson, as Ruth was simply hearing the children read.

Suddenly he said: 'When I breathe in I breathe in God, and when I breathe out I breathe out God.' Some other children asked him, 'Is God everywhere?' He said, 'Yes.' 'Is God in every colour?' 'Yes.' And he went on to insist that God was even in black.

Now here is a child who may well become a social problem in his teens, in view of his background. Of course we know that many young children have this awareness and lose it, but nowadays it would seem that more have it than ever; these are the incarnating 'old souls' who have the *potential* to bring in the new age.

Fortunate children are born into understanding homes, but such homes are rare. Those born into the other kind may suffer a kind of death of all that inwardly they feel they are, because it is not recognized or affirmed. Yet, if they are still strong enough to be true to themselves, perhaps even this suffering may be a part of the pattern.

What they need is validation of their perceptions. Many of us are in some position to help, whether as parents, teachers, tutors, clergy, counsellors, psychotherapists, social workers, doctors, Samaritans.

So, to de-limit my field :

I am not dealing here with the majority of people who are stabilized at the ordinary level of functioning. To awaken them to further awareness is the field of psychological, psychic an spiritual *education.*

Nor, at the other end of the scale, am I concerned with those progressive souls who have won through and are stabilized at a higher level of awareness. These are balanced, in so far as they are healthily in touch with mystical experience of great truth and beauty, and yet can earth their findings wisely; for the greatest seers are often also the most practical people. They have gone beyond most of the conflicts and can work sensibly and objectively at helping society to change itself.

What I am concerned about is the middle range : the unstable, unbalanced people; those who are in process of change, one bit of the personality trying to catch up with another. For often these people have a great inner stretch between the different parts of their personalities. And sometimes the stretch becomes a split, with inevitable conflict and misery.

I met them as children when I was working in child guidance. I meet them now as students and older persons. They have immense potential. Usually they are acutely sensitive; they perceive far more than do most of us, but as yet they cannot reconcile what they perceive with living in our present society. And they haven't reached the point where they can work with detached objectivity to educate that society. They present us with a tremendous challenge in sorting out the true from the false. So I want to look at:

WHAT are the special problems that they bring to us in the helping professions?

WHY is all this happening? What explanations can we offer them so that they can accept their experiences and stabilize afresh? And, finally:

HOW can we (very tentatively) adjust our own attitudes in psychotherapy and counselling to meet the new needs?

WHAT are the problems (as I see them)?

We cannot deny the recent explosion of psychic 'powers'; the rapid emergence of spontaneous clairvoyance, telepathy, purported messages from U.F.O.s, automatic writing and painting —all the E.S.P. phenomena. The trouble is that we haven't a framework to contain it all. Students in hostels play around with ouija-boards or séances, often at a low level and with no safeguards, and the casualties come to us. We need adult education courses in the training and discrimination of psychic faculties but, apart from the College of Psychic Studies and the Arthur Findlay College, where are they?[1] What are we to do about these faculties? What are the criteria of assessment?

As a result of lack of knowledge, the sensitives may go to extremes in their attitude towards their gifts, either swallowing them whole, uncritically, or else rejecting them and even (still more dangerously) repressing them completely, with compensatory neurotic symptoms.

Someone dealing with such matters wrote to me: 'There seem to be two clear-cut reactions in people to the manifestations of E.S.P. They either think they are mad or God. I get more of the God type, you more of the other.' She went on, 'It's very rewarding if one can reassure them that they are neither, though they don't always take kindly to the fact that they are not God, and that this may not be their last incarnation.' Not God? I know what she means, but this assumption needs very subtle discernment. Let us look at each type in turn.

---

[1] [Note, 1976]: I am glad to see that extra-mural and other evening classes of this kind are now being established and are usually well attended. Two courses have run recently in Leicester, and there is a demand for more

(1) *The 'God' type.* Sometimes I am asked to comment on scripts or tapes received in trance or telepathically. Of course we all know that neither the medium's nor the sitter's mind can ever be entirely eliminated, even in the purest channels, so it is a question of assessing the *degree* of validity.

Personally, I always see a red light when people's guides come through with high-sounding names such as the numerous and very different Winston Churchills we have known! So many manifest as Jesus, the Virgin Mary, various Apostles, Masters, and so on. And yet, even here, one can never be quite sure; there's a *quality* in the purest channels which makes even these sources possibly authentic—to some degree. More suspect, I think, are the mediums who identify their own egos with the high-sounding names; their messages tell them that they *are* the Christ or some other great figure reincarnate.

Yet, it's easy to laugh, but even these examples are rarely a hundred per cent false. Often such people are perfectly sincere, open and honest *consciously,* absolutely dedicated. They may have gone through great tests and trials (though not always on the faculty of discrimination). And who is to say that they are not inspired at the highest level by such sources? It is possible that the inspiration, stepped down through intermediaries to a relatively untrained channel, has become distorted by the personal unconscious mind and used to inflate the conscious personality. There is, I find, usually a grain of truth, and it all needs very fine tuning on everyone's part to gain a true assessment.

One of the first things that I watch for in the personality is a paranoid pattern : a repressed sense of inferiority, of being badly done to, which means that the individual needs to overcompensate by these grandiose inflations. (This mechanism is, of course, always unconscious and therefore strongly denied.) If we find sensitives complaining bitterly that everyone is against them, that no one appreciates their divine messages, then there is usually some degree of paranoid neurosis. On the other hand, our spiritually defective society encourages in such people a sense of being alienated or even persecuted, so we must sift carefully. In my own practice, I try first to work on the neurotic mechanisms so as to get the personality cleared as far as possible, or else the individual may take his scripts from one 'authority' to another, rejecting all criticism and hence feeling himself increasingly rejected.

Then, when the ego-defences are more or less out of the way, I try to validate the intimations by looking at them in a deeper, universal way, as archetypal subjective experiences rather than as external facts. For example, in the case of those who have been 'told' they are the Christ, born to redeem the world, one can suggest that perhaps the 'Christ' signifies the Christ principle within all men; that on the path many of us go through the great initiations of crucifixion, resurrection, and the influx of the Holy Spirit in order to transmute and make 'Christed' our own 'world' or patch of life—a unique task which only each individual can perform. This approach does not deny or diminish, so much as put in perspective. To use other idioms, we help (as far as we are able) the sensitive to grow beyond the lower psychic level to the spiritual; or beyond the astral glamour to the white light of truth.

Another example is that of a woman who had been told through automatic writing that she was to become heir to all the world, and the only heir, too. Now, often the highest truths can be expressed most perfectly in paradox; so, after some work on the personality, I used a well-known passage from the seventeenth-century mystic Traherne, which throws light on this intimation. He writes:

> You will never enjoy the world aright till the sea itself floweth in your veins, till you are clothed with the heavens and crowned with the stars, and perceive yourself to be the sole heir of the whole world, and more than so, because men are in it who are everyone sole heirs as well as you. Till you can sing and rejoice and delight in God, as misers do in gold, and kings in sceptres, you will never enjoy the world.

To summarize: the criteria of assessment, as I see them, are:

No grandiose inflations or identifications. The real teachers are humble.

Commonsense in the messages; a quality of quiet strength, harmonious, not frenetic.

The *quality* of what is given. This is the ultimate test; for we have that faculty within us which recognizes and responds to the purest degree of truth that, as yet, we are capable of perceiving.

(2) *The 'mad' type.* I am not dealing with temporary disorientation induced by drugs; that is a different subject [*see Chapter 17*].

Among those who have never touched drugs are those whose sensitivity terrifies them; they fear they are abnormal, 'going mad'. Indeed, if their ego-boundaries are frail so that their experiences cannot be contained, they may indeed go over into neuroses if not psychoses.

When the phenomena are quite mild, especially in the early stages, simple first-aid and common sense may suffice. Thus, under the strain of imminent final examinations, a student developed 'second-sight' of rather an alarming nature (to her), which kept her awake at night. Probably she was innately psychic. I did not reject the experience, for already she 'felt odd'. I appreciated it as a natural gift, common to some other people, which one day she might possibly develop and educate. But I did suggest that there was a time and a place for these things, and strongly advised at present that she practised sealing the solar plexus with the cross of light within the circle of light, also surrounding her whole aura with light, before sleeping. This temporary closing down did the trick.

Some, however, have gone further, and one cannot deal with them in this way. In any case, advice is something which I give only in emergency; mostly all one can do is to go alongside and try to understand. Take those introverted sensitives [*see Chapter 14*] who live largely in the other world anyway; who withdraw and are labelled 'schizoid'. Indeed the ego may shatter, and they may go over temporarily into schizophrenia. Then, for safety and healing, their experiences are damped down with drugs in mental hospitals, and this may be a temporary necessity.

It is the *quality* of their inner perceptions, which helps us to draw a line between madness and sanity. My own criteria are:

(a) The meaningful quality of the inner experiences, their consistency and continuity. But if the images are bizarre,

235

confused, disordered, like a television screen wrongly tuned, then the individual is sick.[2]

(b) Whether the ego is strong enough to tolerate and integrate the experience, to earth it in the here and now, and to live a so-called 'normal' life alongside, however inadequate the outer world may seem to be at first in comparison with the inner. (Ultimately, of course, the two are perceived as parts of the same total pattern.) But if the individual is at the mercy of his inner images, then he *has* gone over the edge; the ego must keep realistic control.

Yet not all are schizoid types. The more cycloid personality types go in for manic-depressive swings. One man had a fortnight of feeling complete unity with God and the cosmos, paid for by months and years of severe depression. Mental hospital treatment including ECT did not help because (so he said) no one there accepted the validity of his 'high' state.

Those are the more severe cases. But an increasing number of others who do not break down may well be living consciously in higher realms. They *know* the eternal quality of love; they are in touch with some of their former lives; they find it agonizingly painful when they meet a soul in incarnation whom they have known and loved with that quality previously, but he is so boxed down that there is no mutual recognition. Too easily, then, they become over-intense and even neurotic.

One student wrote a verse to a man she recognized, though of course she never showed it to him, in fact hardly dared to speak to him, for if she did :

> Would that estrange you ? Could you tell
> It to your heart and care
> For all that is to come,
> If you had known that I was
> Long before you came,
> Richly swathed in antique mysteries ?
> Would you want that intense mystic
> Knowledge, contained in the embryo
> Of Time, here ?

[2] For the difference, see Morag Coate: *Beyond All Reason*, Constable, 1964.

Now the psychotherapists among us will be thinking: 'Ah! But this is just projection—seeing the idealized animus-image with all its glamour in this particular man.' Yes, that also may be true, but isn't this another razor's edge? May the answer be not 'either/or' but 'both'? Why are we drawn by these especially strong magnetic attractions to certain people and not to others? (That they resemble 'Father' is too easy an explanation). If we are to be new age counsellors don't we need to look very deeply at the *degree*: how much is projection, how much recognition?

Some of the stronger and otherwise mentally healthy people of all ages seem at the present time to be broken right down and tested to the nth degree, shaken right to the roots, re-formed from the depths of being. They may feel disintegrated into nothing, like a caterpillar dissolving into the jelly of the pupa. A few may go back even beyond the ego-personality to the primal unity and share in the cosmic experience of becoming. Those who have been through a very deep analysis may have had something of this experience. Yet they are not 'mad' since they can hold the experience and ultimately be enriched by it. In certain cases such major restructuring takes the form of journeys in inner time and space; these journeys are usually redemptive, consistent, and very meaningful.[3]

Even if there is no illness, all these experiences take a great deal of energy. How can we best help?

First, I think, by relieving any unnecessary extra anxiety about having the experiences at all. Just accept that the condition is increasingly common, potentially valuable, and will pass.

This attitude assumes our own freedom from anxiety. We need to be very sure, from our experience of many examples, that the process, however strange and painful, will constellate so much energy from the deep centre, as the work of transmutation proceeds, that it is all immensely worth while and positive. Increasingly, there will come periods of great joy and peace as well as the preliminary suffering, and in the end the individual will have achieved a new, fuller pattern of wholeness.

Mostly, I think, we help by simply *being there*, alongside, without invading. After all, Bunyan in his *Pilgrim's Progress* had Faithful and Hopeful with him. A companion, or a group,

[3] For a detailed analysis see Chapter 1 of *Seven Inner Journeys*.

on any of these creative 'trips' helps immensely. For instance, a friend in later middle life wrote to me that karmic work from past lives was coming up spontaneously, at first in dreams and later in conscious awareness. What worried her was that she was temporarily losing grip of the outer world, suffering from acute fatigue, memory loss, and needing a good deal of sleep. Although she was not ill, and could cope adequately with outer life, she felt 'bad' about having these very natural symptoms; of course, this guilt increased her anxiety and set up an unnecessary vicious circle. She needed the reassurance that, as in the case of any sudden spurt of growth (e.g. adolescence), such symptoms were perfectly foreseeable and would pass when the next phase of consolidation was gained, as indeed they did. But to go to the kind of psychiatrist who does not understand (though mercifully many more do understand, these days) would not have helped.

I see three important needs for people undergoing these phases of rapid change, in whatever form:

(a) On the physical level: plenty of *contact with nature*—earth, water, air and sun.

(b) Plenty of *psychological space and time*: room to grow and to *be*, with time to give the process due, though not undue, attention. Not too many extravert activities, but enough to keep balanced and in touch with the outer world. If we trust the process, the extravert phase will follow naturally in its own rhythm. After the withdrawal comes the true return.

(c) *Sleep.* The subject of sleep provides a useful example of the application of new attitudes to something we don't yet fully understand, despite all recent research. Moreover, it is a practical issue, for we are often faced with clients whose problem is that they sleep too little or too much, even allowing for wide individual variations within the norm.

Do we not have to ask first: what is sleep *for*? Quite apart from the obvious part it plays physiologically in resting and restoring the body and nervous system, what do we do during sleep? And do we make the best preparation beforehand so that we get the best quality of sleep?

Do we accept what the ageless wisdom teaches: that we

can live far more fully during the sleep of the body? That a great deal goes on in the inner world which we do not usually recapture in the waking state, except occasionally in distorted dream-fragments? And that, after right commitment and orientation, we may well profit by considerable learning in the higher worlds when out of space/time, even engaging in healing, helping and teaching others, and possibly in rescue work?

I am just throwing out these ideas to suggest that if someone comes to you with a sleep problem, it needs careful investigation. Inability to sleep *may* indicate fear of death, or an avoidance of the inner life, which then may display its negative aspect, producing nightmares. On the other hand, too much sleep *may* be a form of escape the other way round : from the 'hard world' to a womb, or to an illusion of perfection. Such people may have considerable potential; they may want to incarnate their creativity in outer living, but it seems too difficult to bring their fourth-dimensional insights into three-dimensional form, and so they retreat into sleep.

To summarize: The most frustrating experience for all these so-called 'mad' types is to be surrounded with 'helpers' who do not know from their own lives even a little of what these experiences *feel* like; who therefore tend to explain away the phenomena, or regard the subjects as 'sick'. We need a new philosophy to contain the new perceptions. We need new bottles for new wine.

WHY is all this happening?

Our present conceptual framework is too limited. What theories have we?

First, as a Jungian myself, I must pay a tribute to C. G. Jung, who led us so far in the dark years and is leading us even further since his death, as more of his writings are released. He had been himself through extreme heights and depths, for in the early years he was pioneering alone into uncharted realms. In his autobiography[4] he tells the whole story of his psychic and spiritual

4 *Memories, Dreams, Reflections*, Collins and Routledge and Kegan Paul, 1963.

explorations, especially the amazing experience of near-death in 1944. Afterwards, making use of it in writing to those who were dying, or in letters of condolence, he said:

> What happens after death is so unspeakably glorious that our imagination and our feelings do not suffice to form even an approximate conception of it.

Often he spoke of the changes and the new age, and there is one remark recorded from oral conversation that is particularly relevant:

> It seems to me that we are at the end of an era. The splitting of the atom and the nuclear bomb bring us a new view of matter. As physical man cannot develop any further, it would seem that this particular evolution ends with man. Like the caterpillar dissolves and turns into a butterfly, it is conceivable that the physical body of man could change into a more subtle body. It might not be necessary for him to die to be clothed afresh and be transformed.[5]

I have just reviewed for *The Science of Thought Review* the first volume of Jung's *Letters*, and it seemed to me that a conceptual basis for many of our psychic problems is expressed in a nutshell in one letter. This was written as long ago as 1939, and to a Pastor of the Church who was having conversations with his dead brother (a difficult position for an orthodox Pastor in those days!)[6] Jung writes:

> The capacity to nullify space and time must somehow inhere in the psyche, or, to put it another way, the psyche does not exist wholly in time and space. It is very probable that only what we call consciousness is contained in space and time, and that the rest of the psyche, the unconscious, exists

[5] Margaret Ostrowski-Sachs: *Conversations with C. G. Jung*, trans. David Wheeler, p. 63. (With acknowledgement to the C. G. Jung Institute, Zurich.)

[6] C. G. Jung: *Letters, Vol. 1: 1906–1950*, Routledge and Kegan Paul, 1973, pp. 256, 257 and 258. See also: 'The Soul and Death' in Vol. 8 of *Collected Works*, Routledge and Kegan Paul; and Chapter XI: 'On Life after Death' in *Memories, Dreams, Reflections*.

in a state of relative eternality and a relative non-separation from other psyches, or a oneness with them . . .

Naturally, we can form no conception of a relatively timeless and spaceless existence, but, psychologically and empirically, it results in manifestations of the continual presence of the dead and their influence in our dream life. I therefore follow up such experiences with the greatest attention, because they show many things we dream about in a very peculiar light, where 'psychological' structures appear as existential conditions . . . The connection is not without its dangers because it entangles the consciousness of the living too much in that transcendental state, resulting in unconsciousness and dissociation phenomena . . . It should not be experimented with because of the danger of a disintegration of consciousness. To be on the safe side, one must be content with spontaneous experiences . . . All the signs indicate that your conversation with your brother is a genuine experience which cannot be 'psychologised' . . . There are experiences which show that the dead entangle themselves, so to speak, in the physiology (sympathetic nervous system) of the living. This would result in states of possession.

Three aspects of this passage are particularly relevant to my theme :

First, Jung recognizes as valid 'a genuine experience which cannot be "psychologised" '. His approach not only underlines all I have said about the need to discriminate, but it goes further, because it raises the question of distinguishing between the objective and the subjective modes of perception : what is existential and what psychological? How to reconcile them?

Jung has been accused both ways on: by the more materialistic scientists of objectifying what is subjective (i.e. seeing 'mind-stuff' as 'reality'); and, on the other hand, by spiritualists and U.F.O. fans of subjectifying what to them is objective (i.e. seeing as mind-stuff what are here and now objects). Any of us who are working in this borderland will have suffered in a similar way; you can't win! So here is another pair of opposites which needs synthesis.

I suggest that, seen from a higher level, these two modes of perception are only apparently in opposition. As Lawrence Hyde used to say, the higher you go in awareness, the more the subjective and the objective come closer until they are perceived as one and the same. After all, when we raise our own frequency —when we get 'high'—the corresponding environment appears solid and real to us *on the equivalent level*; for us, in that condition, it is objective. Further, the subjective *acts upon* the objective; 'thoughts are things'; what we create mentally in mind and feeling comes into being 'right down through'—and very rapidly these days.[7] To illustrate with a bit of light relief—though it wasn't light relief to the person concerned—here is a story contributed by one of the readers of the Gildas teachings, who wrote to tell us of what she called a 'salutary lesson' she had learned:

> After my father's quiet and unobtrusive funeral, which was his and the family's wish, there was a desire from the town for a large memorial service, which filled me with horror, but my mother thought it was my duty to go. One day I said to myself very consciously, 'If I fell down and broke my leg, *I couldn't go.*' Need I tell you that the next day I fell in a perfectly simple place and broke my leg and my heel! I have often had prayers answered fairly dramatically, but not quite so much as this. When people asked me how I did it, I could quite honestly say I broke it myself.

The second point I want to pick up from Jung's letter is that of the dangers of dissociation or even of possession by other entities; this problem concerns psychotherapists very much. When we meet a patient whose ego-boundaries are weak, unformed or shattered, and whose personality appears to have changed, there is always the *possibility* of invasion and possession by a discarnate entity. I know there are psychological theories to explain this: a 'Shadow' side which has been rejected and has become an autonomous complex; or a multiple personality. But let us just keep an open mind in certain cases, for one theory does not

---

[7] See Douglas Fawcett's theory of 'Imagining' as described in: Victor Goddard: *Flight Towards Reality*, Turnstone Books, 1975, and Raynor Johnson: *Nurslings of Immortality*, Hodder and Stoughton, 1960.

necessarily preclude another. Indeed, like attracts like, and if the individual has a definite personality weakness he will attract similar thoughts and entities. So the first thing is to help him to integrate himself, to become strong and whole, so that he cannot become invaded. It is essential to build a strong, four-square personality *to sustain the charge* of the higher energies; for only then is it safe to transcend the personality and surrender to the higher self. And always in this life, I maintain, the ego must take responsibility for choice.

Regarding possession: up until the era of materialistic science, possession was recognized, and I am glad to see that it is becoming at least mentionable once more.[8] If the case is severe, we need *wisely trained* exorcists and rescue circles first, before we can get to work to strengthen the cleared personality.

Thirdly, let us look again at Jung's first paragraph, in which he suggests a conceptual basis for the relation of the eternal to the temporal: 'The capacity to nullify space and time must somehow inhere in the psyche ...' This insight is completely fundamental to new age thinking. The practical application to living has immense possibilities.

For example, if one is bereaved and wants to contact the person who is now out of our time/space continuum, the obvious task is to work on extending one's own consciousness beyond the three-dimensional limits, in order to contact him.

And dare we stretch this idea to imply that, beyond time, we can meet other incarnations of our own fuller selves, other personalities existing in what we have been conditioned to call 'past' or 'future'? For, if the fuller life takes place beyond time as we know it, then it is not necessarily true to speak of past or future lives; such a concept *could* be restricting reality into our narrow concept of linear time.

To enlarge on this: I would recommend Jane Roberts' books *Seth Speaks* and *The Seth Material*.[9] Seth is a teacher in much the same way as Gildas, but he is more concerned with the higher philosophy and cosmology, providing a conceptual framework. Beyond time, he suggests, all these lives, our own and

[8] See R. K. McAll: 'Demonosis or the Possession Syndrome', *International Journal of Social Psychiatry*, Spring 1971, p. 150.
[9] Prentice Hall, Englewood Cliffs, New Jersey, U.S.A.

those of others, may be happening in the eternal now. This means that we can redeem the so-called past, and even the so-called future. Seth says, 'Events and objects are not absolute but plastic. Events can be changed both before and after their occurrence.'[10]

He stretches our faculty of imagining still further to conceive of what he calls 'probable lives'. Every time we make a choice, he asks what happens to the other lives we would have lived had we made the other choice? This is not so difficult a concept if we remember that he explains: 'Anything of which you are aware in 3D existence is only a projection of a greater reality into that dimension.[11] In other words, we are conscious only of a fragment of the total truth—just those limited aspects which obtrude into our present mode of consciousness.

In practical psychotherapy, I have found that some such philosophy which underlies theories of reincarnation is an immense relief to sick and seeking souls. It makes more sense of life; it provides some incentive to go on struggling in what otherwise would (for them) be a meaningless existence.

It has struck me recently that what used to happen in dreams or (so we are told) after death seems now to be happening in our conscious lives. To put it another way, as our frequency-rate rises, we are extending our consciousness to take in more.

For example, Jane Sherwood's *Post-Mortem Journal*.[12] Surely much of what T. E. Lawrence seemed to be experiencing, in the early stages after dying in a state of confusion, is experienced by some people here and now, and in many ways resembles deeper psychotherapy. Further, more and more people appear to be working on their other (past?) lives in order to heal the patterns and relationships of the present.[13] We need still more

[10] *Seth Speaks: The Eternal Validity of the Soul*, 1972, p. 169.
[11] *Ibid.*, p. 170.
[12] Spearman, 1964. See also her *The Country Beyond*, Spearman, 1969.
[13] Joan Grant and Denys Kelsey: *Many Lifetimes*, Gollancz, 1968. Here a psychiatrist and a psychic, who can 'key in' to far memory, combine to study in practice the relation of reincarnation to the origins of mental illness. For overwhelming documentary evidence, by a psychiatrist, of group reincarnation and healing, see Arthur Guirdham: *The Cathars and Reincarnation*, Spearman, 1970, and *We Are One Another*, Spearman, 1974. See also the work of Edgar Cayce (Association for Research and Enlightenment, Virginia Beach, Virginia, U.S.A.) especially as studied psychologically by Gina Cerminara in her *Many Mansions*, reissued by Spearman, 1967.

research. This is where P. W. Martin's pioneer work *Experiment in Depth*[14] was such a helpful guide many years ago, because it established recognition and pointed out landmarks.

Is there, I wonder, a sequence, paralleling the development of our conscious perceptive field? For instance :

> What used to manifest in dreams and visions now becomes inner (sometimes even outer) waking experience.
> Then come inner journeys and work on this-life problems *in their deeper context.*
> Then far memory—other-life work.

And then what? Is this as far as we have gone? What lies beyond is a fascinating conjecture. Beyond the personality : living experience of group union, unity with all life, cosmic consciousness? Who knows?

Regarding the recognition by science of new age awareness, it is essential for new age counsellors to have at least a nodding acquaintance with what is going on in the academic departments of *some* universities and elsewhere. I am no scientist, nor am I (now) an academic, but I am delighted to see academic psychology becoming less interested in rats and mazes, and more in human parapsychology, especially the physiological feedback experiments which can be done relatively easily on the states of mind in meditation.

Then there is the rapidly expanding work on energy fields in which the energy-surround (aura) of living plants and human fingertips (especially when giving healing) has been photographed. The work is going on not only behind the iron curtain but also in the U.S.A. and in this country—it is a lovely thought that research at such levels transcends national boundaries.

The experiments—which I can only touch on here—are beginning to 'prove' the existence of what the ageless wisdom has known as the 'subtle bodies'. And when they are gloriously visible in the forms of clear electroencephalographs and incredibly beautiful colour-plates, then the doubting Thomases among us say at last, 'But this is *real*!' To some of the more intellectually

14 Routledge and Kegan Paul, 1955. Re-issued in paperback, 1976.

critical of disturbed seekers, such evidence can be most reassuring. So they should be referred to the relevant books.[15]

HOW can we adjust our own attitudes to meet the need?

First, I suggest, by working on ourselves, for most of us have had *some* degree of neurosis which precipitated self-work, and now we need to re-form at the next level—or in relation to a more comprehensive pattern of the *gestalt*. If we stretch our minds and hearts as far as we can, so as to live and move and have our being in the 4D world ourselves, then we can say to the sufferers, 'You are not alone'. Thus, in a very realistic way, the process of change can be set going in individuals and in society.

In this way, the so-called *para*normal becomes understood and accepted as *normal*. Then anxieties about feeling alienated and consequent resentments are removed.

And, finally, we come to see the E.S.P. problems, however distorted and extreme, not so much as clinical symptoms but as embryonic *faculties* which need education, training and discipline just as other ordinary faculties do.

Such a movement from the attitude of sickness to that of health is paralleled in many fields; for example medicine, where we move from hospitals to public health, from the remedial to the prophylactic, from concentration on the deviate towards health and wholeness for *all*. Healing—wholeness—education.

Thus, whatever symptom is brought to us, we learn to look at it with a 4D eye. I have already taken as an example the problem of excessive sleep. Take any other specific one that interests you and practise the 'new look' on it !

---

[15] Mary Scott: *Science and the Subtle Bodies: Towards a Clarification of Issues*, C.P.S. Paper No. 8, 1975, 75p. (Obtainable from the C.P.S., 16 Queensberry Place, London, SW7 2EB. A very clear introduction to the subject.) Adrian Parker: *States of Mind: ESP and Altered States of Consciousness*, Malaby Press, 1975. (A valuable summary of recent research, especially in the U.S.A.) Charles Tart: *States of Consciousness*, Dutton, New York, 1975. Charles Tart (Ed.): *Transpersonal Psychology*, Routledge and Kegan Paul, 1975. Claudio Naranjo and Robert E. Ornstein: *On the Psychology of Meditation*, Allen and Unwin, 1971. Harold Saxton Burr: *Blueprint for Immortality: The Electrical Patterns of Life*, Spearman, 1972. Dennis Milner and Edward Smart: *The Loom of Creation: A Study of the Forces and Purpose which Weave the Pattern of Existence*, Spearman, 1976. Peter Tompkins and Christopher Bird: *The Secret Life of Plants*, Allen Lane, 1974.

Then there is the question of *levels of manifestation* in the total pattern. The 4D attitude implies our realization that neurotic symptoms or disturbed behaviour may well be saying the same things as does physical illness, but each in its own idiom according to the 'body' in which it is expressed. By now, this knowledge is elementary in psychosomatic medicine, but let us push it one degree further. According to your craft, you can tackle a psychosomatic symptom physically, psychologically, *or spiritually*, so that there is room for all approaches. And the higher the level of resolution, the less likely is recurrence of the problem, perhaps in some other form.

For instance, take the gastric ulcer syndrome and personality pattern. One can tackle this physically with suitable diet or operation; one can tackle it psychologically, perhaps finding that the person has repressed his dependency-needs and is over-responsible. But if he can find his true source from which to draw nourishment, and which he can trust in the spiritual sense, then there is less likelihood of manifestations on the personality and physiological levels.

So we come to see that there is seldom a single linear cause, but rather a multiple causality: not 'either/or' but 'all-and-everything'. For example, here is a boy with a problem: is it attributable to a 'bad' father, *or* to his own inner, introjected father image, *or* to his karma? Wrong question! Probably all. For we *did* ask to be born; our higher selves *did* select our parents so that we should constellate these personality-lessons to be learned in this day of life.

The new counsellors practise what we may call 'see-through' technique; not trying primarily to cure the symptom, nor even its social cause alone, but rather asking what it is all *for* at the level of soul-learning; why the individual must live it through. And if we hold such an attitude in our work, it is felt by the inner self of the client to be far more deeply accepting.

In this way, we learn to 'see through' the changing forms of 3D life to the universal realities; beyond the temporal to the eternal and permanent patterns. The old, limited attitude was to see an inner image as a symbol given to us (perhaps in a dream) for material living: to give us a hunch for the Derby, or warn us not to travel, and on a certain level these may have their place. But with the 4D eye we reverse the way of looking; we recognize that the archetypal patterns *are* the realities, and the changing forms of daily living are but signs and symbols of something far more total—the playthings by which we learn—the coloured counters which help us to do our sums. For the counters themselves are not intrinsically as significant as are the principles of number which we learn to perceive as eternal laws pervading form.

We need a team of counsellors who are themselves experienced in such attitudes. At present there are still too few.

I realize that I have put an awful lot of responsibility on to the counsellors! However, a corollary of the assumption that incarnate counsellors should have some degree of 4D vision is that we then discover that we ourselves have infinite help from the higher counsellors in the fourth dimension—and beyond it. So we, the counsellors, are not alone. Less and less do we work from ourselves. We find our inner guides and teachers; our higher self—our source—whatever we may care to call it. And in this way we cannot help reflecting what we find, whether explicitly or implicitly, on to the people with whom we work. With due respect *always* for the particular path and idiom of the individual, we help those who come to us to learn to rely in a sound way on their own inner sources, so that eventually we can hand over and become thankfully redundant.

*　　*　　*

Some sources of information (apart from special references already given in the text):

(1) *New Age groups, centres and courses*

There are now so many of these (to suit all tastes) that many pages would be required to list them. An invaluable quarterly newsletter, keeping the reader up to date with all new developments, is *Trans-Group News*, obtainable for only £1 per annum from John Sinclair, 16 Great Ormond Street, London WC1N 3RB.[16]

[16] See also Stephen Annett (Ed.): *The Many Ways of Being, A Guide to Spiritual Groups and Growth Centres in Britain*, ABACUS and Turnstone Books, 1976.

Two groups, which I should like to recommend personally, may be of particular interest to professional readers of this book :

(a) *The Scientific and Medical Network* is an informal group, founded in 1972, of men and women holding university degrees in science or medicine, having a personal interest in a non-materialistic world outlook and in promoting studies of and research into paraphysical, parapsychological or spiritual matters and action that can usefully flow from these. Facilities include conferences, seminars for young people, and a residential centre at Sidmouth for small seminars and group meetings. Write to Mr. G. B. Blaker, Lake House, Ockley, Surrey RH5 5NS, or Dr. Patrick Shackleton, Sidmouth House, Cotmaton Road, Sidmouth, Devon EX10 8ST.

(b) *Centre for Transpersonal Psychology*, 26A Gilston Road, London SW10 9SS. Ian Gordon-Brown and Barbara Somers run workshops in Transpersonal Psychology. Deriving from the work of Maslow, Frankl, Assagioli, and Progoff, the term 'transpersonal' describes a broad movement within psychology that accepts the reality of a deeper or higher Self within man, and the need to find ways of relating that Self to ordinary everyday awareness and making its energy available for our use.

(2) *Libraries*

Two first-class libraries (both with postal services) cater for psychical research, parapsychology, esoteric and spiritual studies:

(a) *The Library of the College of Psychic Studies*, 16 Queensberry Place, London SW7 2EB, has 11,000 books and is the most extensive library of its kind in Great Britain. (Members only.) There is also a book-sale service.

(b) *The Lucis Trust Library*, 235 Finchley Road, London NW3 6LS. This is a free lending library giving excellent service to all. (No membership required.)

Conclusion

I ended the last chapter on the note of redundancy. To learn to be redundant economically is a bitter test for many people at present. As we grow old, it is a test for nearly all of us on other levels as well. I recognize the fear, depression and sense of being unwanted that it can bring when familiar patterns of work and habitual supports crumble away. But have we thought of the positive aspect : the freedom and joy as the old dies and the new breaks through? The relief from over-anxiety and exaggerated responsibility when ego-living becomes subsidiary to a wiser form of life?

Psychologically and spiritually it would seem that there is no other way through to the fuller life. We have to let go the ego-cares, and allow the minutiae of every day and hour to be directed from the higher self—the Christ self within us all. When we do, we find wonderful help; we see how much better our lives are run than they used to be. I cannot give detail about methods, partly because each must find his own unique way, partly because this is a lesson I am only now learning (with many lapses!) Writing this book, in itself, has been a great help in shedding the past like an outgrown snake-skin. All I can say is that *it works*, and that I see it as the essential pattern for the new age.

I realize that throughout the book I have stressed the importance of building a strong and balanced ego during the first part of life. This is not a contradiction. Until one *is* a person, one cannot surrender the personality. The two go hand in hand. A well-established ego can form a stronger channel through which the higher self can operate. Although it is not the prime mover, the channel is important.

In recent years of counselling, more and more I have found

myself saying, 'I simply don't *know*'. I have just allowed things
to happen. I well remember one session immediately after lunch
(a bad time for the ego!) when a very withdrawn girl talked
more freely than ever before, her head bent, her face hidden
behind her dark curtain of hair. She never looked up to notice
that I had slept throughout most of the hour. 'Dr. Swainson,'
she said as she left, 'that was the best session yet.' This taught
me a good deal. Seriously, though, in many instances I have
deliberately given up and 'handed over'. This is not necessarily
opting out, although it can be so; but I feel that many counsellors will understand, for then things went much better. So
much change and redemption takes place anyway at other levels;
and when we find that the ego can do no more, the higher power
works in both of us, and we can safely trust it. For:

> In Great Eternity every particular Form gives forth or
> Emanates
> Its own peculiar Light, & the Form is the Divine Vision
> And the Light is his Garment. This is Jerusalem in every
> Man,
> A Tent & Tabernacle of Mutual Forgiveness.. [1]

As awareness increases, co-operation with the timeless realm
becomes more conscious. Deliberately we work from the higher
dimension in ourselves, and thus with the equivalent level in
others, so that counsel takes place from the apex of the tent or
triangle—the peak of the 'holy mountain'. This is why, at the
beginning of this book, I quoted from that well-known passage of
Isaiah which forecasts the new age. Only when we look down
from the holy mountain, with the 'unfallen' vision of a child,
can we transcend ego-judgement based on the ordinary senses
and the lower mind; only then can we perceive the apparent
opposites as reconciled in harmony. This insight is the spirit of
counsel.

[1] William Blake: *Jerusalem.*

INDEX